1001
HIGH PERFORMANCE
TECH TIPS

WAYNE SCRABA

HPBooks

HPBooks
are published by
The Berkley Publishing Group
A division of Penguin Putnam Inc.
375 Hudson Street
New York, New York 10014

First Edition: April 1995

The Penguin Putnam Inc. World Wide Web site address is
http://www.penguinputnam.com

© 1995 Wayne Scraba

Printed in the U.S.A.

18   17

Library of Congress Cataloging-in-Publication Data

Scraba, Wayne
    1001 high performance tech tips : engines, drivetrain, chassis,
suspension, power tuning, body, interior, workshop / Wayne Scraba.
        p. cm.
    ISBN 1-55788-199-5 (trade pbk.)
    ISBN 1-55788-020-4 :
    1. Automobiles—Maintenance and repair.   2. Automobiles—
Performance.   I. Title.   II. Title: One thousand and one high performance
tech tips.
    TL152.S425   1995   94-24716
    629.28′72—dc20   CIP

Book design & Production by Bird Studios
Interior photos by the author unless otherwise noted

CONTENTS

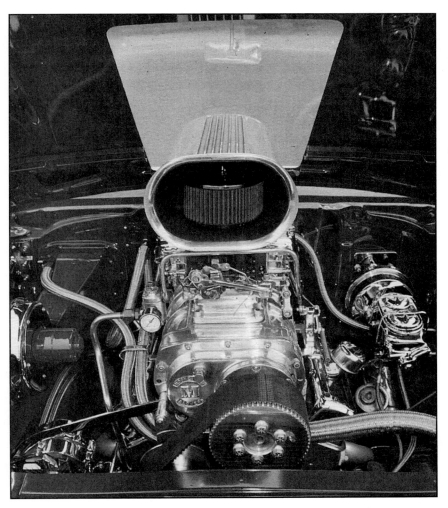

Years ago, while toiling behind the counter of a speed shop, I came to the realization that more than a few of our customers were in need of technical support. Although many of the products we sold came complete with instructions, it was often generic in nature. Many of the bits and pieces of hardware produced by the various manufacturers proved to be universal in make-up. As a result, these components weren't exactly tailored to the individual needs of the customer.

Most of the questions that I encountered were intricate (and varied) but all came down to one basic ingredient: The customer needed a technical tip or two to help him or her through a project (whether it was a simple header installation or something more involved like setting up piston-to-wall clearances). Just as important, I came to the realization that the customer didn't want to wade through one, two, three or more automotive service manuals to find the answer to his or her dilemma. In the end, we began to compile our own technical tips in loose-leaf format. But there was a distinct need for a much larger compilation of technical tips—bound together and cataloged to make it easy to find and just as easy to understand. Unfortunately, I never have had the opportunity to present the tips in such a format. In the end, it became a service born from need.

Over a decade later, I found myself behind a computer keyboard instead of a speed shop sales counter. My second freelance magazine assignment was a short series of tech tips for a monthly drag race publication. Within a couple of years, tech tip format articles became a rather healthy portion of my repertoire. But there was a difference between the old "system" I incorporated at the speed shop and the new one. Now the demand for information became so much larger (with the quantities of the tips growing proportionately) that I had to go beyond my own resources. Because of this, I began to call upon friends, racing buddies, acquaintances and business people in the performance automotive aftermarket for their assistance. Just like myself, they too had stockpiled tips based upon their own needs along with the needs of their customers and specific usage. Without the help and input of these individuals, a book containing this many tech tips simply would not have been possible. You'll find a complete list of the companies who have helped with these tips in the Source directory at the end of the book.

Just like you, these people (and yours truly) spend as much time as possible working on their personal toys. Every once in a while, tips and tricks are found that simply make life easier in the garage. Some of the ideas are time savers, some are performance shortcuts and others are simply the result of trial and error (and yes, even mistakes). Of course, necessity is sometimes the mother of invention and because of that, we've even found a few new ways of doing old things. Check out the tips that follow. There's something here for every gearhead, pro and amateur alike.

—Wayne Scraba

ENGINES

1 PICKUP TUBES: Do you have a problem with pickup tubes cracking inside aluminum oil pans? Under certain conditions, the resonance inside an aluminum oil pan can cause the pickup tube to crack. Initially, the problem was thought to be unique among racers and hi-po street machiners, but even Detroit has had problems. At this point, oil pan resonance that cracks pickup tubes is a hit and miss science. Because of that, check your pickup occasionally. It works better when attached to the oil pump.

2 PISTON-TO-VALVE: How much piston-to-valve clearance is required? In an over-the-counter piston, the figure is often 0.100" or more, but the actual number you use depends upon the combination. As an example, engines with steel rods can use a smaller piston-to-valve clearance figure—simply because the steel rod doesn't "grow" like an aluminum job. Some engine builders have gotten away with figures as small as 0.030", but that's living on the edge. One mistake (like a bit too much rpm on a gear change or a missed shift) and it could mean a bucket of bent valves. More realistic clearance figures are a minimum of 0.080" on the intake side and 0.100" on the exhaust side.

3 VALVE ANGLE: Valve "angles" are the hot topic in today's hi-po powerplants. What is the valve angle stuff all about? The valve angle is defined as the angle between the valve stem and the cylinder bore centerline. As an example, a stock small-block Chevy has a 23° angle. The trend in competition engines is toward shallower (smaller) valve angles. This produces a smaller, more efficient combustion chamber. A small chamber allows the use of a lighter piston that has a smaller dome. By the way, heads that are listed as "rolled over" feature smaller valve angles.

4 VALVE SPRINGS: In order to increase valve spring life, the end faces of the spring should be dressed before you install them. Although it sounds exotic, it isn't. Simply polish the ends of the spring smooth on a flat piece of 200-grit wet-and-dry emery paper. Most experts agree that holding the spring upright

and using a simple "figure eight" pattern works well for this job. Just be certain that your motion covers all portions of the spring end face. If the surface looks too coarse for your tastes, you can repeat the process on 400-grit paper.

5 HEAT SHIELD: Most of you have seen those funky tin oil shields that Chevrolet rivets to the bottom of iron intake manifolds. Do they do anything? We didn't think so, but Jere Stahl (Stahl Headers/Cams, 1513 Mr. Rose Ave., York, PA 17403) added one to a 350 Chevy truck engine equipped with an Edelbrock Performer intake manifold and found that part throttle fuel distribution improved 50%. With the shield installed, the average cylinder-to-cylinder temperature variation went from 200° to 100°.

6 HEADER TUBE SIZE: Thanks to Stahl Headers, here's how to determine header primary tube size: "Header primary tube size is a function of the horsepower the cylinder is producing, fuel efficiency and manifold vacuum or throttle area.

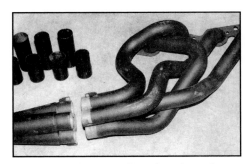

Primary tube length requirement is generally a function of rpm range."

7 TAMING VALVE LASH: Does your ride constantly need attention to the valve lash? Of course solid lifter cams need regular maintenance, but if you chase the lash much more frequently than the next guy, have a look at the tips of your pushrods. There's a good chance that the press-in ends are "moving," which in turn makes the lash change regularly. The solution? A set of the new one-piece pushrods.

8 VALVE SPRING TRAVEL: According to
Crane Cams, the valve spring travel on late-model Ford engines with exhaust rotators is very short. Sometimes the spring travel is so small that there is barely enough for a stock cam, much less an aftermarket cam with considerably more lift. Measure the spring travel with the spring on the head. There must be at least .060" more travel than the net valve lift of the cam you are using.

9 AIR CLEANER SIZING: Just how big should
your air cleaner be? K&N supplies the following formulas to put you in the right filter ball park:

$$A = \frac{cid \times rpm}{25,500}$$

A = the effective filtering area.

To find the total height (including the rubber sealing edges) of the filter needed, use the following formula:

$$H = \frac{A}{D \times 3.14} + .75$$

D = The estimated maximum diameter that will fit unobstructed in the vehicle. H = The height of the filter.

10 VALVETRAIN GEOMETRY: In order
for an engine to run properly at high rpm, the valve-train geometry must be absolutely correct. That, of course, isn't a big secret. But what affects the geometry? There are a number of factors, but the following is a place to begin: Changes in valve stem length, lifter length, block height (includes cylinder head and block milling), and camshaft base circle diameter all are critical when it comes to valvetrain geometry.

11 PUSHROD CUPS: Rocker arm pushrod
cup breakage is pretty common—especially when the engine has several thousand miles of use on the stock rockers. Crane Cams examined this problem and found that the breakage usually occurs when a cam is installed that has a higher lift than the earlier cam. The additional amount of travel required of the rocker arm tends to relocate the load generated by the valvetrain and concentrates it partially in the already worn area of the rocker arm pushrod seat, and partially in the area not yet worn. The result, according to Crane, is a concentration of loading on an area of thin metal and breaking through the pushrod seat often occurs. The solution? Install new rockers.

12 NO SYNTHETIC OIL: Virtually all of the
major cam grinders (and more than a few oil companies) discourage the use of synthetic oils during engine break-in—particularly those with flat-tappet (solid or hydraulic) camshafts. Instead, use a quality grade of naturally formulated non-synthetic oil for the break-in. You can safely use synthetics following the proper break-in period. Besides, synthetics are pretty pricey and you'll have to drain it out after the first 20 minutes or so anyway.

13 OVERSIZED PULLEYS: Once upon a
time (before serpentine belts), racers and go-fast street enthusiasts were plagued with alternator and water pump belts that went missing the moment the engine rpm skyrocketed. The aftermarket responded with large diameter, deep-groove alternator pulleys. Cast from aluminum, the pulleys measured a full 5.0 inches in overall diameter. Compared to a factory hi-po pulley (which typically measure a paltry 3-3/16"), the aftermarket pulleys were huge. Not only did the new pulleys solve the missing belt syndrome, they also slowed down the alternator and water pump, which in turn freed some extra horsepower. Racers and savvy street freaks picked up on the idea quickly. Then serpentine systems were introduced and everyone forgot about the big alternator pulleys. But they're still available and yes, they still work. Moroso, B&B, Canton and other companies stock them.

14 COGGED BELTS: Have you noticed the
alternator and fan belts that have "cogs" on the outer surfaces? Dayco manufactures one. They've been around for a while, and not only are the cogged belts slicker looking, they also run cooler and last longer!

15 WRIST PIN LOCKS: Wrist pins can be held in check via two different methods—pressed in place or floating (with various lock arrangements). A pressed pin simply means that the piston, wrist pin and connecting rod are assembled with a press. In essence, the pin can't move because of the interference fit in the connecting rod. Floating wrist pins are more convenient, but they always add another problem: The pin locks must stay in place until you decide to remove them. Typically, performance pistons are machined for one of three possible pin lock systems: Tru-Arcs, Spirolocks or buttons. Pin buttons are the least common, and in most cases, they're only found on fuel and blown alcohol combinations. On the other hand, performance pistons will often feature Tru-Arc retention. Tru-Arcs are basically circlip devices that can easily be installed with a pair of snap ring pliers. Spirolocks are another matter entirely. A Spirolok is basically a spiral clip that is "wound" into the retainer groove. It is almost impossible for a Spirolok to back out in a running engine, but it is also extremely difficult to install or remove when you're working on the powerplant (let's just say you need a lot of patience, strong fingers and a stronger will to get them in or out).

16 BENT PUSHRODS: If you bend one or more pushrods for no apparent reason, Crane Cams suggests that you are experiencing some form of mechanical interference in the valvetrain. The places to look include the rocker arm-to-stud clearance, valve spring coil bind, interference between the retainer and the valve seal or retainer and the valve guide. In addition, high engine rpm might be causing the valves to whack the pistons, which in turn bends the pushrods. Check out the problem before it becomes real serious.

17 INSTALLING DIPSTICK: Dipstick tube installation should be easy. But in some oil pans (or blocks) it doesn't always work that way. Instead, they require no end of smashing, bashing and "persuading" to get into place. Rather than beating the dipstick tube to death with your largest hammer, try covering the block-end with a bit of silicone (or other slippery sealant). Then slip a run-of-the-mill header bolt into the tube and tap the works home.

18 HOT DRAIN PLUG: Magnetic drain plugs aren't new. But the SX CHP-1 magnetic chip collector is. It provides a slick 'n easy way to monitor your engine without the hassle of draining the oil (or worse yet, tearing down the engine). By design, this drain plug features a self-sealing housing with a powerful magnetic probe locked in place. The main body incorporates a sealed port which closes every time the center chip collector is removed. The magnet collects metal debris which in turn is your signal that something isn't right inside the engine. A neat idea, and it works too!

19 K&N's STUBSTACK: The air that flows into your carburetor often takes the form of a tumbling, turbulent mess instead of a straight and calm entry. And the root of this problem isn't the carburetor. It's the choke horn and the air cleaner which surrounds the carburetor. That's why racers invariably remove the carburetor choke horn and smooth the entries into the carburetor venturis. Unfortunately, milling a choke horn isn't very practical in a street car. K&N Engineering's "Stubstack" solves the problem. The Stubstack is designed to decrease the airflow restriction around a stock Holley choke horn. In practice, the polyurethane Stubstack fits inside the air cleaner housing and slides down tightly over the choke horn. How much is it worth in terms of performance? In a typical application, a Stubstack will increase the carburetor airflow by as much as 40 cfm (on an 850 cfm Holley carburetor). Smaller carbs, such as 650 cfm models, will see gains of approximately 28 cfm. Typically, a 450 cubic-inch powerplant with an 850 cfm carburetor will see gains of six to seven horsepower along with similar torque gains when the Stubstack is installed.

20 ROCKER STUDS: Stock big-block Chevy rocker arm studs are too short. There isn't enough thread on the bottom of the stud to anchor the stud in the cylinder head, and there isn't enough thread on the top side to accommodate a longer valve stem. This isn't a big problem with iron heads and stock valves but it becomes critical with aluminum castings. ARP offers a wide range of aircraft-quality studs to solve the problem. Check your local speed shop or auto supply for ARP bolts, nuts, studs and other assorted fasteners.

21 CARB SPACER CLEARANCE: When adding a carburetor spacer, think about the overall air cleaner height. Now, it should come as no surprise that hood clearance is critical—especially when a spacer is added. Under no circumstances should the carburetor-to-hood clearance be sacrificed. If the carburetor air horn is moved too close to the hood, then the airflow and fuel metering can become restricted. In simple terms if a shorter air cleaner is used with a spacer, then you are gaining in one area and losing in another.

22 SPRING DAMPER FAILURE:
Valve spring damper failure is more common than we'd like to think (especially on high lift, radical-profile camshafts). Occasionally, a damper will physically "unwind" and the lower portion of the assembly will work its way between two lower coils of the outer spring. Naturally, this stacks the spring into coil bind. One easy solution to this problem is to inspect the spring, inner spring and damper carefully before installation. You might find that some valve springs have added "flashing" on the spring ends (this is quite common on some dampers). If that's the case with your spring(s), use a small die grinder and very carefully smooth over the burrs. Similarly, some dampers have very sharp edges on the "flats." The life of the damper can be improved by gently deburring and chamfering this section.

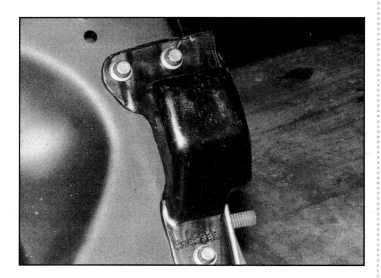

23 TAPERING MOTOR MOUNTS:
The next time you have your engine out, take the time to taper the ends of motor mount bolts. When tapered, they slip in (actually thread in) much easier. Bolts with conventional flat ends take forever to install through the motor mount holes. To obtain the taper, simply dress the bolts in your bench grinder. Many new OEM motor mount bolts are tapered just for this reason.

24 CAM BOLTS:
Here's a little tidbit for you: Check each bolt that is used to fasten the cam gear

to the cam to ensure that it doesn't bottom-out in the cam. If it does, you know what happens next: The cam sprocket wobbles and takes an unscheduled vacation. In most cases, the threaded holes in the cam are the right depth, the sprocket is the correct thickness and the bolts are correct when they come out of the box. The problem usually occurs when a cam or gear is re-machined for a button or a thrust washer.

25 TRIAL-FIT HEADERS:
Before you send off a new set of headers for coating, test-fit them in your car! Not that long ago, we received a set of name brand, high quality headers for a very common application (first-generation Camaro with a big block). Unwittingly, we didn't trial-fit the headers before they were sent off for coating. When they returned, we found that our new headers hit (a) the starter (b) the passenger side bellhousing (c) the steering pitman arm (d) the clutch linkage. By the way, another set of headers from the same manufacturer fit like a glove.

26 MAGNAFLUX PULLEYS:
It's not a bad idea to Magnaflux crank pulleys (or even water pump pulleys). We've seen them cracked or broken before. And we just had a call from a buddy who lost a pulley (along with the radiator hoses, belts, water pump pulley, and the water

pump) when the crank pulley exploded on his Crew Cab dually (on the way home from the U.S. Nationals, no less). Naturally, the pulley decided to take its vacation in the middle of nowhere.

27 INSULATED SPACERS:
Some carb spacers are manufactured with materials that have an insulating effect. These spacers decrease the amount of heat that is transferred from the intake manifold to the carburetor

(particularly the throttle plate and main body). The use of an insulating spacer reduces the fuel temperature inside the carburetor. The end result, of course, is a denser fuel charge to the manifold, which in turn creates more horsepower. And one of the best insulating materials to use for a spacer is plywood. The thin layers of laminated wood, bonded together with resin, form a natural heat sink. The spacer offered by Moroso features top-quality hardwood plywood with a sheet of phenolic resin-impregnated paper bonded to both sides. Finally, plywood spacers are easy to modify to suit a given manifold for optimum performance.

28 REMOVING ALTERNATOR: Over

the years, it's been common practice to ditch the alternator if a car was set up for drag racing. Trouble is, most of us followed the trend like sheep—blindly. If a battery is fully charged, then the alternator only has to supply enough current to maintain the charge. Typically, this amounts to 7-8 amps or less. Translated into horsepower loss, we're talking about something in the neighborhood of 1/3 horsepower to turn the thing. Of course, there's a bit more. And that's the situation that exists with the latest high-powered ignition

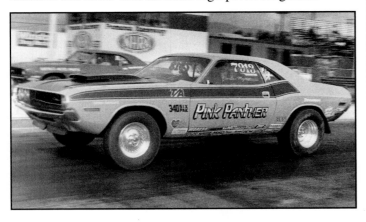

systems. Without an alternator, they can take a fully charged battery (13.6 volts) down to less than 10 volts in one quarter-mile pass. It doesn't take a brain surgeon to figure out that an alternator can maintain the battery voltage that allows the high-powered buzz boxes to maintain the highest levels of horsepower. This is probably why more and more Pro Stock racers are adding alternators to their cars. Think about it before you remove yours, or consider putting it back on.

29 COMPRESSION LIMITS: When

thinking about the compression ratio of an engine and the octane of gasoline, there are some variables that you should consider. Here's the rundown:

• A higher compression ratio requires higher octane fuel
• More spark advance requires higher octane fuel
• Lower humidity requires higher octane fuel
• Higher altitude allows the use of lower octane
• Leaning of the air/fuel ratio requires the use of higher octane

30 ALCOHOL FUEL: When selecting cylinder

heads for an alcohol-fueled application, remember that the volume of alcohol required to maintain a 1.00 brake specific number on the dyno is much greater than the fuel volume for a gasoline powerplant (which typically has a .40 brake specific). Because of that, heads with a greater runner size compensate for the oxygen that is displaced by the alcohol flowing through the ports.

31 HEADER BOLTS: After you've installed

new headers (and especially gaskets) on your engine, warm it up and re-tighten the header bolts. Do it again after another cycle. Once the engine has been through one or

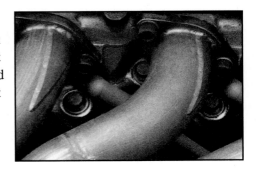

two heat & cool cycles, the bolts will always loosen because the gasket is compressing and expanding while it sets. Once it sets, the gasket will remain a constant width.

32 PREHEATING OIL: The diesel truck

bunch has been doing this for years, but only recently have enthusiasts caught on. The idea is to preheat the engine oil before the engine is fired. Even multi-grade oils can become tough to pump when cold. Because of this, the pressures can be out of control. Things like oil filters can blow off, bearings can be scuffed due to lack of lube and countless other problems can creep up. A preheater solves the problem (and in many applications, saves tremendous grief and aggravation) by warming the oil. Hamburger Oil Pans sell a slick glue-on "blanket warmer" that fits to the bottom of the pan, while Moroso and other companies sell warmers that can be installed inside the pan or sump. Once installed, simply plug 'em into the closest 110-volt outlet. In about 1/2 hour, the oil will be up to operating temperature.

33 VALVE STEM SEALS: You've just spent megabucks for a perfect cylinder head redo. You specified close tolerance bronze guides on both the intake and exhaust side. No problem. Simply button up the heads and run them. Unfortunately, valve stem seals come into play. When bronze wall guides are installed, some applications don't require seals. Others do. If you're in doubt, consider this: The exhaust valve runs hotter than the intake. Because of that, oil seldom leaks by the bronze guide into the combustion chamber. On the other hand, the cooler intake does allow some oil seepage into the chamber. The result can be minor oiling or worse, detonation. From past experience, we've found that a quality (conventional) valve stem seal on the intake guide is all that is required. No seal is used on the exhaust guide. The engine won't rain oil, but on the other hand, the guide will not be starved for lubrication.

34 PUSHROD LENGTH: Never overlook the fact that pushrods of the wrong length can wreak havoc on the rocker arm geometry, adversely affect the amount of lift and even contribute to valve guide wear in the engine. A number of factors can influence pushrod length and valvetrain geometry. Included are the installation of a smaller base circle cam, a decked block, installation of lash caps, installation of non-stock length lifters, custom length valves, altering the valve seat depth. If any of these items have been included in your engine, then the pushrods could be far too short. To measure the correct pushrod length, try a set of adjustable measuring pushrods.

35 1320 PISTONS: Before you spend big dollars on pistons for your street car, remember that many aftermarket forged pistons are designed for drag racing *only*. Not only are these pistons extremely light, they also often use different alloys of aluminum and may need large piston-to-wall clear-ances. As an example, a factory-type forging will normally have a piston-to-wall dimension of between .005" to .006" (or less). Because of the expansion rate of the aluminum used in some aftermarket pistons, the piston to wall dimensions may

exceed .010". What's wrong with this figure? The engine can literally rattle itself to death when cold. Skirt wear increases and ring sealing fades.

36 REPLACING CLUTCH FANS: Before you contemplate swapping your genuine, made-in-Detroit clutch fan for a generic version, give this some consideration: Many OEM clutch fans not only de-clutch with speed, they have a built-in thermostat that senses heat, which in turn de-clutches the fan. The majority of aftermarket jobber fan clutches do not have this provision.

37 FAN DISTANCE: The distance between the radiator and the fan is more critical to cooling than you might first think. How close to the radiator should the fan be? The distance from the forward edges of the fan blades to the radiator should not exceed two inches for proper cooling. In short, the closer you come (say, one inch), the better the cooling will be.

38 LUCKY CARB SPACERS: Dart Machinery offers a slick line of cloverleaf--shaped carburetor spacers that combine the best features of a four-hole and an open spacer. The cloverleaf shape closely matches the shape of an open plenum single plane intake manifold and provides a smooth transition from the carburetor base plate to the runners. Check it out. It might combine the best of both worlds for your application.

39 WRIST PIN LOCKS: Here's another tip on wrist pin locks or retainers: Never, ever, reuse them (Tru Arcs or Spiral Locks) once they have been run. You're gambling thousands of dollars' worth of engine components against hardware that costs nickels. By the way, if your pistons have been prepped for use with double Tru Arcs, install them with the sharp edges facing out.

40 UPSIDE-DOWN COOLERS: Did you know that there's a right and a wrong direction to mount coolers (engine oil, transmission, etc.)? Cooler mounting is particularly critical when it comes to the location of the inlet and outlet ports. No heat exchanger (radiators included) works well if the liquid side is filled with air. Coolers should never be mounted so that both the inlet and outlet ports are on the bottom. The best method is to have the ports on the top. If this isn't possible, the next best scenario has

the cooler mounted on its side so that the ports are arranged horizontally.

41 OIL SEPARATION: If you've set up your car for corner or cone racing, you might find that the lateral acceleration forces can overcome a breather's ability to control oil. In short, oil can pour into the intake manifold through the breather lines. To solve the problem, try stuffing Scotchbrite® into the breather hose (or metal pipe). The

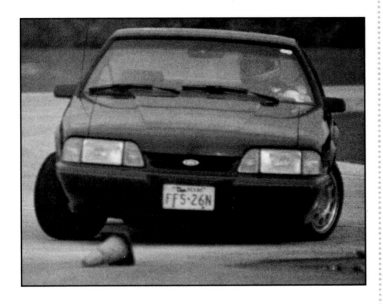

Scotchbrite® acts as an oil separator and your engine won't rain oil. By the way, this tip also works for drag race cars with oil pan evacuation systems which rain oil on burnouts (in this case the oil actually fills the lines while braking after the burnout).

42 TORQUING HEAD STUDS: Head studs should never be installed with more than 10 foot-pounds of torque (five foot-pounds is usually the practical limit). More than that will distort the deck and create head gasket problems. Install the stud with a correct stud and bearing lock (or mount) epoxy.

43 HOT HEADED: When installing a thermostat with a rating of less than 180° in a late-model fuel-injected automobile (it doesn't matter if it's a mass flow or speed density system), keep in mind that the computer will compensate for cold running and adjust the mixture. And yes, it will make the mixture "fatter," hence a poor running combination. When changing to a thermostat colder than 180°,

then the chip has to be changed.

44 STEEL MOPAR CRANKS: Scouring the wrecking yards for a steel 440 Mopar crank? Try looking under the hood of 1973 and earlier New Yorkers and Imperials. They came equipped with them and we all know that a 440 from a big old New Yorker costs a lot less than one from a GTX (same crank though!).

45 CAM LUBE: Most cam break-in lubricants contain molybdenum disulfide. This is the best stuff for cam break-in. But remember that they can easily plug an oil filter within 20 minutes of operation. When the filter is plugged, it will typically bypass, and the result will be problems for the engine. After breaking in a new camshaft (or a new engine), replace the filter after about 20 minutes of running time.

46 SEAL HEAD BOLTS: On engines such as the small-block Chevy, cylinder head bolts thread directly into the deck surface. And the majority of these head bolt holes are exposed to the waterjacket. Don't forget to apply sealant to the threads. Otherwise, you'll have a coolant leak that will be impossible to find.

47 RUST NEVER SLEEPS: If you have a cam or a crankshaft that has been sitting dormant for some time, you might find a bit of rust on the journals. But before you throw it in the garbage, consider that, according to Stahl Cams (1513 Mt. Rose Avenue, York, PA 17403), the rust can be polished off using 600-grit sandpaper. Use even, gentle pressure to prevent scouring.

48 CHECK COIL BIND: Before installing a set of larger-than-stock ratio rockers in your engine (as an example, adding 1.6:1 rockers in place of 1.5:1 rockers), carefully check for coil bind at the valve spring, especially in applications with stock or stock spec valve springs. You need at least 0.40" clearance between the springs at maximum lift.

49 OIL PAN TRASH: Before you install your brand-new oil pan, have a look inside the pan. You might be surprised to find a considerable amount of welding trash inside the pan. Clean it carefully and when you think that

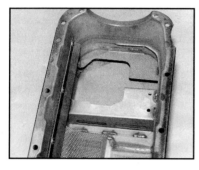

it's clean enough, run a magnet around the inside crevices. If you find metal junk inside, it's not clean enough. Do this on OEM-built pans as well as aftermarket steel and aluminum units. Obviously, a magnet won't work on an aluminum pan, but be sure to clean out any oil pan trash you find.

50 HEIGHT MICS: Need a height micrometer and can't afford one? Although they are very useful tools, some are pretty expensive. If you don't have enough in your budget, take a close look at the back end of your dial caliper. The ruler can be used as a height mic in a pinch.

51 ROCKER ARM SLOTS: When installing an aftermarket, high-lift camshaft on an engine with stamped-steel, stud-mounted rockers, be sure to check the rocker arm slot that allows the rocker to pivot at maximum lift. According to Crane Cams, there should be approximately 0.60" of additional travel left in this slot when the valve is at maximum lift. At the same time, be sure that the rocker arm contacts only the valve tip, and not the valve spring or retainer.

52 CRANE'S PUSHRODS: When buying pushrods, bigger isn't always better. You have to consider the overall weight of the pushrod—and that includes

the oil pumping through it. For example, a large 7/16-inch pushrod has a larger inside diameter. When you consider that Chevrolet pushrods are always full of oil when the engine is in operation, the larger pushrods also increase the weight of the oil alone by 17%. So what's the solution? Take a look at the new one-piece pushrods from Crane Cams. Cold forged from aircraft-quality 4130 chrome moly steel tubing, the "Pro Series" pushrod does not have press-on or welded tips. This technique creates an end that is actually heavier in thickness and stronger than the tubing wall itself. In terms of size, the new pushrods feature .083-inch walls with a finished length within + or – .005-inch per pushrod. In the end, the new wave pushrods are lighter and stronger.

53 MINI STARTERS: If you need some extra room in your engine compartment and want to eliminate some excess weight, check out the new high-torque mini starter. Many enthusiasts and racers are switching to them for these advantages. But there has been some concern as to whether or not they can be adjusted like conventional starters. Well, they can. The new mini starters also include shim packs to move the pinion up and out, just like the big ones.

54 CHECKING MANIFOLD BOLTS: How many of you check the bolts on your intake manifold after the engine has been heated and cooled several

times? If you have, you might find that several of the bolts are simply finger-tight. No, you didn't forget to torque them. As the engine cycled, the gasket compressed and the bolts loosened. To prevent this, re-torque the hard-ware after the engine has heated and cooled down a couple of times.

55 CARB SET-SCREWS: If you have a weird combination of spacers and/or gaskets under your carburetor and can't find a stud of the correct length, try using set screws. They are available in varying lengths, making them ideal for carb stud use. On the plus side, set screws are easy to install—simply because they come equipped with a female Allen-head hex on one end. On the minus side, set screws must be coarse thread to match your intake manifold (regular carb studs have a coarse and a fine thread end). As a result, you'll have less clamping power at the carburetor base.

56 ROCKER NUTS: Tucked away in the Crane catalog are rocker nuts, and if you run a stock stamped-steel rocker arm, they should be right up your alley. The idea behind them is to deflect the pressure-fed oil to the rocker arm pivot ball. In the end, the pivot ball runs cooler and has superior lubrication. By the way, the correct name for these is "Posi Stop® with Oil Deflectors." They're available in both 3/8-inch and 7/16-inch sizes.

57 INSTALLING CAMS: Some guys are always playing with camshafts—advancing them, retarding them and generally messing around to find the right combination. There's absolutely nothing wrong with that, except it takes a bunch of trial-and-error to get right. A good shortcut is to hook up a compression gauge to the engine once you've advanced or retarded the cam. With the carburetor locked in a full open position, move the cam timing around until you obtain the highest cranking pressure on the gauge. In most cases, this means that the cam is installed in the best position.

58 SPRING HEIGHT: Different retainers can mean different valve spring installed heights. And different valve locks can move the spring height up or down. Because of the variables involved (retainers-locks-springs-shims), the whole valve spring installed height situation can get real murky. Fortunately, the folks at Crane have come up with a retainer height checking tool. It allows you to determine which retainer and which locks can be used on your application. By using this system, you can adjust the spring height to suit your combination. It's another one of those "why didn't I think of that" tools.

59 VITAL VISCOSITY: Which oil viscosity is right for your car? According to Torco Racing Oil, the following is the right lube for the specified situation:

Race Application	Viscosity
Blown Nitro	70
Blown Alcohol	60
Blown Gas	50
Normally aspirated alcohol	50
Normally aspirated gasoline	20W50
Circle track alcohol	50

Drag racing w/pump gas	10W40
Propylene oxide enhanced gas	20W50
Nitrous oxide and gasoline	50
Endurance road racing	20W50
Endurance off-road racing	20W50
Circle track endurance events	20W50
Maximum horsepower, normally aspirated gasoline **	5W30 or 5W40
Maximum horsepower, normally aspirated alcohol **	5W50

**NOTE: In these maximum horsepower applications, the suggestions are based upon the fact that synthetic oils are used.

60 ROCKER RATIOS: One area many enthusiasts tend to forget about are the rocker arms. In most cases, however, the ratio of factory rocker arms will often be way off. Using a small-block Chevy as an example, OEM specs call for a rocker ratio of 1.5:1. This simply means that the rocker arm will multiply the camshaft lobe lift by 1.5 times. If the lobe lift on a small-block camshaft is .400" on both the intake and exhaust lobes, multiply it by the rocker ratio of 1.5. The gross valve lift should be .600". Unfortunately, a stock stamped-steel rocker ratio might only

be 1.43:1 or less. As a result, the gross valve lift works out to .572". The valvetrain effectively lost about 5% of the lift. This only gets worse as the lobe lift numbers increase (camshaft becomes more radical). The least expensive option is to check a bunch of available rockers until you find 16 that have the highest effective ratio and are relatively close to one another. To do this, you'll have to install one solid lifter on one camshaft lobe. Slowly (and carefully) tighten the rocker arm to

zero lash. Next, install a dial indicator to read off of the valve stem side of the rocker arm. Manually turn the engine through one complete revolution. Compare this gross (zero lash) figure to your camshaft specifications. You might be surprised to find that the numbers don't correspond. To verify the figures, either check the number with your cam spec card or check the lift at the lifter and multiply the number by your rocker ratio. This number is the theoretical gross valve lift. In many situations, a factory rocker arm will have a ratio that is significantly less than you imagined. As mentioned previously, most small-block rockers check at between 1.4:1 and 1.47:1. Few attain the advertised ratio of 1.5:1. To correct the problem, you can either rummage through boxes of new rockers until you find a a perfect set, or you can install a set of aftermarket rockers from a reputable high performance manufacturer. If you install aftermarket rockers, be absolutely certain to verify the ratio. Hi-Po parts aren't always perfect either (see Tip # 147).

61 SETTING VALVE LASH: Is there a difference in lash procedure between an engine equipped with stock rockers and one equipped with roller rockers? None in terms of lash numbers, but there is one thing you have to remember. When lashing valves with OEM rockers, you can sometimes fudge and slide the feeler gauge in on a bit of an angle (although we don't recommend it). This isn't possible with a roller tip rocker. If your engine has roller rockers, be certain that you slide the feeler gauge in a straight line between the rocker tip and the top of the valve. In any case, the idea is to use a "Go-No-Go" system. In other words, if the cam company calls for .024" lash, then a .024" feeler gauge will fit, but a .025" gauge won't. After some practice with your particular combination, you'll get a real "feel" for the correct lash. Some people like a "tight" pull on the feeler gauge, others don't. It's a matter of personal preference.

62 MORE VALVE LASH: When dealing with aluminum cylinder heads and/or aluminum cylinder blocks, cold lash numbers can vary greatly from the hot figures. Why does this happen? Simply because aluminum expands much more than cast iron when hot. Because of this, valve lash figures are decidedly different with aluminum engines. Although it's difficult to provide hard and fast numbers for all cam and engine combinations, Chevrolet offers this advice: "Cold lash all aluminum engines .010" tighter than hot lash specifications." Generally speaking, you can use this as a starting point. Some aluminum head/iron block combinations are very close to an all-iron engine in

terms of cold lash while others might be anywhere from .005" to .010" tighter. Your best bet is to contact your cam grinder and ask for a specific cold lash number for your exact combination.

63 HARMONIC BALANCERS: A balancer is a balancer, right? Wrong! Harmonic balancers or torsional dampers are precision pieces of equipment. Because of NHRA regulations, a large number of race-bred harmonic balancers have been introduced into the performance community. One of the slickest aspects of these trick dampers is the fully degreed main body. This allows for very simple valvetrain adjustment and makes ignition timing a snap. Unfortunately, these balancers might be too expensive for many street/strip enthusiasts. Is there another option? Years ago, racers had their balancers degreed. This was a machining process where the external ring of the balancer was either partially marked off and numbered or totally marked and numbered. B&B Performance manufactures fully degreed Chevrolet balancers—all based upon new Chevy cores. The B&B pieces are machined so that they are perfectly concentric. Next, the balancers are indexed—with marks in 1° increments. Bolder lines are added for 5° and 10° increments and then the actual numbers are stamped into the unit. And if you do your homework, similar balancers (from other sources) can be found for FoMoCo and Mopar applications. Although a degreed balancer installation will not allow for any fresh horsepower output in your personal combination, you can count on the fact that ignition timing and valve lash adjustments will be right on the money. And that will allow your combination to produce the serious horsepower that it was capable of all along.

64 BEADING SPRING DAMPERS: So you still have a valve spring problem. You've checked installed height, hand detailed the springs, pre-stressed them and done all of the other tricks but the springs still die. Now what? Try this old racer trick (it's been around for about twenty or more years): Try glass beading the damper after it has been deburred and chamfered. The glass

beading relieves the stress in the damper. As a result, the spring lasts longer.

65 SPRING TENSION: While installing the springs on the cylinder heads, have a close look at the relationship between the inner spring and the damper to both the cylinder head seat and the valve spring retainer. Because of different designs in springs, retainers and spring seats, there might be coil bind at these locations, but no coil bind on the outer spring. Have a close look as the engine is turned through a cycle (by hand). In the case of a poorly selected spring (or spring retainer), don't be surprised if you see coil bind on the inner spring(s). If that's the case, you have to tear everything apart and install an inner spring that suits both the application and the spring retainer.

66 SEAT PRESSURE: While you're at it, regularly check the springs with a seat pressure

tester (inexpensive models such as this Moroso unit are readily available). These testers simply slip over the rocker arm. Add a bit of muscle power and pull down on the tester. The number that appears on the beam scale (it's like a beam torque wrench) is the spring seat pressure. If the seat pressure is down from the specs, you can bet your boots that the valve springs are tired. Make it a practice to check the spring seat pressure every time the valves are lashed. The checking process adds about 15 minutes to the routine maintenance process.

67 WRIST PIN CLEARANCE: Wrist pin clearance is critical to piston (and pin) life. When it comes to wrist pin clearance, most production cast pistons operate with a figure of 0.0002-0.00025". Pistons forged with the TRW type high silicon alloys can have a hot running clearance of between 0.0015-0.0020" (the cold, installed numbers begin at 0.0002"). On the other hand, some engine builders recommend a cold clearance of as much as 0.0008" between the pin and the pin bore. Generally speaking, the correct pin-to-bore clearance figure depends upon the piston type, the form of pin retention and the operating

circumstances. In short, double check the number with your piston manufacturer.

68 POWER PAINT: The debate over painting internal engine surfaces will probably rage on forever, but if you do decide to paint the lifter valley, timing chain valley and other portions of your race engine, try the following: General Electric makes a wonder paint called Glyptal. This paint is designed for use as electric motor case paint. It is available in the common red primer color and is nearly indestructible. We've tried Glyptal and the more common anti-rust paint and from our investigations, we feel the GE product is far superior. To find it, try calling your local electrical company wholesaler and ask if they stock General Electric products. By the way, Glyptal is available in aerosols as well as the more common brush-on variety. They both work great.

69 HEADER COATINGS: If you want to wring every bit of performance from your engine, consider coating your headers. Companies such as HPC offer coating services, or companies like Hooker sell them coated.

Not only are the headers good looking and won't peel or fade, but the coatings offer better heat isolation than common paints. How good are these coatings? The high-budget Indycar guys can't be wrong.

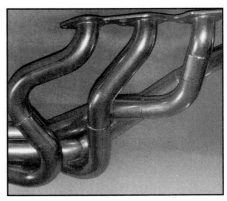

70 MANIFOLD END SEALS: Anyone who plays with Chevy V8 engines knows about the end seals for the intake manifold. They have a very nasty habit of slipping out as you torque down the intake. To solve the problem, trash the end seals completely. In their place, simply apply a thick bead of silicone. Be nice to the silicone as you install the intake (we normally let it set up slightly) and torque the manifold to specs. The result? No leaks and best of all, no goofy end seals.

71 UN-ANODIZED: Anodized aluminum engine accessories look trick. But after a few seasons of use, frequently removed pieces like air cleaners and

valve covers can get old-looking in a hurry. The anodizing is scratched and scuffed. Worse yet, you don't have access to a shop that can re-anodize the pieces. Now what? If you need to remove the anodizing, simply coat the parts with household oven cleaner. It strips the anodizing and underneath, you'll find nice virgin aluminum. You can either polish or leave it natural. Either way, it beats the look of scratched, scuffed and weathered anodizing. Just remember to wipe the oven cleaner off after a couple of minutes. Otherwise, the aluminum will be etched and therefore ready for paint only (not a bad alternative either).

72 BROKEN BLOCKS: Do you have a crack problem with your small-block Chevy—especially on the deck surface (heads & block) between the center exhaust ports? This is a common problem spot on blocks and cylinder heads, but there is one other common denominator: The place of casting. You see, blocks cast with "Hecho en Mexico" on the bellhousing flange are made in—you guessed it—Mexico. Now there's nothing wrong with that, except the grade of iron used in those south-of-the-border specials isn't up to our standards. In fact, it's lousy and because of that, Mexican-cast small-blocks should be avoided.

73 BALANCER LEAKS: If you have a leak at the nose of your engine, it may be coming from the front crank/balancer seal. What's happened is this: The spinning balancer has a groove worn on it by the oil seal.

Fortunately, you don't have to replace the balancer. Many companies (even gasket manufacturers) offer sleeve kits designed just for this dilemma. In essence, the sleeve slides over the snout of the balancer, effectively covering the groove. No major machine work is necessary. In addition, the parts are relatively cheap, and best of all, the leak will be banished forever.

74 PRESS-ON PICKUP TUBE: Installing a fresh pickup on an oil pump can be a curse—especially if the pickup tube is a press-fit such as those found on most Chevy V8 engines. While there are special tools available to press the pickup tube into the pump, you can

get your kitchen to help in the installation process. Spray the end of the pickup tube with an aerosol lube and slide it inside your freezer for an hour or so. In the meantime, slip the bare oil pump body in a pan of water and household cooking oil. Bring the pump to a boil and with the help of some oven mitts, quickly slide the cold pickup tube into the hot oil pump body. It slips on easily and usually doesn't require the use of a hammer or any special tools.

75 HEAT-TREATED PUSHRODS: So, you've found a great deal on pushrods. They are straight, look new and the price is downright reasonable. But how do you tell if they are trick, heat-treated models? Use a sharp pocketknife and scrape the wall of the pushrod. A heat-treated pushrod won't scratch, but a run-of-the-mill cheapo will.

76 RTV O.D.: RTV silicone is a versatile material. We use it in a variety of applications, but there is a point where too much is just too much. When using the stuff, be sure to use enough of the sealant, but not so much that it gums up the workings of a component you are assembling. As an example, if you use the sealant in place of intake manifold seals and use too much of the RTV, a big chunk of the silicone can dry and fall into the oil pan. As a result, it might eventually work its way into the main oil galleries and that can spell trouble. The same applies to RTV on transmission pans, rear axle covers and other locations. Use it, but don't use it to excess.

77 HEAD GASKET CHECK: You suspect that you've wiped out a head gasket in your street machine. How do you check to see if it's history? Allow the engine to cool naturally (don't try flushing it with cold water if it has overheated—you'll only aggravate the problem). When cool, fire it up and remove the radiator cap. If you spy bubbles or foaming inside the radiator, there's a good chance that a head gasket has gone south, but which side? Try removing the fan/water pump belt and drain the radiator. Remove the thermostat and start the engine again. Coolant bubbles should

appear from the side that has the wasted gasket. Now you can get to work yanking the head.

78 OIL FILTER O-RING: If you've ever had the misfortune of an oil filter leak (especially at high rpm), you'll appreciate this tip: When you remove the oil filter during an oil change, be absolutely positive that the rubber O-ring (gasket) hasn't stuck to the block surface. If it has and you install the new filter (complete with a new O-ring), you'll have an immediate, high pressure leak.

79 ANTI-SEIZE: Anti-seize compound is pretty common stuff—especially now that aluminum cylinder heads have gained widespread use (anti-seize on the spark plug threads stops galling and thread damage). But one place where it can be put to good use and seldom is, is on the water pump bolt threads. If you've ever had to remove the pump bolts on a well-used, high-mileage engine, you'll know exactly what we're talking about. Try anti-seize compound.

80 NOT-SO-MINOR PINHOLES: Before you purchase a used aluminum intake

manifold for your Chevrolet (or any other car with a built-in water cross-over), take the time to look inside the thermostat housing passage. Give it a close examination. Aluminum erosion is a problem, especially if the car in question was operated with straight water instead of contemporary coolant. Severe use (or use on a salt-water ski boat) can wreak havoc on the crossover passage, rendering it paper thin. The result can be pinholes and constant puddles of coolant on top (inside and underneath) of your intake manifold.

81 LEAKY OIL PAN: Many a rear main seal has been replaced due to leaks, but at the same time, many of those seals weren't faulty. Instead of quickly blaming the rear main seal on a leak, have a close look at the oil pan seals and gaskets. If your car leaks oil at the back of the engine, examine the main seal closely before giving it the

heave-ho. If it's dry, it might not be the culprit. We've seen a good number of oil pans that were overtightened, warping the pan rails. Go easy on that wrench when tightening pan bolts.

82 MILLING EFFECTS: When the cylinder heads on a Chevy engine are excessively milled, or if the cylinder block decks have been milled considerably, the length of the distributor is also affected. By the same token, if you use extra thick intake manifold gaskets (or spacers), the relationship between the distributor and the intake manifold changes. If that happens, then the distributor gear might not engage the camshaft gear and the oil pump driveshaft. An easy solution is to use a distributor with an adjustable collar (MSD sells them). Otherwise, you'll have to play with distributor height by milling the pad or adding spacers between the distributor and the intake manifold.

83 FROZEN DISTRIBUTOR: If you encounter a frozen distributor body, it can become an immediate source of frustration. Just how do you un-stick the thing—let alone move it to set the timing? Try wrapping an adjustable band-type oil filter wrench around the body of the distributor for more leverage. Next, squirt a small amount of penetrating fluid around the base of the distributor. Allow the penetrating fluid some time to work and then use the oil filter wrench to break it free.

84 ANTI-FREEZE MESS: No matter how careful you are, when you pull an engine out of a car, there's going to be some (and it could be a bunch if you're not careful) anti-freeze coolant that leaks out. It makes a massive mess. It's slippery. It stinks. It's hard to clean up. And your dog will die if he drinks it. To solve the problem, drive a large freeze plug into the end of the lower radiator hose and clamp it with a conventional hose clamp. If you really want to out-trick yourself, make up a special "short hose" and install it.

85 PUSHROD ENDS: Everyone knows the tip about rolling pushrods on a piece of plate glass to ensure the rods are straight. But while you're checking,

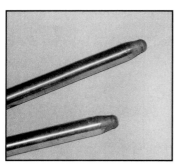

inspect the pushrod ends very carefully. The majority of pushrods feature press-in tips or ends. In some cases, these ends can work their way loose. The result is erratic valve timing and in a worse-case scenario, outright failure. If you have a pushrod that even looks slightly suspect, toss it in favor of a new one. They're too important to valvetrain life to take a chance.

86 WEEPING PLUGS: If you have a problem with block or core "soft" plugs popping out or "weeping," try this: Take some emery paper to the core plug bore in the casting. Then apply Permatex hardening sealant to both the block and the plug before installation. The result is a "glued" in place soft plug that is resistant to minor leaks.

87 PRIMING THE SUMP: If you've just rebuilt an engine with a front sump (i.e., most Fords) and you can't get the oil pump to prime, try adding some extra oil. A couple of quarts over full will work while you spin the engine over. After the oil system primes (and before you start the engine), climb underneath and drain out the extra oil.

88 STABILIZING VALVE LASH: If you have installed roller rockers or a poly-lock kit to your rockers, the lash should remain stable. Sometimes it doesn't. In most cases, it's caused by the rocker stud. Most OEM (as well as many Jobber replacement) rocker studs are not machined on the top end. High-quality aftermarket studs from fastener experts ARP have fully machined tops, while OEM studs have irregular top surfaces. As a result, the Allen head set screw can never be accurately tightened and the lash never remains stable. If you're tired of constantly setting valve lash, replace your OEM studs with high quality units.

89 RING CLEARANCES: How close can the top piston ring be relative to the piston deck surface? The actual location of the ring grooves is often

dictated by the compression height of the piston, the size and depth of the valve notches, and of course, by the overall size of the ring package. Most passenger cars will have the top ring 0.300-0.400" down from the deck surface. In an endurance engine, the top ring is typically 0.125-0.150" down while drag race applications can vary from 0.060-0.100" down from the deck (although 0.060" is cutting things close). Moving the top ring closer to the piston deck has a number of advantages, not the least of which is the "dead air" space between the top ring land and the deck. As this space is reduced (by moving the ring up), the amount of trapped combustion gases is also reduced. In the end, the combustion process is cleaned up considerably when the rings are moved upward. Horsepower increases, and by coincidence, the amount of unburned hydrocarbons goes down.

90 OILING SEIZURE: If you have experienced a seized oil pump, the root of the problem might not be so obvious. In most engines, the oil pump drive is connected to the distributor. If the distributor clamp is over-tightened (entirely possible with heavy-duty aftermarket clamps), it can physically seize the oil pump. Further to this, too much clamping power might not seize the pump, but it can cause excessive wear on the intermediate shaft.

91 JAMMED HEADS: Removing the heads on a well-used engine can be a real chore. And if you run into this problem (if you work on engines, you will), be absolutely certain that you have removed all of the head bolts before dragging out the pry bar and other heavy artillery. With the intake manifold removed, tap a large screwdriver between the block and head deck surfaces (near a dowel pin). A few taps and the screwdriver should wedge the head free from the block.

92 KNOCKING NOISES: If your Chevy V8 (or small-block Ford) has the sick sound of a knocking rod, don't be too quick to tear the engine down. Late-model Chevys and Windsor Fords don't have the world's best timing chains. Check the chain first. The sound of a loose chain whacking the chain cover is very similar to a rod knock.

On a similar note, a Chevy mechanical fuel pump can also create similar noises. Check the easy stuff before you tear down the engine.

93 CLACKING LIFTERS: You've finally determined after a lot of hunting that the clacking under the hood is a bad hydraulic lifter. But how do you know which lifter is the guilty party? It's easy to pinpoint. Shut the

engine off and yank the valve covers. Push down on each rocker arm (backward toward the pushrod). When you come to a soft rocker, you've found the problem lifter. Chances are the lifter is either starved for oil or it is bleeding down far too quickly.

94 RING GROOVE CLEARANCE: The clearance between the ring and the ring groove in the piston is extremely important. During the compression stroke, the ring drops to the bottom of the groove, eventually sealing against the machined surface. During the power stroke, the piston moves down in the bore. The ring then moves up in the groove and eventually seals against the top of the machined surface. As you can well imagine, a poor finish in the groove will not allow the ring to seal tightly. Because of this, the pressure will leak past the rear (or back) portion of the ring. Evidence of this leakage can be found in excessive heat discoloration or carbon buildup in the land area between the top and second rings.

95 MORE RING CLEARANCE: Another area that affects the above ring seal dilemma is the vertical clearance of the ring. Typically, a race or high performance piston should not exceed 0.002" vertical clearance (street cars often have clearances of between 0.002-0.004"). More than that and the ring will leak. Less than that figure and you run the risk of seizing the ring in the groove. A ring that can't turn freely in the groove will not clean carbon out of the groove, and will not be free to expand when combustion pressures enter the groove. If the piston has tight vertical clearances, then the ring back clearance figures become more important. As indicated previously, gas pressure enters the area behind the ring during combustion. In turn, this gas pressure forces the ring out, against the cylinder wall. If

there is too much back clearance (which in turn creates too much volume for the combustion gases to fill), then it takes too long for the pressure to build and force the ring outward. Naturally, a lesser amount of back clearance will increase the speed and the force at which the ring will exert pressure upon the cylinder wall. Typically, a production piston will have as much as 0.040-0.050" of back clearance. In a high performance application, the backside clearance figure can be reduced to as little as 0.020" (depending upon the ring configuration and the piston design). On the other hand, the back clearance cannot be so small that the ring protrudes past the ring land.

96 KEEPING KEEPERS: When you're removing and replacing valve springs, the biggest piece of aggravation has to be the keepers or locks. They always seem to wiggle their way out of the groove in the valve stem before you can release the spring compressor. In a worse-case scenario, the valve keepers can drop down an oil passage and be lost inside the engine forever. You know what happens next. To solve the problem, you have two choices. One is to keep a magnet close to the keepers during installation. The other is to apply a light coat of grease to the valve stem. Install the keepers in the normal fashion. They won't move because the grease holds 'em in check.

97 OIL GALLERY: The oil gallery plugs found at the back of Chevy blocks must be installed by Arnold You-Know-Who. There is no way to get 'em out without pain. Unless, of course, you take the time to heat the plugs with a torch. While they are still hot, give 'em a shot of WD-40. Once they cool, you can unscrew them with a meek 1/4-inch ratchet. At least this tip saves having to use easy-outs.

98 DAMPER BOLTS: The folks at B&B Performance offer a massive damper bolt. This doesn't seem like a big deal until you have to manhandle that big-block while precisely setting the valve lash! The B&B "Super Duty Crankshaft Snout Bolts" positively retain the Chevy damper and also feature a massive one-inch hex head. Wrenches can't slip off and neither will sockets. The internal threads are rolled rather than cut and an integral washer is incorporated into the design. The unit is manufactured from premium 4340 steel and finished with black oxide for protection. Both big- and small-block versions are available. You'll soon come to appreciate it.

99 **BLOCK CLEANING:** Once upon a time it was common to recommend laundry detergent such as Tide™ for final block cleaning. But have you ever tried rubbing wet laundry soap on your hands? The granules remain coarse for a very long period of time. Use a quality liquid dish soap instead. It has far less grit and is much friendlier to both your block and your hands while you clean up the casting. Also, try wiping the block dry with clean white (and soft) paper towels. If dirt remains on the paper towels, the block's internals are not clean enough. When finished, rinse the block with clean water, blow-dry with compressed air, and re-wipe the block with clean paper towels lightly oiled with automatic transmission fluid.

100 **HIGH GRADE FASTENERS:** Be very careful when purchasing engine hardware such as fasteners. There has been a proliferation of garbage hardware made overseas masquerading as high quality (and not cheap) grade 8 equipment. Two safe bets for items such as rod bolts, head bolts, main cap bolts, etc., are Detroit vehicle manufacturers and ARP. ARP's products are manufactured to meet rigid aerospace standards and are highly recommended.

101 **SPARK PLUG REACH:** Many cylinder heads are designed to accept 0.460" reach, tapered 14mm spark plugs (e.g. AC R45T or Champion BL-series plugs). Even though these spark plugs are all designed with a reach that measures 0.460" in length, some, such as the AC models, are actually 1-1/2 threads longer than the Champion examples. Check your heads before installing the plugs. If they're machined for AC spark plugs, then a Champion will be too short.

102 **ROCKER SHAFT SHIMS:** When using shaft-mounted rockers in an engine, the height of the shaft determines the geometry of the valvetrain. The shaft height is adjusted by adding or removing shims between the cylinder head and the rocker arm mount. Pushrod length is still important with a shaft system, but don't be tempted to make up the length difference with the shaft lash adjusters! You're just asking for geometry problems.

103 **PISTON SKIRTS:** Pistons are available with two different types of skirts— *full* skirts and *slipper* skirts. The slipper skirt piston configuration has been popularized by TRW. TRW did extensive research into the design—beginning with the vintage Offenhauser Indycar motor and extending into Detroit production (hi-po Chevys in particular). The slipper skirt has a smaller contact area (with the cylinder wall), but can be made lighter than a full skirt piston. In the case of a full skirt piston, you'll find that the skirt isn't actually round. Instead, the shape is such that only the faces on the thrust axis of the piston actually contact the cylinder wall. When compared to a slipper skirt, however, the full skirt piston will still have more contact area. Because of this, the full skirt is often easier on cylinder bores.

104 **CARB STUDS:** Have you ever considered carburetor studs? There is no question that they are required for racing, but you probably use bolt on your street machine like most people. Unfortunately, bolts that are constantly threaded in and out of a relatively fragile aluminum intake manifold are not the hot tip. ARP offers a slick stud with a quick fastening end. This piece is like a miniature NASCAR quick-start wheel stud. The threads don't get damaged during the many remove-and-replace operations and best of all they don't cost an arm and a leg. Lock washers and nuts are commonly used to secure the carb body to the stud. Unfortunately, these aren't the best

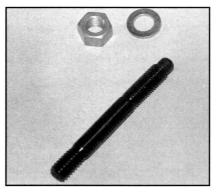

components available to fasten the carburetor. A common split lock washer doesn't do nice things to an aluminum or pot-metal carburetor base. Instead, try swapping your conventional carburetor lock washer setup for a "spinlock" nut. These flanged nuts have serrations machined into an integral washer. They don't vibrate loose and there's one less piece that can wander into the intake manifold when the carb comes off for service.

105 **BLOCK DRAINING:** The process of draining a cylinder block prior to teardown between rounds can be difficult when the engine is hot. In most cases, the factory uses a common pipe plug in the waterjacket core. More times than not, the pipe plug hex head will become rounded and you'll have to use heavy-duty vise grips to break the thing loose, often at the expense of a knuckle or some skin. To make matters worse, the plug is normally in a hard to reach location—especially in the case of a doorslammer. The solution? Swap the pipe plugs for a set of common radiator drain petcocks. Draining the water will be easier to do.

106 PORTING HEADS: When porting intake ports, use a round-headed, straight tapered burr and set the head so you can access the intake port inlet at a comfortable angle. Protect your eyes and mouth, and slowly grind the intake ports out to 1/32" of your scribe marks, extending into the port about 1". Do one side of the port at a time, and do all of the ports on one side before moving to another side. Compare your work as you do each port, taking regular measurements for comparison. For an amateur porter, this will prevent overdoing any single port and will generate a more consistent port job. Be very careful around the pushrod holes. Casting shifts may limit porting there. Once you've

ground out to within 1/32" of the scribe marks, use a pair of screw adjustable calipers or dividers and measure the width every 1/4" of each port where you have ground. Check the length and width. Carefully balance each port to one another by grinding any additional amount necessary to achieve that relationship, while working your way back to the valve bowl. Basically, you will be squaring the intake ports to increase their volume.

107 STUDS VS. BOLTS: Are studs better than bolts? Actually, both studs and bolts have advantages. Bolts are often more convenient, especially in space-restricted applications. On the down side, bolts are more likely to damage the threads in components such as cylinder blocks. Why? Simple. The torque is carried down through the body of the bolt and into the block threads. With studs, torque is applied to the nut and tends to remain there instead of being transmitted through the body of the stud into the block threads. While the tension load is still carried in the body of the stud, the additional stress due to torque is not held by the block.

Finally, bolts can cause damage to threads due to repeated teardowns and reassemblies.

108 THERMOSTAT BYPASS: Big-block Chevys are probably the second most popular powerplant in the world (second only to their little brothers, the small-block). If you run a rat motor and you don't use a thermostat, you can eliminate one extra hose on the powerplant. The thermostat bypass hose that normally runs from the intake manifold to the water pump can be disconnected. Aside from cleaning up your act, it allows for easier water pump removal if you tend to play with camshafts on a regular basis.

109 CRANK RUN-OUT: It is generally believed that if a crankshaft can be turned in the bearing saddles (with the bearings and main caps in place), it is straight. Maybe so—if you're lucky. Don't bet your engine on a quick test like this. Instead, do it the right way: Measure the runout with a dial indicator. It guarantees that the crank is straight (or bent!).

110 VALVE COVER DRIPPERS: If you have a big-block Chevrolet and you run stock (or stock-type rocker arms), you should definitely use a set of valve covers with "drippers." These are the funny-looking pointy objects spot-welded to the top of the valve cover. Their purpose is to direct excess oil that splashes onto the rockers to the rocker arm balls. When the drippers are removed, the rocker balls can become starved for oil. The result is

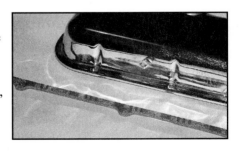

usually complete rocker arm failure (sometimes the rocker arm becomes so hot that the pushrod end fails first). Of course, if you have roller rockers, you don't need them.

111 GUIDE PLATES: Hi-po "stepped" guide plates should not be used on Dart 220 small-block Chevy cylinder heads. Dart recommends the use of Iskenderian adjustable guide plates for small blocks with stud-mounted rocker arms. Adjustable guide plates solve the problem of aligning the pushrods and valve stem tips with wider-than-stock intake ports.

112 WET SUMP:

Oil moves around a lot inside a powerplant. At any given moment in a stock, unmodified engine, there might be one quart of oil in the filter, one quart in the valvetrain, another quart thrashing around in the crankcase and at least one quart "glued" to the crank due to a phenomenon called "the rope effect." Now, if you've been keeping count, that means that there could conceivably be less than one quart of oil in the crankcase or oil pan sump. But that's not all. A dyno test is a static evaluation. The engine doesn't move. In a vehicle, it does—moving with the car as it accelerates. Depending upon the application, this creates a whole new set of variables—things like oil never returning to the sump, oil climbing the back "wall" of the oil

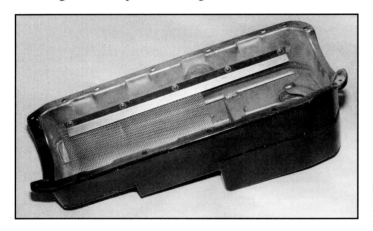

pan into the cam gallery and oil being trapped in the lifter or valve cover valleys. Because of these facts, a properly designed, state-of-the-art wet sump can solve most (if not all) of these problems. Currently, custom pans designed to combat these problems are available from Hamburger, Moroso, Canton, Milodon and others. Horsepower will increase and so will reliability.

113 OIL LEVEL:

Have you ever checked your dipstick? Sure you have—every few days if you are a fanatic about your pride 'n joy. But have you ever checked to ensure that the dipstick is correctly marked? Next time you do an oil change, fill the filter completely before you screw it onto the block. Add the appropriate amount of oil to the crankcase (obviously taking the amount the filter holds out of the equation) and let the oil drain into the sump. The drain time can vary but give it an hour to be safe. Then pull the stick and see what it says. If it's out a bunch, remark the dipstick. If the oil level is right up there, an extra quart should be perfect. Wrong! Too much oil is just as bad as too little oil, and when the oil level is too high, it can interfere with the crankshaft

counterweights. This results in excessive drag and also creates foaming inside the oil pan. Foamed oil does not lubricate as well and as a result, your engine could be an accident waiting to happen.

114 BLOCK HONING:

When power honing a cylinder block (especially big-block Chevys), consider the following tip courtesy of Kip Martin Racing (Phoenix, AZ): Mill a relief (approximately 5/8 inch) around the bottom of each cylinder bore. This allows the hone to make a full pass through the block without bottoming, but only if the CK-10 (Sunnen Cylinder King) hone bronze guide shoe is ground flush with the bottom of the guide holder. If you don't believe us, examine your big block. You will find that it is virtually impossible to make a complete pass down the cylinder bores without this minor modification.

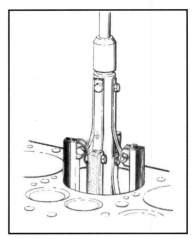

115 VALVE LENGTH:

Many aftermarket exhaust valves for the big-block Chevy are not stock length—even if they're advertised as such. Instead, they are 0.050 inch longer than stock. When using a dished aftermarket retainer with OEM Chevy valves (which feature a 0.220" tip instead of the more common 0.250" tip), there is a chance that the rocker arm will physically hit the retainer. Keep this in mind when checking rocker arm geometry.

116 CRANK MODS:

If you have a crank with skewed dimensions but it is still considered salvageable, let an expert tune it up. Crankshaft

Specialists (280 Tillman, Memphis, TN 38112) can repair little problems using a hard chrome process. In essence, they can bring a damaged crank back to standard (or custom) dimensions and at the same time can improve the structural integrity of the assembly. They can also offset grind (for a stroke increase or decrease) or rework the crank in a special "NHRA Stock/Super Stock legal Rules Rider" configuration (which amounts to indexing the crank with .013 inches more stroke). We've used this company before and the work is top notch.

117 VALVE GUIDES: A valve guide's sole purpose in life is to guide the valve as it moves up and down. In doing so, it takes quite a beating from the valve stem. Using high lift camshafts only serves to compound the problem. The sideways movement of the valve will cause a stock guide to wear quickly. Because of this, bronze wall guides are extremely popular with performance enthusiasts. Winona and K-Line both offer outstanding bronze

guides for any Detroit application. Wear is reduced significantly and excessive guide oiling is stopped.

118 DUAL-PURPOSE RINGS: The hot tip as far as street 'n strip piston rings are concerned is as follows: In a hi-po application, stick to the basics—a plasma moly top ring, a cast-iron second ring and a standard tension oil ring. If you want to get "racy," there's a great option that you might want to consider. Try using Speed Pro's "back-cut second ring." This operation reduces the radial dimensions of the ring slightly, which in turn provides for less drag. This can correspond with better ring sealing and more horsepower. As far as the oil ring is concerned, don't mess with any of the special drag-race-only, low-tension pieces— they don't work well on the street.

119 OIL PAN STUDS: One of the neatest ideas to come along over the years are oil pan studs. Anyone who's pulled a pan while the engine is still in the car can attest to the grief of re-fitting the thing to the engine. With studs in the place of regular bolts, lining up the pan is much easier. No more fighting with bolts and misaligned threads. Not only do these slick little kits make pan installation a breeze, they also help prevent warped pan rails.

120 TORQUING HEAD BOLTS: When torquing head bolts on an engine (in fact, this applies to all fasteners), it is advisable to torque the fastener on the last full rotation of the nut or bolt. Using a socket wrench, tighten the fastener until you feel there is approximately one more full rotation left before the fastener becomes fully secured (in this case it's better to have an estimate that's looser rather than tighter). If you are using a click-type torque wrench, set it for a figure that is less than the required torque. All fasteners should be brought up in equal torque values in stages. Pick a set of figures such as 20%, 40%, 60%, 80% (these are percentages of the full torque figure) and then full torque. Be sure to follow the torque

sequence determined by the OEM manufacturer. The idea is to equally tighten the fasteners (such as those found in a cylinder head or intake manifold sequence) in a similar manner, effectively sneaking up on the desired torque value.

121 SUPERCHARGER BACKFIRE: A common problem with supercharged engines is a violent backfire that hammers the pop-off valve open—occasionally flames shoot out. According to some high performance engine experts, the cause could be insufficient spark lead. Try locking out the centrifugal advance and running 32-34 degrees of initial timing. Since supercharged engines usually have compression ratios of less than 8:1, the starter shouldn't have any trouble cranking the engine over. If it does, an adjustable timing control can be added to retard the spark during timing.

122 BLOWER PULLEYS: Before you blast off to test your newly installed supercharger, check the pulley alignment between the super-charger and the crankshaft pulleys. Factory machining tolerances and cam chain gears can cause slight misalignments that guarantee drive belt trouble. Correct any misalignment by

machining the pulley spacer or shimming as necessary. Shown here is the 8-groove pulley drive from Vortech. If you have been having problems keeping the belt on, you will need to contact a Vortech dealer for this upgrade.

123 BELT ALIGNMENT: Because of their high performance nature, many a street/strip car has pitched its fan belt in the upper reaches of the rpm range. Don't be too quick to blame either the belts or the various pulleys. It could simply be a matter of alignment. Sight down the respective pulleys and if they are out of alignment, the pulleys can be shimmed (from the backside) to perfection. Vary the washer thickness to compensate for the mismatch—it will work wonders for alignment and belt life.

124 AIR FLOWING CLEANERS: Over 20 years ago, Chevrolet spent quite a bit of money researching airflow and how it relates to induction systems. While there were many production lessons learned,

the big news for the racers concerned the air cleaner. Everyone knows that the fourteen-inch open element Bow Tie air cleaner is an efficient piece—there are at least a dozen aftermarket clones of that very same stock unit. Unfortunately some of these clones aren't as efficient as the real thing. Before purchasing an air cleaner, compare the shape to the vintage Chevrolet design. It might be worth your while to use the aftermarket lid and filter, but combined with a legit, high-flow Chevy base.

125 USING HEAD STUDS: Are you fed up with head bolts? Are you going to make the switch to head studs and eliminate the wear and tear on the cylinder block deck threads? Before you lock the

bottom row of bolts onto your engine, check the fit of the headers. In many cases (especially those without trick "high port" exhausts), the bottom row of head studs interferes with the header flange. This makes it virtually impossible to completely tighten the header bolts. The only solution is to shorten the studs slightly (in most cases the studs are actually longer than a conventional bolt) or to replace the bottom row of studs with standard bolts.

126 SUPER BELT: Like other components in the automobile, the lowly fan belt can be found in varying stages of quality. Most vintage applications still rely upon V-belts—the industry standard for decades. Fortunately, Dayco decided (a number of years ago) to use NASCAR as a test bed for new V-belt technology. Different configurations as well as various materials were tested, with the result being the latest Dayco production belt assembly. These belts are manufactured with special synthetic fabrics in the tension area. Additionally, they have a high tensile strength and feature a "greater compressed area" (in English, this translates into less slippage at high pulley speeds). All of this adds up to a belt that is less prone to turning inside out or flipping at high rpm. Once a belt has flipped, it will soon depart, and you know what happens next.

127 DUAL-PLANE MANIFOLDS: Dual-plane intake manifolds have made a serious comeback, and they are the hot ticket for many street applications. They make terrific low-end torque in the bottom of the powerband. If you find that your combination has plenty (or too much) torque on the bottom end, you might consider milling the plenum. This operation sacrifices bottom-end torque, but at the same time, it moves the powerband upward. When remov-ing the plenum, make sure you leave at least .250" of material at the plenum floor. In addition to this, the jetting will likely require some fine tuning. The result? A major improvement in top-end horsepower.

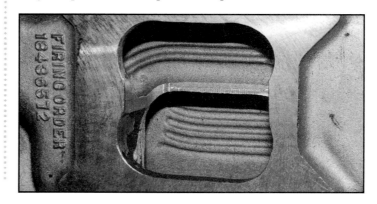

128 **ALIGNING PORTS:** Let's assume that you've just port-matched your intake manifold to the gasket. Similarly, the heads have also been matched to the shape of the gasket. But how do you guarantee that the intake ports will line up with the head ports? Carefully enlarge all of the intake manifold bolt holes by two drill size numbers (a steady hand is required). Next, fashion a "tool" from a piece of welding rod or coat hanger. This "tool" must have a small J -shaped hook at one end. Install the manifold in the normal manner—sans bolts. Before the sealant has time to dry, run the J-shaped tool through the plenum into each runner/port. By carefully feeling the port alignment, you can then shift the manifold fore and aft to obtain the perfect match. A small flashlight can also be used on some of the more accessible ports. When the match is complete, install the hardware and torque to specs.

129 **TIMING CHAIN WEAR:** Before you purchase a trick timing chain, give this some consideration: Roller timing chains are subject to a phenomenon called "chordal action." Basically, the chain turns into an "S" shape during operation. As engine speed increases, so does the chordal action. The result is often shortened chain life and worse yet, inaccurate valve timing. Further to this, the chordal action is enhanced by stiff valve springs. What's the solution? Try one of the inexpensive, large pin link-belt chains that are currently available. Not only are they less costly, they live longer!

130 **LIFTER VALLEYS:** Lifter valley trays have been around for years, and they're still a great idea for a street or strip machine. In essence, these trays or baffles isolate the base of the intake manifold from hot oil in the lifter valley. The result is a cooler intake charge and of course, more available horsepower. Installation is literally a snap—the trays simply snap into place. We should point out that trays or baffles are available from Moroso for small- and big-block Chevys as well as LA series Mopars. The Moroso trays also retain the lifter in the event of failure. In addition, GM sells a one-piece tray for big-block Chevrolets.

131 **FUELING NITROUS:** The limitation of any nitrous system is the stock fuel delivery system. As horsepower increases, so does fuel volume requirements. Bolt-on nitrous kits are typically designed to operate "on the gas" at a fuel ratio of 8.75:1. This means a bsfc (brake specific fuel consumption) rate of about .69. At this bsfc, your fuel delivery system must be capable of delivering a minimum of 148 lph (liters per hour) of fuel, at an elevated pressure, to handle a 150 horsepower kit (this is on a stock 5.0-liter Mustang engine, but similar thinking applies to all other types). Shown here is a nitrous upgrade system for 5.0 Mustangs that upgrades the fuel

system and doubles the horsepower of the basic N.O.S. 5.0 kit. It includes a Bosch fuel pump, a larger nitrous jet, and all necessary hardware. Contact your local N.O.S. dealer.

132 **VALVE COVERS:** Yanking the valve covers can sometimes be a pain: Unfasten the bolts, grab the little load bearing washers, pull the covers, run around the valve lash, re-install the covers and then fight with the hardware. Usually, it takes longer to properly line up the valve cover bolts than it does to lash the valves on a solid-lifter cam. Worse yet, too much torque on 1/4-inch bolts can either bend a steel or stamped aluminum cover into a pretzel shape, strip the threads or snap the bolt. In any case, oil leaks at the valve cover are common. Fortunately, there's a better system— one that's been around for what seems like forever. They're Dzus valve cover fasteners (sold by Moroso and other companies). Once set up, they take a quarter turn with a Phillips screwdriver to remove or replace. Due to the integral spring design, the torque numbers against the valve cover are exactly the same after every installation. Plus, the valve cover gaskets are always held in check on the cylinder head. Because of that, a normal set of cork valve cover gaskets will often outlast the engine.

133 **BEST OIL FILTER:** All oil filters are not created equal! Some filters (including some respected "name" products) are simply junk. If you don't believe us, try cutting apart three of the top name brands. Then cut apart an AC-Delco PF35 and compare them. You won't believe what you see! OEM filters are without a doubt more durable and better at sifting grit from your oil than quite a few of the popular types hyped by racing drivers. (With all that sponsorship money, wouldn't you do the same?) Bottom line?

Save yourself some money and buy some peace of mind by going with the OEM units.

134 SLICK FILTERS: More on oil filters: If you want the ultimate filter for your Chevy, check out the General's latest PF35L (P/N 25013454). This is a synthetic oil filter that can replace any conventional AC PF35 or PF25 unit. It has a 100% synthetic element which is rated at 12 microns. Compared to some of the "name" aftermarket filters, this filter can actually reduce engine wear by 75% without creating any added oil flow restriction.

135 PORTED HEADERS: Before you install a fresh set of headers on your car, take a close look at the port flange on the headers. Many models (particularly the cheap jobs) are full of welding trash and junk inside the ports. You'll find some power lurking in the engine if you take the time to deburr the header ports. This problem is actually very common, so check your headers.

136 CHECK PARTS FIRST: Recently one magazine made a bit of a flap over the poor quality of Chevy's over-the-counter crankshafts. Seems the writer was building a big-inch big block and ordered a finished 4.00-inch stroke steel crankshaft. After the crank was polished, deburred and had its oil holes chamfered, he decided to install it in the block to check dimensions. What happened? The connecting rod side clearance was completely out of whack—even though the width of the connecting rods was

right on the money. Guess what? Chevy would have gladly exchanged the crank if it had not been played with. The idea of any good engine building project is to dimensionally check your parts first. If they are right, then go on to the blueprinting and modification procedures.

137 PUSHROD FACTS: Chevrolet has recently released four new pushrods for the "rat" motor. Available in either 3/8-inch or 7/16-inch diameters, the pushrods are manufactured from case-hardened 1010 steel tubing and feature a .080-inch wall thickness. The pushrods are one-piece designs that do not have a pressed-in end. The 3/8-inch versions are available under part numbers 10134307—intake and 10134308—exhaust. 7/16-inch examples are available under part numbers 10134303 and 10067333 for exhaust and intake rods respectively. Guide plates are required.

138 MORE PUSHROD FACTS: The "ultimate" Bow Tie pushrod for the big block is a special 7/16-inch version that is manufactured from a premium grade of chrome moly steel (4130 alloy). The tubing is .080 inch thick and features one-piece construction (without add-on tips). In addition, the pushrod is case hardened. Part numbers for the pushrods are as follows: Intake—1013406; exhaust–10134305. Guide plates are required.

139 PREMIUM PUSHRODS: And finally, the last word on factory pushrods: Chevrolet has released a set of "premium" one-piece 4130 chrome moly pushrods for use in the small-block engines. These pushrods are .100 inch longer than stock (helpful when using taller than normal installed valve spring heights) and feature similar construction to the previously described fat block pieces. The small-block parts are slightly smaller in ID at 5/16 inch, but when compared to past heavy duty small-block examples, are a whopping 35% stiffer! The part number for this spring is GM #10134309.

140 ALL LOCKED UP: I once read a magazine article that mentioned that thread-locking chemicals can be used in internal engine components such as main cap fasteners, rod bolts and the like. In 20 years of racing Chevrolet V8's, this writer has never seen a Chevrolet spec advocating the use of these chemicals inside the powerplant. In fact, we have examined a small block with the red sticky goop on the connecting rod bolts and main cap bolts. The engine was very fresh but had failed because of foreign material in the oil. A close examination found rather large pieces of red thread-locking compound in the oil galleys, inside the oil pump, inside the oil pickup screen and jammed in the bearing oil holes. During disassembly, several connecting rods had to be cut off the crank with a torch. The thread-locking compound simply worked too well in an area where it was not intended. Take it for what it's worth, but only use the super goop where it is called for—such as on external studs and fasteners.

141 BORING TIPS: Contrary to what you
may have read elsewhere, you should always have the cylinder block *decked* and *qualified* before the block is nestled against the boring bar! Many boring bars register against the deck surface of the block. If the deck is out of whack, then the bores will not be straight.

142 MORE BORING TIPS: Most
engine machinists know to use torque plates when boring cylinders. But be certain that you use torque plates that are compatible with the cylinder head type that is to be used on the engine. If you run aluminum heads, be positive that the torque plate simulates the stress imposed by aluminum. If the heads are iron, use a plate that simulates an iron head. BHJ Products (37530 Enterprise Court, #3, Newark, CA 94560) can set you up with some of the best equipment in the business. If you're not doing the machining yourself, make sure your shop knows the type of head you'll be using. They should ask as a matter of course, although they may forget.

143 VALVE NOTCHES: There has
always been quite a bit of discussion regarding the valve notch found on hi-po big-block cylinder blocks. Some magazine articles advocate grinding out the notch to match the head gasket. But before you grab the nearest die grinder, think about this: By grinding out the notch you reduce the overall compression ratio (and due to the size of the notch, it can be significant). Furthermore, if a piston with a higher than normal top ring location is used, you run the risk of hanging a ring up in your new notch (especially if it is too deep). Last but not least, you could go too far and "strike water" if you are not careful in this area. In essence, you are compromising the integrity of the casting. If Chevrolet thought a major notch was required in the block, they would have made the hi-po notch larger. By the way, a large overbore of approximately .060 inch almost eliminates the OEM notch.

144 MODIFYING CHEVY RODS:
Some folks like to criticize stock Chevy connecting rods, but unless you are about to lock fenders with the road race crowd or go on to a career in professional drag racing or Winston Cup racing, using anything but stock Chevy components amounts to overkill. Obviously, connecting rod length enters the equation, but if you have no need to stretch the center-to-center length, you can easily fortify the stock connecting rods for most amateur and street high performance use. The rods should be straight before they are

Magnaflux inspected for cracks. Once they pass this test, polish the beams (to eliminate stress risers), have the rods shot-peened, have the center to center specs checked and adjusted, and finally, add a set of quality rod bolts. What about bearing pins, pin oilers, pin bushings and the like? Frankly, all three modifications are a waste of money for mild use. If a bearing turns on a steel rod, you have a problem much larger than the connecting rod! At the same time, full-floating pins work well in the high oil concentration environment underneath the piston.

Adding bronze bushings only serves to weaken the connecting rod. The same applies to extra pin oilers. If the engine is oiling correctly (and in a Chevy it's very hard to screw up the oiling system), there is no need for added holes in the small end of the connecting rod.

145 CHEVY ROD LENGTH: If you
insist on altering the length of your connecting rods (center-to-center dimension), keep in mind that the relatively short connecting rod found in Chevy V8's was designed for a purpose. Connecting rod length is tied into port volumes and camshaft profile. A well-flowing cylinder head (such as the big-block hi-po heads) allows large volumes of air and fuel into the combustion chamber. The very short connecting rod (compare the 6.136" OEM rod length to FoMoCo and Mopar engines) balances the very good intake breathing (and large intake volume) against the exhaust flow (which in all normally aspirated powerplants is traditionally lazy or inefficient). Generally speaking, as the length of the connecting rod is increased (versus crankshaft stroke—this is called rod ratio or l/r), the powerband of the engine is raised upward. In other words, it will make horsepower in a higher rpm range. Keep in mind that the big block can easily function in the 7000-8000 rpm range with the stock 1.63:1 l/r. As the ratio is increased, the powerband rises, negating bottom-end horsepower. This can be compensated to some degree by altering the camshaft lobe displacement angle, but these variables become very involved and are beyond the scope of this tip. Suffice to say, it's tough to beat the OEM rod length in a street application.

146 COMPRESSION & GAS: Lately

there has been a rather large smoke screen created over compression ratios and gasoline. Before you lay down some of your hard-earned cash on ultra-low compression ratio pistons, give some added thought to the equation. Detonation is certainly created (to a degree) by available gasoline quality and compression ratios, but is there a way to increase the compression ratio and still live with today's fuels? Certainly! Just have a look at the Corvette ZR-1 powerplant. It has more compression than we ever dreamed possible two years ago. Obviously, a modified pushrod Chevy engine will not have the luxury of computer controls to monitor detonation, but with current technology (and recent advances in unleaded gasoline quality), we feel that many a car can easily get by with more than 10:1 compression ratios. How is this possible? Although it is simply a theory and would require testing, a flat-top piston (without any dome or dish) could provide the answer. In a typical "old-fashioned" hi-po

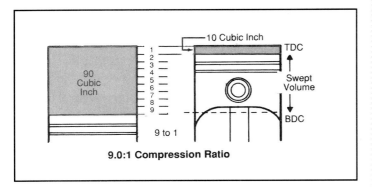

9.0:1 Compression Ratio

Bow Tie, the pistons were always domed to increase the CR. When an engine is run and then disassembled, a distinctive pattern around the piston dome will have developed. Sharp tuners will observe that the factory dome was a compromise between production costs and performance. As a result, a good portion of the dome is not "colored"—indicating that the combustion occurred on only a segment of the piston surface. By blending the domes on past race engines (smoothing them to promote the travel of the flame front), the engine horsepower levels increased, the actual compression ratio decreased and the appetite for extremely high octane race fuels diminished. The dome of the piston then became more evenly colored, indicating that combustion was actually taking up more room in the total chamber. If the dome were eliminated completely, obviously compression ratios would decline, but in powerplants with relatively large swept volumes, even a flat top can create rather large compression ratios—especially if a thin head gasket and a small combustion chamber volume

enter the picture. Our guess is that a similar engine might make between 10:1 and 11:1 in the compression ratio department, but at the same moment stands a very good chance of running reliably on available pump gasoline.

147 RAISING ROCKER RATIOS:

Dave Emanuel, author of *Small-Block Chevy Performance*, has this to say about rocker arm ratios: "Increasing rocker ratios increases power potential, but it does so at the expense of valvetrain durability. In most applications, the trade-off in favor of power is a good one because the increased valvetrain stresses aren't large enough to make much of a difference in durability. However, for some types of endurance racing, the possibility of premature valve spring failure cannot be tolerated, so rocker arm ratios are sometimes on the conservative side. In fact, some engine builders use ratios lower than stock. However, most drag racers and circle track racers use higher-than-stock ratios. There is little problem because the valvetrain is thoroughly checked before running. Remember, raising rocker arm ratios is like putting in a cam with greater lift—stress on the valve springs and pushrods is increased. Most problems occur when rocker ratios are changed on a running engine, when checks for coil bind, retainer-to-seal interference and piston-to-valve interference aren't done. That's when problems occur."

148 INSTALLING CLAMPS: More

clamping tips: If blown hoses are plaguing your motorized toy, give the installation of the clamps some consideration. If you carefully examine the nipple of the component to be clamped (e.g. the thermostat housing), you will note that the actual "nipple" is pronounced. The idea is not to clamp the hose directly over the nipple, but rather behind it so that the hose is properly sealed. If you want added insurance, take a tip from the roundy-round crowd and double clamp radiator hoses. Simply add a second clamp that has its screwdriver slot positioned 180 degrees from the first clamp

slot. Also, not all hose clamps are created equal. Some imported versions are pretty shoddy, and not up to the added stress of high performance use. Use high quality clamps such as those from Earl's. It'd be a shame to lose a big money event over a $1.00 piece of equipment.

149 OIL PRESSURE: How much oil pressure is required in a high performance application? According to the major engine building gurus, a Chevy will live a long and happy life with 10 psi for every 1000 engine rpm. In other words, if it runs a maximum of 7500 rpm, it needs 75 pounds of oil pressure at that rpm level. How do you achieve this figure? By using your head during assembly! Don't run excessive clearances as suggested by some publications. Stick to the Chevy recommendations for connecting rod and crankshaft main bearing clearance numbers. Next, use a standard volume oil pump! There is absolutely no need for running a super high pressure/high volume pump! Simply check the oil pump end clearance to determine if it is on the money and use it. There is no need for exotica in a Bow Tie oil pump—especially if you did not goof up on the clearances!

150 OIL PUMP SHAFTS: Oil pump driveshafts are not all the same! If you are worried about the spindly plastic collar that comes as standard equipment on many Chevy V8's, simply swap it for a steel collared heavy-duty version. Versions are available from your local Chevy dealer, and from aftermarket companies such as TRW, Speed Pro, Moroso, Hamburger, B&B and a host of others.

151 FOUR-BOLT BLOCKS: Some people have been advocating the use of Chevy's over-the-counter big-block, four-bolt main caps.

These have been available almost forever, but pro racers and knowledgeable engine builders have avoided them like dirt. Why? There seems to be a problem getting them properly registered and they don't hold up like the caps normally installed on four-bolt main engines (production line four-bolt main engines). So what should you do if you want to four-bolt a two-bolt big block? Run down to the nearest volume engine rebuilder and grab a grenaded 427 truck block. Pirate the caps and have them installed on your cylinder case. Obviously the block will require a proper line bore, but these caps are structurally superior to the over the counter stuff—plus they cost a bunch less.

152 TWO-BOLT BLOCKS: Are four-bolt main caps really necessary? A top northeast drag race engine builder did some dyno testing on the subject. Seems the magic number is 600 horsepower. Below that figure, the factory two-bolt equipment will do just fine.

153 VAPOR LOCKS: Vapor locks are a pain in the you know where. And most of the time, they happen when you're miles from the safe environs of your garage (and your toolbox). If you need quick relief, try this: Soak a couple of towels in cold water and wrap them around the mechanical fuel pump. Repeat the process until the pump is cool to the touch. The car should start since the pump is the most likely culprit.

154 BEARING BLISTERS: Engine bearings often require extra attention during engine assembly. The "hot tip" as far as conventional bearings (such as the Morraine versions used in all Chevy engine, see below) is to polish the bearing surface lightly with green Scotchbrite®. This removes the protective shipping coating, allowing you to hold the bearing up to a bright light for examination. What you have to look for are obvious "blisters" which can appear as circles in the bearing material. If a bearing is blistered, put it aside and try another bearing. A bearing showing blister signs can fail unexpectedly.

155 BEARING DOWN: The very best bearings made by any North American car manufacturer were the Morraine "500" versions, followed by the "420" series. Unfortunately, these bearings have been discontinued for a number of years. On the plus side, many Chevrolet main bearing sets still make use of the "500"

bearings for the thrust bearing. In most cases, this bearing will outlive your engine! In the aftermarket, the best bearings available are the Vanderville units manufactured in England. Custom examples complete with specialized prep work are available from Childs & Albert or Crower in California.

156 TEFLON SEALED: Without question, racers have flocked toward the Fel-ProTeflon head gaskets. These are Teflon coated and feature solid wire O-rings around each cylinder. They do not require a hot retorque and in most cases are available with compressed thickness figures in the .040" range. Fel-Pro offers gaskets for both big and small block examples and in the case of the mouse motor, an identical gasket is offered through General Motors' Parts Division.

157 HAMMERED HARMONICS: Using a big hammer to install a harmonic balancer or damper is a surefire way to create irreparable damage. The right way to install the balancer is to pull it onto the crank. Unfortunately, if you use the damper bolt to pull on the assembly, you run the high risk of stripping the crankshaft threads. In either case it gets expensive! The best method of installing a damper is with a tool designed specifically for this purpose. In essence, it's a pilot tool that threads fully into the crank snout. The damper is then installed over the crank snout (over the pilot tool). A special bearing then presses the damper onto the crank—properly installed and in less than a minute. Where can you get such a tool? B&B Performance.

158 SLIM WRIST PINS: Wrist pins are critical components in a high performance engine. As you might expect, not all wrist pins are the same. While drag racers lighten their pins to radical levels to reduce bottom end rotating weight, this type of pin will not work on the street, especially if subjected to severe detonation. On the flip side, many pins supplied with replacement or OEM type

pistons weigh as much as bricks. A good compromise are the tapered pins offered by aftermarket sources such as Wiseco (7201 Industrial Park Blvd., Mentor, OH 44060). Basically, these pins have outer shapes that resemble a conventional pin, but the ID takes on a definite taper. This design configuration reduces weight significantly without sacrificing strength.

159 OIL SEALS: The folks at MSD have done a considerable amount of R&D on oiling between the cam gear and the distributor gear. What they have found is a need to seal the distributor gear. Their in-house distributors feature a pair of O-rings on the shaft—one above the location of the cam oil gallery (in the block) and one below it. These O-rings keep oil from leaking internally along the clearance between the distributor housing and the block. In addition, MSD added an oiling hole that sprays oil against the distributor gear. The result of these efforts? Much improved gear wear on the distributor.

160 CLEAN MACHINE: When rebuilding an engine, have you ever tried to clean the oil pump pickup screen? It's next to impossible—unless, of course, you leave the thing immersed in a bucket of carb cleaner. A few hours in carb cleaner and the thing will come out squeaky clean.

161 FILL FILTER: This should be common knowledge, but whenever you change the oil filter on your car, fill the new filter with clean (and correct grade) oil before installing it. Make sure you deduct this amount from the total amount required to fill the oil pan. For example, if the motor calls for 5 quarts, and you add a pint to the filter, then you only need to add 4-1/2 quarts to the engine. If you leave the filter empty, oil will be directed to fill the filter before it circulates throughout the engine, which basically means the bottom end is spinning around without oil until the filter fills. This ensures that at least some oil will get to the bearings when the engine is first fired up.

162 CHOOSING VALVE GUIDES: According to Dart Machinery (manufacturers of high tech race heads and induction systems), different types of valve guide material should be used with different engine compression ratios. Engines with 9:1 or lower compression ratios should use phosphate bronze guides while higher compression ratio engines should make use of magnesium bronze guides. Why the difference? On a low-compression

ratio engine, exhaust gas temperatures are higher. As a result, valves can seize in the magnesium bronze guides.

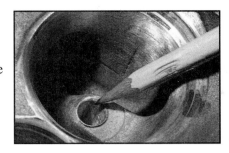

163 VALVE STEM SEALS: Dart
Machinery offers this tip on valve stem seals: "If you're concerned about the seals coming off the guides, we suggest that you thread the outside diameter of the guides with a 1/2" NC die. The threads will positively retain the seals."

164 CHAMFER CRANK HOLES:
When chamfering an oil hole in a crankshaft, grind the chamfer on the trailing edge of the oil hole, relative to the direction of the crankshaft rotation. The idea behind this is to create a negative pressure that physically pulls the lubricant out of the hole. If you chamfer the crank holes opposite to this, oil can actually work its way back into the crank. And as you might have guessed, that isn't conducive to long engine life.

165 DRAIN-BACK HOLES: If you
examine different pistons, you'll find that two types of oil drain-back holes are commonly used—drilled round jobs and slotted grooves. In most cases, the drilled type provides for a stronger piston, but it also allows more heat to enter the skirt region. You'll find that most race and high performance pistons use the drilled hole format. The reason, of course, is strength, since the slotted drain-back system allows the skirt to become more "flexible."

166 CRANK WEIGHTS: Radical "knife
edge" crankshaft counter-weights might not be as important as you think. Dry sump engines see little if any gain, but in a wet sump application, the best crank

counterweight shape is probably a tear drop. In this configuration, the counterweights are shaped like an airplane wing. Naturally, the overall size of the crankcase, the size of the oil pan and the size, length and shape of the connecting rods influence the power gains when dealing with special crankshaft counterweight shapes.

167 TIMING SOLUTIONS: If you play
with camshaft timing, here's something to think about: If the car constantly picks up in performance when the camshaft is advanced, the cam that's in the car is too big. If the performance improves when the camshaft is retarded, the camshaft is probably too small.

168 PISTON CHOICES: Pistons can
either be manufactured by forging or by casting. In virtually all race and high performance applications, a forging is preferred. Cast pistons are designed for quiet operation. Typically, they include a steel strut next to the wrist pin boss so that expansion can be controlled (the steel strut holds the piston in a permanently expanded state). Although this type of piston will live a long life in a low horsepower, daily driver application, it was never intended for performance duty. Needless to say, cast pistons have serious limitations when it comes to racing or high performance. What about a forging? During manufacture, a forged piston begins with an aluminum billet. The billet is placed in a die and stamped into the basic form by a punch. By design, forged pistons have a much denser molecular structure than their cast counterparts. Because of this, heat can transfer through the piston at a much quicker rate. This also means that the piston will be noisy when the engine is cold. As the engine reaches operating temperature (or more accurately, as the piston reaches operating temp-

erature), it will expand, creating the correct operating clearances. We should point out that different parts of the piston "see" different temperatures. Due to this temperature differential, certain parts of the piston expand at varied rates (hence the cold "rattle").

ENGINES

169 GASKET GOOP: Should gasket sealer be used on head gaskets? It depends. Today's high tech, Teflon-coated head gaskets should be installed dry. When it comes to steel shim gaskets or soft copper head gaskets, spray-on sealers should still be used. In addition, a small amount of silicone around each of the water passages is also important with the steel or copper head gaskets.

170 DECK CLEARANCE: In an engine, the quench area is where the flat part of the combustion chamber meets the flat part of the piston. During operation, the piston and head come together. When this happens during the compression-to-power portion of the operating cycle, combustion gases are forced into the open sections of the chamber. The result is more turbulence and better combustion. In order for the quench to operate at its peak, the clearance between the cylinder head deck and the piston deck surface should be as close as possible. In simple terms, the closer the quench figure, the greater the compression ratio and the greater the turbulence (and horsepower). So how close can you come? Keep in mind that the overall compressed gasket thickness enters this equation, and so does the overall deck height of the powerplant. Aluminum rods and engine rpm also influence the quench clearance figure. When all is said and done, there is no ideal deck clearance, but numbers that approach 0.060" (including the compressed gasket thickness) are probably just right for aluminum rods and probably too large for steel rod engines. Look for a clearance figure of 0.035"-0.045" for steel rod combinations, but remember that these aren't absolutes! Generally speaking, the idea is to have the deck clearance as close to zero as possible while the engine is operating at the proper temperature and rpm range. If it's too close, the piston can smack the cylinder head and pinch the top ring land. The end result, of course, could be catastrophic.

171 GASKET USE: Whenever you reuse a gasket (head gasket or any other gasket), you run the risk of premature gasket failure. Why? When a new gasket is installed, it conforms to the irregularities found on the sealing surfaces when compressed. Regardless of the type of gasket material used, the gasket is permanently compressed. Typically, this is called "taking a set." If the gasket is re-used, it is almost impossible to reinstall it in the position it was originally installed in. Since the material has already been compressed, it cannot "readjust" to the sealing surface irregularities. The result is gasket failure and a leak.

172 BOLT HOLE CARE: Before any components (such as cylinder heads, main caps, intake manifolds, etc.) are fastened to the block, you have to be sure that both the bolts (or studs) as well as the actual bolt holes are in good condition. In many cases where the head or block has been resurfaced, then some extra work on the bolt hole will often be required. In these situations, there's a good chance that the bolt hole threads run right up the surface. When the threads go to the surface, the threads can be pulled or drawn up as the bolts are being tightened. This slight irregularity is enough to cause gasket failure. To solve the problem, chamfer the tops of the bolt holes. Next, tap and clean the threads to the bottom of the hole. Remove all loose material from the bottom of blind holes. If these steps are not followed, the bolt might bottom out. The result can lead to a loss in clamping force and, of course, gasket failure.

173 THREAD LUBE: Thread lubricant is extremely important. Lubricants reduce the amount of friction between the fastener and the surfaces it comes in contact with while being pre-loaded. Increases in friction carry with them corresponding increases in torque to achieve proper fastener pre-load. A good thread lubricant reduces the amount of torque required and also reduces the amount of distortion found in the parts being clamped together. Finally, a quality lubricant will also provide a constant friction factor from one fastener to another (critical when you're dealing with a bunch of similar fasteners such as head bolts).

174 THREAD SEALANT: In many applications, head bolts or studs will penetrate the coolant passage(s) in the cylinder block deck surface. If that's the case with your engine, some form of sealant must be used. This sealant must be non-hardening (Fel Pro offers a product called "PLI-A-SEAL" for this job and ARP sells a product simply called "Thread Seal" that works well). The idea is to stop coolant from seeping around the bolt threads. Eventually, this coolant will migrate to the oil or will begin to corrode adjacent engine parts. In the end, if a proper sealant isn't used, you can expect some engine damage or possibly outright failure.

175 ROD SIDE CLEARANCE: How much side clearance should an engine with aluminum rods have? As expected, the side clearance dimensions for most aluminum rod engines vary significantly from those fitted with OEM steel connecting rods. Generally speaking, aluminum expands at about twice the rate of steel. Unfortunately, many aluminum connecting rods are constructed with dimensions that take the expansion rates too seriously. You see, some aluminum rods have out-of-the-box side clearances of close to 0.045". While the engine will operate with this huge side clearance, it will also excessively oil the cylinder walls, which will eventually lead to oil contamination in the combustion chamber. And more important, there simply isn't any power gain when you use excessive clearances. Most engine builders will agree that a side clearance figure of 0.016" to 0.020" is sufficient with aluminum connecting rods (and if you check those figures against many factory specs, you'll note that these numbers are very close to those used with steel connecting rods).

176 VALVETRAIN WEIGHT:

Reducing valvetrain weight improves performance. Unfortun-ately, reducing the weight of the valvetrain isn't a particularly easy task, but there are a couple of areas that you can concentrate on. Testing by several well-known sources has shown that removing weight from any of the components on the valve side (valve, spring, retainer, lock) of the system significantly increases the maximum rpm limit

of the valvetrain. On the lifter side, very light pushrods, lifters and rocker arms have little effect on the engine rpm limit. It should be noted, however, that the weight of the lifter or pushrod is not without consequence. It is important because a very heavy pushrod will ultimately reduce the engine speed limit (but in this case, we're talking about "conventional" 5/16" and 3/8" pushrods—not sewer pipes). All of this simply means that the best (and easiest) place to reduce excess baggage in the valvetrain is the valve itself or the valve spring retainer. Unfortunately, lightweight titanium valves are often over the budget of most enthusiasts—they're expensive with a capital "E." Lightweight retainers aren't. Because of that, you should give lightweight retainers some consideration when you're building your next engine.

177 ALUMINUM RETAINERS:

Instead of titanium retainers, how about using aluminum jobs? It might not be such a good idea. According to most experts (and that includes virtually all camshaft companies), the maximum spring rate should not exceed 300 pounds when an aluminum retainer is used. Any more pressure and you can expect the service life of the retainer to decline rapidly. A major point of wear or erosion is usually found where the flat damper coil contacts the aluminum retainer. If you see specks of aluminum floating around the oil (the oil will look like metallic paint) or deposited on the head when you remove the valve covers, there's a very good chance that the retainers are being "eaten" by the springs. The only solution is to replace the retainers. And constantly replacing retainers (or living with aluminum chunks floating in your oil) might not be so cheap in the long run.

178 VALVE SEAT PRESSURE: You

might find this hard to believe, but high open spring pressure really has nothing to do with controlling valve bounce or "float." It's the spring seat pressure which keeps the valve from bouncing on the seat. Of course, there are other factors that influence valve float on the seat—cam-shaft lobe profile, valve weight, guide design, and others—but maintaining

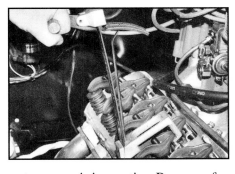

adequate valve spring seat pressure is imperative. Because of this fact, virtually all camshaft manufacturers will readily provide you with a minimum spring seat pressure for a given cam profile. On the average, a street car needs between 110 and 130 pounds of seat pressure. A typical small-block race car can get away with a minimum of 220-250 pounds of seat pressure while a large-valve, Pro Stock big block will usually require 300 to 350 pounds of seat pressure.

179 RING GAP: There are a number of

gapless piston rings available on today's market. Unfortunately, these rings should not be used in high output, high rpm engine combinations. Why not? Because the gapless ring configuration is prone to fluttering at higher engine speeds. In the end, this costs a bunch of horsepower on the dyno (more than the superior ring seal is worth). The moral

of the story is simple: Only use gapless rings on engines that do not make high rpm horsepower. For high performance, stick with gapped rings, and check them while installed in their respective bores as shown.

180 FREEZE PLUGS: If you examine engines that have been professionally built, you'll find that the vast majority of the pros use brass freeze or core plugs. Yes, they look neat, but there is another reason for their almost universal appeal: They don't corrode like common steel jobs. Besides, they're relatively inexpensive and we think they add a bit of flash and professionalism to your engine.

181 WASHER LOWDOWN: How important are hardened washers under fasteners such as head bolts? Washers should always be used unless otherwise stated in specifications or hardware instructions. Hardened washers tend to protect the spot face surface and prevent galling from the rotation of the bolt head or nut against the material face. Of course, washers are absolutely mandatory when aluminum is used. In this case, a washer reduces the bearing stress which occurs at the head.

182 OIL PAN SIZE: The shape of a vehicle's engine "cradle" is the determining factor when it comes to oil pan size and shape. In the case of virtually all production pans, the shape is compromised in the name of universal fit. In other words, the vehicle manufacturer creates a given oil pan for a powerplant and that pan is designed to fit a broad range of chassis configurations (trucks, passenger cars, vans, etc.). Given these parameters, almost all (if not all) production oil pans are size compromises at best— they're too small—especially in the area under the nose of the engine. So what's the point? For maximum performance in a

wet sump oil pan arrangement, use the largest oil pan that will fit within the confines of your engine compartment cradle. There's a bunch of horsepower to be found when the oil pan size is increased.

183 VALVE FLOW: Low lift valve flow is extremely important to performance, although it often isn't considered. Low lift flow centers upon the valve seat. If it isn't right, then the flow cannot be initiated properly. Close attention must be paid to the angles which lead up to the seat, and the only way to determine what's right for your combination is via a flow bench. What you have to look for is a valve seat that minimizes reversion (backwards flow) on the intake side. Any seat configuration that promotes early outward flow on the exhaust side is also important. In the end, this simply means that high performance valve jobs shouldn't be left up to the amateur.

184 EXHAUST VALVE SEATS: Typically, exhaust valve seats that are found on older heads will see some recession (and in some cases, the recession will be healthy). The exhaust valve and valve seat combo is particularly prone to this problem due to the heat the valve and the seat see. The reason for this is simple: The use of unleaded fuels with engines designed to operate on leaded

gasoline eliminates the lubrication factor. In the old days, tetraethyl lead was effectively deposited on the valve and the seat. These lead deposits typically occurred at the same rate as the inherent wear process. In the end, the seats and valves escaped relatively unscathed. Not so when unleaded or even low lead fuel enters the picture. Even the use of valves with modern alloys doesn't totally solve the problem. When all is said and done, the old style "soft" seat will simply be pounded away. There is only one solution: Install hardened seats in any cylinder head that will be exposed to unleaded fuels.

185 CAM DEGREE: When you start to degree a hydraulic camshaft, don't attempt to run through the steps with a hydraulic lifter in place. It's a game of futility, because the clearances inside the lifter are too large. As a result, accuracy is impossible. Yes, you can make a special "solid" test hydraulic lifter by reworking the piston and cup, but why bother? Instead, use a new solid lifter for the job, then simply replace it when the degreeing job is done.

186 DISTRIBUTOR GEAR: If you've ever messed with steel billet roller camshafts in your car, you know how important a bronze distributor gear is. When a conventional iron distributor gear is used, the compatibility of materials isn't very good. In fact, you'll be replacing gears in short order. That's why bronze distributor gears were introduced. They worked well—for a short period of time. Unfortunately, bronze gears wear out too. So what's the solution? Shop carefully when you're in the market for a steel billet roller cam. Many of today's rollers either have tempered surfaces or have trick composite construction (steel cores, iron gears). In either case, you can use a stock distributor gear with no worries about short life expectancy.

187 INSTALLING RODS: If you have a close look at all V8 engines, you'll find that the connecting rods can be installed in one of two ways. The big end (crank pin) of the rod has one side finished with a healthy radius. The other side doesn't. In operation, the end with the radius matches the fillet radius on the crank. The flat end faces the other connecting rod it's paired with on the journal. To install them correctly, always face the radius end toward the crank fillet.

188 REAR MAIN SEAL: This is an oldie, but a goodie. When installing the rear main seal on an engine, offset it slightly so that the seal parting line doesn't match the parting line on the rear bearing cap. Add some sealer to the edges of the seals as well as the edges of the main cap. Leaks will be banished permanently.

189 INSTALLING RINGS: Piston rings can be installed upside down, which is not a good thing. To prevent this, you have to identify the rings. If the ring has a dot stamped onto the surface, the dot faces up. If it has a chamfered edge on the inside of the ring, then the chamfer always faces up (usually a ring with a chamfer is a second ring). If the ring doesn't have a dot or a chamfered edge, then it can be installed in either direction.

190 ROCKER WEAR: When a stamped steel rocker arm bites the dust on a Chevy V8, it's usually an exhaust rocker. This is because the exhaust side runs hotter. But when it comes time to replace the rockers, swap a good used intake to the exhaust side and install a new rocker on the intake. That way, the new rocker won't be pounded before it's "seasoned."

191 INSTALLING ROLLER CAMS: When installing a roller camshaft in an engine, you absolutely must install some form of cam thrust bearing (e.g., a cam button). A conventional flat-tappet (hydraulic or solid) camshaft has a lobe taper. Flat tappets pull the cam in against the front of the block. Roller tappets don't have this luxury. If you don't use a button, then there is no rearward pressure and no means to maintain desirable relationships between the distributor gear and the cam as well as the top timing gear. In the end, the block gets chewed up, parts wear out and the engine is down on horsepower. Use a button. And if you can, use a real roller cam button and wear plate. They're not expensive.

192 TIMING GEARS: If you want to improve the life of your roller timing chain and gearset, try this: With an abrasive cartridge roll slipped

into your die grinder, lightly deburr and smooth the cam and crank gear teeth. Then have both gears glass beaded. This helps the gears retain oil. Naturally, the gears will have to be cleaned before installation, but you can be assured that the durability of the timing gears will be extended with a deburr and bead job.

193 LIFTER ALIGNMENT: Many

engines can have lifter bores that simply are out of alignment in relation to the camshaft lobes. The misalignment can create varied valve timing from cylinder to cylinder. In addition, the out-of-whack bores can create significant lifter wear since they can't rotate properly in the bore. The fix isn't as easy as the diagnosis: The lifter bores will require sleeves. It's not cheap, but once done, you can bet your boots that the timing will be accurate from hole to hole. Besides, it makes for much improved valvetrain life.

194 HONING CYLINDER BORES:

What is the correct procedure for honing an engine? According to several professionals, all honing should be done on a Sunnen CK-10 machine and the block should be fitted with torque plates. As many of you are aware, the use of a torque plate simulates the same amount of stress on a block as a torqued-in-place cylinder head. Different plates are used for aluminum and iron heads. A gasket that is identical to that used during final assembly is sandwiched between the block and torque plate. Once the honing begins, the bore size is brought to within 0.0010-0.0015" of the final size using #525 stones. Following the initial hone, the equipment is set up with #625 stones and honed to within 0.0005" of the final bore size. The last step involves the addition of much finer #800 stones set on a light load. The end result is a nearly perfect, round cylinder bore that is ideally suited for use with moly-type piston rings.

195 TORQUE PLATES: As described

above, torque plates are necessary for honing cylinder bores, but did you know you should also use them for grinding valve seats? In order to maintain concentricity in the

valve seats, Kip Martin Racing always uses torque plates when grinding the valve seats on cylinder heads. Like an engine block, the torque plate simulates the distortion when head bolts are tightened.

196 ALIGN HONING: Believe it or not,

it's a good idea to align-hone a brand new block. In a normal production atmosphere, small amounts of misalignment are easily handled by the installation of hand-selected bearings. These bearings make up any discrepancies in the main bearing bore alignment. As the crank and bearings wear together, the variation is accommodated. When a new crank is installed (along with fresh bearings), the minute differences between the bearings will be eliminated. In other words, the factory can make up the clearance differential with special bearings. In the real world, these bearings simply aren't available. Prior to align-honing a block there are some steps that should be taken: Clean the main bearing cap parting line with a fine file. The main caps can then be ground absolutely

flat and deburred. Next, the main fastener holes are cleaned with a bottoming tap and the caps are properly registered in the cylinder block. Finally, the main caps can be torqued in place. Then and only then can the main bearing bores be honed with Sunnen align hone equipment.

197 LEAKING EXHAUST: One of the

things that robs horsepower is a leaking header gasket. When installing new headers or new header gaskets, be sure to soak the header and collector flange gaskets in water for 6 to 8 hours before they are used. This will improve their sealing ability and significantly extend their lives. Also spread a small bead of high temperature RTV silicone around the port outlets on the gaskets.

198 HEAD CHAMBER VOLUME:

How much volume will a head lose when milled? Generally speaking, a Chevy engine will lose 1 cc of volume from the combustion chamber for every 0.004-0.005" of material removed through a standard milling operation.

199 OIL FILTER BYPASS: Most Chevy

engines use a special oil filter adapter sandwiched between the block and filter. This adapter also happens to have a bypass valve inside it. If you want all oil to run through the filter, the valve should be punched out. Drill and tap the hole for a pipe plug. With the plug in place, all oil will go through the filter. Unfortunately, you have to monitor the filter carefully with this modification. The oil can't bypass the filter at high pressure. And if it can't bypass the filter, it could explode the thing if it's plugged.

200 GROOVY CAMS: Big-block Chevys

manufactured in 1965 and 1966 usually have a fully grooved rear camshaft bearing journal. The purpose of the groove was for lifter oiling. That's cool, but if you use an early cam (with the groove) in a later block, you can expect a serious internal oil leak. To solve the problem, the oil hole in the rear cam bearing must be soldered closed, then redrilled to 0.060" in diameter. What about using a late cam in an early block? The only real answer is to have a groove machined into the rear cam journal.

201 OIL DRAIN PLUGS: Not that long

ago, most GM and aftermarket oil pans were equipped with a nylon washer that sealed the oil drain plugs. These washers worked well—until they cracked (which was normal). You can replace the junk washer with GM part number 23011420 (the last time we checked). You'll receive a composite metal-neoprene washer and the General will throw in a magnetic drain plug in the bargain. These metal washers work far better than the old nylon washers.

202 THERMOSTAT SEALS: If you are

tired of the old seal-the-thermostat-neck-with-silicone routine, try this: GM has released a neat housing gasket that has a bead of silicone on both sides already applied. It's available under part number 10105135 (again, the last time we checked). Just be sure to install it dry. No additional sealers are required.

203 HEAD BOLT WASHERS:

Hardened washers are a good idea under head bolts (we've already covered that subject). But when you buy head bolts, be sure that they are long enough to handle the added thickness of the head bolt washer. Typically, the bolts will have to be approximately 3/16" longer than stock if head bolt washers are used. Otherwise, you'll be short-changed in the thread engagement department and clamping load will be decreased.

204 INTAKE PORT LEAKS: On

aluminum big-block Chevy cylinder heads, you'll find that two of the intake runners have holes in the runner floors. The reason for this is that the heads are designed to accept extra head bolts used on aluminum blocks. If these heads are destined for use on iron-block motors, be certain that the holes are plugged and sealed (we use a pair of set screws locked together). If you don't, the engine will have a massive vacuum leak inside the lifter gallery.

205 PLUG DETAILS: On the left side rear

deck surface of a small-block Chevy, you'll find a plug. This plug leads directly to an oil gallery. The plug cannot be installed once the heads are bolted in place. If, by chance, the plug goes missing during a hot tank job, you can expect oil everywhere when the engine is fired up.

206 ALIGNING ROD CAPS: In order

to maintain the alignment of connecting rod pairs, always insert a pair of feeler gauges between the rod cap duet while you torque the rod bolts. The feeler gauges will maintain the alignment while the rod bolts are torqued.

207 POWER SECRETS: If there is a

secret to finding power in an engine, it's in the machining and assembly. Without quality, precise work, the engine will never be able to produce substantial or reliable horsepower. Quality machining can add as much as 50 or more horsepower to your engine combination. An experienced, race-oriented shop will ensure that every piston is identical, as is every connecting rod; all of the cylinders are equally round; the decks are perfectly square; the main journals are perfectly round; and the crankshaft is perfectly indexed. Yes, these operations can be performed by many machine shops, but for the most part, volume engine machine shops lack the equipment and the time to do the job correctly. Finally, there's the knowledge factor. A hi-po engine shop has the experience and knowledge gained from years of working with a mix of original equipment, aftermarket and race components. They know what needs massaging and what doesn't.

208 DECK HEIGHT: Sometimes, it's not a good idea to take factory specifications as gospel. You see, many of the factories were looking for an "edge" with specific engine combinations—especially those

destined for racing. One area is the block deck height dimensions. As an example, specifications for a vintage, open chamber, Chevrolet L88 call for a block deck height of 0.008" above the block deck (+ deck height—which is extremely rare). In the real world, this would easily result in pistons whacking the combustion chambers—especially at high rpm. In such a scenario, try a clearance of 0.004" between the piston deck surface and the block deck surface. Naturally, other factors, such as actual connecting rod length, piston compression height, true crankshaft stroke and the compressed thickness of the head gaskets used, also enter the equation. Just use your head when it comes to certain dimensions.

209 OVERBORING: Other than for wear purposes, why should cylinders be overbored? Overbores not only result in perfect, round cylinders, they also increase the displacement and swept volume of the engine. An overbore also unshrouds the valves which in turn allows larger volumes of the air-fuel mixture into the cylinder (and also allows larger volumes of spent gases to exit the powerplant). That's one reason why today's professional racers are searching for ways to increase cylinder bore size (e.g., siamesed bore cylinder blocks, etc.).

210 DEBURRING: When deburring a block, don't forget to spend some time in the lifter valley. The area around the main oil drainback holes is important. Remove all casting flash with a die grinder. Similar attention in the timing chain valley doesn't hurt either.

TRANSMISSIONS, CLUTCHES & TORQUE CONVERTERS

211 FLEXPLATES: According to the folks at ATI and McLeod Industries, you should be careful when buying aftermarket flexplates—even those which carry a SFI label. The SFI certification indicates that the flexplate won't disintegrate. It doesn't determine that the flexplate is concentric. In fact, some flexplates with SFI labels are made "offshore". And the quality isn't—uhh, shall we say great? In the end, they can cause more grief than they're worth. You get what you pay for.

212 COOL LINES: When it comes to cooler lines, ATI advises that you use stock steel lines. Why? If you use AN hose and you're not extremely careful during the hose to hose end assembly, there is a chance that the line will be restricted (simply because the hose end was not installed correctly). In the end, this can result in significantly reduced coolant flow. The bottom line? A fried transmission. Besides, reproduction steel lines are cheap and readily available, two more good reasons to use them.

213 CLUTCH AIR GAP: If you wander through the pits of any big drag race, you'll often see the clutch assembly out of the car. And in the conversations between racers and crew members, the words "air gap" will often come up. What's air gap? It's the distance between the clutch disc and the pressure plate when the clutch pedal is pushed to the floor. While most race clutches use something in the neighborhood of 0.085" gap, streetable clutch air gaps are as follows: Long—0.050"; Borg & Beck—0.040"; Diaphragm—0.030". If you're setting up your clutch, use a common feeler gauge to determine the gap (naturally, you'll need a bellhousing that provides access to the plate and disc).

214 SHIFTER PRECISION: If you're stuck with the stock shifter on your post-'79 Mustang or you are using the '85 short throw shifter, improve your shifting precision by brazing up the holes and drilling new holes with a "P" drill bit. This will allow the lever to be bolted firmly against the shifter, eliminating the mush associated with the rubber grommets. This little bit of advice is courtesy of William Mathis, the author of *Mustang Performance Handbook*. He tried this modification on his Slot Car Mustang project car, and found the resulting shifter action more precise.

215 MYSTERY LEAKS: If you have a mysterious leak near your automatic transmission, take a close look at the dipstick tube. Believe it or not, a well-used dipstick tube will often crack at the O-ring indentation. Check yours before you yank out the autobox to find the mysterious leak. If you're installing a fresh automatic, it's always good insurance to install a new tube.

216 STACKED COOLER: Not all coolers (actually the correct name for them is "heat exchanger") are created equal. The "stack plate" type of cooler configuration is much more efficient than the tube and fin jobs. Typically, a modular cooler or "stack plate" will reject as much as three times the heat (for a given area) than a tube and fin cooler. Then there's oil pressure drop: The modular configuration cooler will have less than half of the pressure drop found in a tube and fin design. When it comes to coolers, check out all of your options before you buy.

217 SECURE DIPSTICK: Here's a slick tip regarding automatic dipsticks: When racing your car, always duct tape the dipstick handle to the tube. If you don't, it could come out on a hard pass. The result is ATF everywhere in your engine compartment (and possibly on your rear tires), and possibly fried transmission components. A bit of perennial racer tape will prevent the problem.

218 CONVERTER SPEED: What's the difference between converter rated *stall speed* and *flash speed*? Foot brake stall is just that. You load the converter by stomping one foot on the brakes and the other on the gas. Watch the tach. The rpm at which the converter overpowers the brakes is "foot brake stall." "Flash speed," on the other hand, is quite different. Flash occurs the instant you release the foot brake and the rotating inertia (which is "stored" in the engine-flexplate converter) is released. In many cases, this flash speed can be anywhere from 500-2500 rpm higher than the foot brake stall speed. Often, a drag racer will stage at idle, hold the brakes and "flash" the converter (flooring the gas pedal) the instant the last yellow on the Christmas Tree comes on.

219 SHIFTER MOUNTING: When mounting an automatic shifter inside your racer, take some time to think about the installation before you start drilling holes. Sit in the car with the seat in the correct position, belts on and move the shifter through the full range of travel. In certain locations, you might not be able to engage reverse or park. If that's the case, the shifter location will have to be adjusted. It's better to find this out before you start drilling holes.

220 RELEASE BEARINGS: Did you know that there's a right and a wrong way to install a release bearing? Sure, they only go on one way, but if you install it with the tabs over the lip of the bearing, you can guarantee an early bearing departure. By the way, installing it the wrong way isn't so tough to do.

221 TRANS PANS: There are a bunch of different options available when it comes to automatic transmission oil pans. On the plus side, trick cast aluminum trans pans run cooler than steel ones. And the cast versions can prove to be significantly stiffer than the stamped-steel jobs. On the minus side of the ledger, cast aluminum pans are much more fragile and far heavier. Weigh your options carefully before you choose.

222 INSTALLING TRANS: If you're installing a new clutch assembly in your ride and the gearbox refuses to move the last inch (or less), don't be tempted to tighten it up with the main transmission-to-bellhousing bolts. If you do, you'll break something (like the ears on the transmission). Instead, hook up the clutch linkage and have a buddy depress the clutch pedal. Guess what? The pressure on the disc will be released and you'll be able to slide the transmission forward easily.

223 FLEXPLATE HARDWARE: In many cases, you'll find that flexplate bolts are held in place with a star-shaped washer. Not so with ARP's line of super-duty flexplate hardware products. They are designed for use without washers. Don't use any washers (star-shaped or otherwise) on ARP flexplate bolts.

224 TRANS SWAPPING: In Chevy applications, there are normally two different torque converter bolt patterns used (depending upon the transmission). But what if you don't know which is which? It helps if you know that GM offers double-drilled flexplates. Also, some converter manufacturers (such as ATI) offer double-drilled converters. In this case, you're covered either way for transmission swaps.

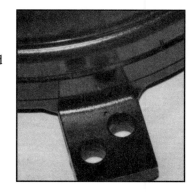

225 HEADER CLEARANCE: Before installing a fresh automatic transmission in your car, think about cutting off the lower tabs at the bellhousing before you install it. Typically, this is the location where the converter dust cover bolts too—and the spot where headers whack the transmission.

226 MONSTER FLYWHEEL BOLTS: Generally speaking, flywheel bolts are held in place by a paltry 60-70 ft-lbs. of torque. Not much for a bolt that has to endure the stresses of a modified powerplant. When the time comes to install a new clutch, replace the bolts with the ones from ARP. Not only are they superior in strength, they're also designed to handle 115 ft-lbs. of torque (each). Install them with engine oil as a lubricant.

227 PILOT BUSHING SWAP: Stick shift artisans are always looking for an advantage. In the case of Bow Tie (and other GM products), you can gain an edge by swapping the bronze pilot bushing in the crankshaft with a roller assembly. As you can imagine, a roller bearing soaks up far less power than a bushing (mind you, we're not talking big overall power numbers here—but every little bit helps). Although there are several good versions available in the aftermarket, you can't do much better than an original equipment GM piece. Originally destined for use behind diesel-powered pickups, the GM unit features a full 17 internal rollers (about 9 more than the aftermarket units). Best of all, the GM part (number 14061685) costs less than ten bucks and is available at your local dealership.

228 SHIFTER SHIMS: Hurst shifters are the standard of performance. What's neat about 'em is the fact that they can easily be tuned up with a "pit pack"—a small package that includes new bushings and new

clips. When you are redoing your shifter (Competition Plus or whatever), try adding an AN washer behind the clip. AN washers are available in several sizes and due to their design, they aren't as thick as standard hardware. The installation makes for a tight fit on the shift rods, but what an improvement in terms of shifter feel. Even the normally tight

Hurst action is improved upon. Be forewarned: Some of the clips will be a bear to install, but it's worth the aggravation.

229 CLUTCH FORK FIX: Many race cars fitted with stick shift transmissions have a nasty habit of pitching the clutch pushrod—especially in the heat of battle. Now this isn't really a fault of the pushrod. It's the clutch fork that is causing you grief. A quick fix is just as close as your nearest dealer. Run over and purchase a clutch fork for an early Corvette (any model from '63-'81). These forks used a clevis arrangement to retain the pushrod instead of the more common recessed ball setup found on the other forks. You'll have to fabricate a new

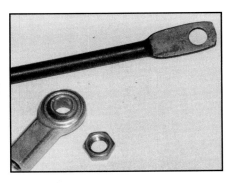

pushrod or you can substitute a chrome moly Mr. Gasket item. In some applications, the vehicle floorboards might require a bit of hammer surgery to get proper clearance, but in most cases it isn't that severe.

230 CLUTCH SWAPPING: Over the years, racers have developed their own preferences with regard to clutch assemblies. The winning hand seems to be the Borg & Beck or Long style clutches. If your car originally came equipped with a diaphragm-type

clutch and you want to make the switch to a heavy-duty model, you're going to find that some bits and pieces of linkage won't line up—especially the clutch pivot ball. Also, swapping an OEM cast aluminum bellhousing for a scattershield sometimes has the same problem. In essence, the clutch fork will hit the pressure plate cover. A quick solution is an adjustable clutch pivot ball. You can crank in the desired length and easily tighten the assembly. Mr. Gasket and McLeod both offer similar examples.

231 TRANSMISSION MOUNTS: In
some instances, a solid transmission mount just does not work. Too much shock and vibration is transferred back to the transmission case and the result is a mangled transmission tailshaft, or worse, a cracked case. On the other hand, some of the stock transmission mounts are far too soft for drag strip duty. Is there a middle ground? Yes. Simply wrap a couple of large hose clamps around a common rubber transmission mount. It tightens up the works considerably, but not to the point of wiping out gearbox cases or tailshafts.

232 EASY CLUTCH ALIGNMENT:
Removing and replacing a clutch can be a pain—especially when it comes time to align the clutch. Sure,

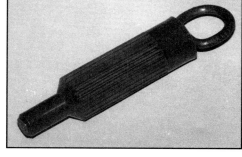

you can make up your own alignment tool from an old input shaft, but Mr. Gasket goes a step further—a special set of dedicated, splined alignment tools.

These trick models are manufactured from high impact plastic and feature a small snout which fits inside the pilot bearing. On the opposite end is a handy handle. Because of the design and light weight, they're extremely easy to use (especially when you're laying under the car in your driveway). Mr. Gasket offers them for 10- and 26-spline GM applications as well as large and small spline FoMoCo applications. Clutch and gearbox swaps will be easier.

233 RECYCLE: The next time you buy (and
use) rear axle or gear lube, save the little filler spout. Not only does it work great for filling rear axles and manual transmissions, it eases the pain of adding ATF through the dipstick tube on your automatic transmission.

234 OIL FLOW: Gear lube (rear axle and/or
manual transmission) is heavy-weight stuff. It doesn't like to pour very well. And because of this, it can be a real pain to install, especially in cramped quarters. To make the stuff pour better, slip each plastic bottle of lube into a microwave oven for a minute or so. You'll be amazed at how easy the 90-weight pours when it's warm!

235 700-R4 VALVE BODY: Many
enthusiasts and racers are finding out that the 700-R4 transmission is more than adequate, and in some cases better, than the venerable TH-400 or 350 trannies. But this is only with modifications. One such modification is the High Tech Valve Body Kit from Art Carr Performance. Essentially,

the kit helps you modify the valve body of your 700-R4 by improving oil flow and pressure by redrilling holes in the valve body separator plate. Also included are a replacement clutch valve and pressure regulator valve. Other items are also available to produce firmer, crisper shifts without hunting between gears. Check you local speed shop for Art Carr's products.

236 ELIMINATING WHINES: Do
you have an impossible-to-find whine originating from the underside of your car. If you do, try adding a small amount of grease to the splines on the transmission slip yoke. This eliminates the metal-to-metal contact from the splines in the yoke to the splines on the output shaft.

237 WATCH YOUR LUBE: If you have
a late-model Warner T-5 manual gearbox in your car, be careful with the lubricant. These new generation transmissions (found in various Camaros, Mustangs & Firebirds) are designed for automatic transmission fluid (ATF) rather than gear lube. If you use gear lube, it will prove too thick to flow through the narrow internal passages. The result? Early transmission expiration.

238 PILOT BUSHING: Sometimes pilot
bushings literally fall out. Most other times, they require a serious amount of persuasion to remove. If that's the case, try this on for size: Run down to the local hardware store and purchase an 11/16-inch coarse bolt. Thread it into the soft pilot bushing material. Keep turning and when the bolt strikes the back of the crank, it should force the bushing out. If it doesn't, you have a long handle to work the bushing out of the crank.

239 FRIENDLY SPLINES: Have you
ever come across a new clutch disc that doesn't want to slide easily over the input splines on your transmission? If you have, don't worry—you're not alone. The problem is a burr on either the gearbox input or on the clutch disc splines. To ease the job, take the time to carefully deburr the splines on both the clutch disc and the input shaft. From now on, the installation will be a snap.

240 HYDRAULIC PILOT BEARING:
Pilot bearings at the end of the crank can sometimes fall out. If you're lucky. We've mentioned a removal method or two before, but another easy way to pull them is with "hydraulics." In this case, fill the cavity behind the bearing with grease. Insert a wooden or steel shaft that is slightly smaller in ID than the bearing hole, and give it a whack with a hammer. The pressure will dislodge the bearing. When it starts to move, remove the shaft and repack the area with more grease. Repeat the process. A few more taps with the hammer and the pilot bearing will fall out in one piece. Hydraulic pressure beats hammering 'em to death with your largest sledge and a cold chisel.

241 STOP BOLT: Stop bolt adjustment on a
Hurst shifter is important. It's also a two-person job. Have an assistant shift the transmission into fourth gear—maintaining a slight amount of rearward pressure on the stick. Be absolutely positive that the transmission is firmly in

fourth gear. Loosen the locknut on the front stop bolt and turn the bolt down until it stops. Back off the bolt by 1-1/4 turns and tighten the locknut. Next, have your assistant shift the transmission into third gear, holding the stick forward with a slight amount of pressure on the handle. Repeat the adjustment process on the rear stop bolt/locknut. Check the adjustment by having your assistant run through the gears. In all cases, the transmission should be firmly engaged. In other words, no excess movement that would cause the gear to be over-engaged.

242 SHIFTER SLOP: Once a Hurst shifter
has seen some use (or you have a heavily used shifter assembly), it may become "sloppy" or wobble around a lot between gates. In most cases, this just means the bushings are worn. Replace them and the excess play will disappear, and the stick will firmly engage gears once more without having to hunt for them. Never tighten the front bolt at the base of the stick. This bolt holds the preload tang. Overtightening this bolt will only accomplish one thing—a bent tang and destroyed shifter preload.

243 SHIFTER ALIGNMENT: Included
with every Hurst manual shifter is a special alignment pin that's used to set the neutral gate in the shifter. The L-shaped nylon pin holds the shifter levers in neutral as you work on the shifter arms. Certain applications (such as vintage 'Vettes) have ridiculously tight quarters around the shifter body. Although you might be tempted to toss the alignment pin, don't! Use of the alignment pin is essential in the total shifter setup!

244 CATCHING OIL: When removing a
transmission, you always run into the problem of oil running out the tailshaft end. Yes, there are special tools to plug the hole, but if you don't have one (or you don't have a spare yoke), try this: Cover the end of the transmission with a couple of sandwich bags. Seal the bags to the back of the tailshaft with several large elastic bands. No leaks, no mess and no special tools.

TRANSMISSIONS, CLUTCHES & TORQUE CONVERTERS

245 SHIFTER BODY MOUNT:
When installing a Hurst shifter body mount plate to the transmission tailshaft, consider adding a small amount of Loctite to the bolt threads. It stops them from backing out (which they occasionally do). Follow Hurst's torque recommendations to the letter. In most cases, you are dealing with an aluminum tailhousing casting—too much torque can strip the threads and too little torque will cause the bolts to loosen with time.

246 SHIFTER SWIVEL:
If you are setting up a shifter, the rod/swivel location is critical. Often though, the swivels will "move" before the assembly is complete. Try this: Once the rod/swivel position has been determined, add a small amount of weatherstrip adhesive or silicone to the threads on either side of the swivel. This will lock the swivel in place, but if further adjustment is necessary at a later date, the adhesive can easily be removed.

247 TH-400 BURNOUT:
Did you know that there's a right and a wrong way to do a burnout with a TH-400? The folks at ATI offer the following recommendations for properly heating tires when your Chevy is equipped with a Turbo 400:

1. Spin the tires slowly in the water to get them wet. Initially spinning the tires slowly avoids soaking the rear wheelwells with water during the burnout. If the wheelwells are soaked

with water, then the water will drip down on the tires after you've heated them.

2. Pull up to the front edge of the water using Low to 2nd to High. Simply stated, this means that you should begin your burnout in first gear, shift to second and then shift to third while the car is still in the water. While you're doing this, remember number one above.

3. When the tires are hot enough (you don't have to melt

them), release the line lock and power the car out of the water 5-10 feet out, then lift off the throttle. Avoid a "hook" that will scuff the tires.

4. Stage immediately. Dry burnouts or "hops" reduce traction and consistency. If you don't believe this, pay attention to the first dry leave after the burnout. The car will hook hard every time. What about the small amount of water that might be left on the tire after you leave the bleach box? Forget about it. The heat inside the rear tires will dry the water completely—long before the green light comes on.

248 TRANS COOLER LOCATION:
Where's the best place to mount an automatic transmission cooler? According to Earl's Performance Products, "the cooler must be mounted in a stream of moving air at ambient temperature to operate efficiently. It is not a good idea to mount the oil cooler behind the water radiator where it will receive only heated air. It is not enough to lead air to the cooler—the heated air must have somewhere to go after it passes through the core. Remember, air always obeys the immutable laws of fluid dynamics. Air will only flow from a region of relatively high pressure to a region of relatively low pressure. Any attempt to convince it to do otherwise is doomed to failure." In other words, mount your cooler in the air stream ahead of the vehicle's radiator. In that way, it will always be subject to high pressure at the front and the engine fan will always provide for a region of low pressure behind the cooler.

249 TRANS BRAKE:
In a stick shift car, the suspension is unloaded before the clutch is dumped. When it is dumped, none of the built-in suspension anti-squat is used up. As a result, the suspension is allowed to work and the tires are shocked properly. In the end, the stick shift car hooks. An automatic car will likely spin the tires. This is where a transmission brake enters the picture. When a car is equipped with a brake, it allows the engine to be brought to a specific rpm level (like a stick car), but the rear suspension and tires aren't loaded. As the tree comes down, a switch is released and the car launches like a stick shift example, shocking the rear tires. Best of all, this allows the car to be very consistent since you can leave at precisely the same rpm level, pass after pass. In operation, most internal transmission brakes work in the same manner: They apply forward and reverse "elements" inside the transmission. This prevents output from a planetary, hence no output at the transmission tailshaft. When the trans brake switch is released, the reverse element in the transmission is released simultaneously. As a

result, the car launches like a stick. Do they work? Definitely!

250 GEAR RATIOS: Should an automatic be fitted with lower (or higher) than stock gears? Lower than stock first gear ratios are best for things like trucks used for towing or for RV vehicles. They are also a good alternative to stiff rear axle ratios in street-driven hi-po cars. Be forewarned, however, that a deeper first gear results in a larger percentage drop between the gears. As a result, the engine will have to operate in a larger (wider) powerband. Higher than stock ratios are well suited to tire limited, high horsepower/high torque applications. In these cases, the car is "on the converter" longer than a standard gear combination. Additionally, there is less rpm spread between the respective gears. Keep this in mind when deciding on what automatic to put in your car.

251 FLEXPLATE BOLT PATTERNS: Some Chevy flexplates have dual bolt patterns, some don't. But if you're in doubt about the pattern, think of this: Some aftermarket converters have dual patterns for the converter legs. This allows the converter to be installed on either of the Bow Tie flexplate config-urations.

252 TRANNY BEARING PLATE: While today's Super T-10 is a relatively beefy piece, there are some minor modifications that can help durability significantly. Perhaps the major troublespot inside these gearboxes is the rear bearing plate. The OE Richmond piece is cast in aluminum. As the car accelerates, the input shaft/first gear combination receives the majority of the

loading. The helical cut of the gears tries to move the mainshaft and the input shaft forward during this acceleration phase. In addition, the helix gear cut attempts to spread the cluster gear and the mainshaft apart. As you can imagine, this force can eat the aluminum bearing plate—often enlonging the bores by as much as 0.020". With this deflection, there is a significant decrease in gear tooth contact (the gear teeth ride on the high side) which in turn creates uneven gear tooth loading. The result of this internal movement? Gear tooth failure and untold numbers of shifting problems. To solve the problem, sharp transmission builders are adding a steel center plate assembly (available from Daryl's Gearbox, G-Force and others) to their T-10 transmissions. Designed to replace the fragile OE component, the steel plate piece stabilizes the case and main shaft. Gear deflection is minimized and component wear is stopped dead in its tracks. Shifting is improved dramatically. Best of all, there won't be transmission parts lying on your garage floor.

253 COOLER LINES: Most transmission cooler lines are pre-bent steel units. There's absolutely nothing wrong with these components (and in fact, they have plenty of advantages). Unfortunately, they're a pain in the you-know-where when it comes time to remove the autobox. To eliminate some of the grief, try substituting a short section of each line with braided hose and AN fittings. In the middle of each stainless hose, add a quick disconnect fitting. Companies like Earl's, Keith Black and others sell slick aluminum or steel couplers that have minimal restriction and can be uncoupled in seconds. They don't drip or leak, but more important, they make transmission swaps a piece of cake. By the way, these same couplers can be used in other applications such as fuel lines or other hydraulic applications.

254 POWERGLIDE YOKE: The stock yoke on a Chevy Powerglide is a pretty dismal piece. It's marginal in many stock applications. And if you add any heat under the hood, the yoke will be on the brink of extinction. To solve the problem, swap the yoke for a new job designed for use behind big-block Chevys with a four-speed manual transmission. You'll need a heavier U-joint, but otherwise, it's a straightforward swap.

255 TRICK ATF: According to people who know about this stuff, you should only use Dexron or Dexron II transmission fluid (here's a tip within a tip—Dexron is always red in color) in a GM transmission. Do

not use type "F" or "FLM." In addition, specialty "trick" oils are actually harmful to transmissions and should be avoided.

256 FILL CONVERTER FIRST:

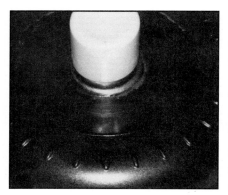

Before installing a torque converter to the transmission, add one quart of fluid to the converter. Simply fill it via the converter snout. Upon startup, the converter will definitely have oil in it to avoid initial wear and tear caused by the rubbing of bare metal surfaces.

257 REVERSE LOCK-OUT:

When shopping for an aftermarket automatic transmission shifter, be sure to consider models with separate reverse lock-out levers. Many of today's shifters have them as standard equipment. Others have lock-out options. Most require two hands to bypass the lock-out. It might sound troublesome, but they're a good idea. Why? Simply because it's no fun shifting into reverse (instead of third) at 100 miles per hour.

258 GREASE Z BAR:

Most cars with a mechanical clutch linkage use some sort of "Z" or equalizer bar that attaches from the engine to the body or front frame rail. Found inside both ends of this equalizer bar are a pair of ball and socket pivots. Some bars have grease zerks, others don't. In either case, don't forget to grease these locations occasionally. It makes shifting a lot easier, and it can be the solution for many mysterious clutch woes.

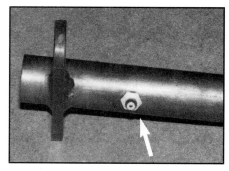

259 INSTALLING CONVERTERS:

Before the final installation of a converter, put the assembly up to the flexplate and make sure that the mounting pads fit flush to the flexplate and are in correct alignment to the bolt pattern. With the pads flush to the flexplate, the converter pilot should be a good fit into the crankshaft with approximately 1/8" minimum extending into the crank below the chamfer. While you're at it, check the bolts that are used to secure the converter to the flexplate. They must fit the flexplate properly. If necessary, the flexplate can be drilled, but no more than 0.010" larger than the torque converter bolts.

260 MUSTANG CLUTCH QUADRANT:

The Fox-chassied Mustangs and T-Birds ('79-'93) equipped with manual transmissions and self-adjusting clutch mechanisms are notorious for developing clutch problems, especially if the driver likes to dump the clutch now and then or is teaching a friend how to drive a "stick." Hard shifting between gears or poor clutch adjustment where the clutch will grab at a

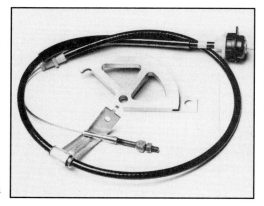

low pedal height (such as right off the floor) are some of the more common problems that occur. But before you remove the transmission and replace the clutch, check the clutch quadrant. The quadrant is located underneath the dash panel directly above the accelerator pedal, and is composed of two plastic pieces with plastic gears that activate the clutch cable. When the clutch pedal is depressed, the gears engage and move the cable, which engages the clutch. As you might have guessed, the plastic gears wear out rather quickly and will either not stay engaged or will slip. Furthermore, the stock setup does not allow for any cable adjustment. Both of these design features can lead to hard shifting between gears, and low pedal grab. The problem has been solved by BBK Performance Parts (Corona, CA). They have designed a replacement clutch quadrant machined from a single piece of billet aluminum that does not rely on gears to activate the cable. The unit will fit any Fox-chassied Mustang or T-Bird with the self-adjusting clutch mechanism. The BBK cable is of a heavy-duty performance caliber, complete with a threaded end that allows for fine clutch pedal adjustment. Installation is relatively simple, with the hardest part being removing the quadrant itself, because it must be done by feel while lying under the dashboard.

261 PRESSURE PLATE BOLTS:
After a number of assemblies and disassemblies, the bolt holes in a pressure plate can open up. To fix the problem, simply use a flat-nose punch to peen the metal over slightly, then reinstall the pressure plate. The bolt shoulder will drive an accurate pilot hole, centering the pressure plate.

262 KEEP IT CLEAN:
Before installing an automatic transmission to the back of an engine block, be sure that the mating surface of the engine block and the transmission case are clean and free from nicks,

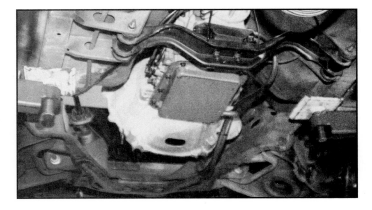

paint, dirt, etc. Use a file to clean and smooth the surface. Further to this, the engine dowel pins must be firmly in the block, in good condition, and long enough to protrude into the transmission bellhousing at least 3/16" of the full diameter, not counting the chamfer.

263 STUCK TRANS:
If the GM automatic transmission in your car refuses to shift out of low gear, the first thing to check is the fluid level. If it's up,

doesn't smell burned and looks red, try this: Climb under the car and peel out the governor (normally found under a small round cover on the side of the transmission case). The governor is likely stuck. Free it up, re-install it and try the transmission. There's a very good chance that it will function correctly.

264 STOP ENGINE MOVEMENT:
You might be surprised at how much fore-and-aft movement an engine has in a car. This is particularly troublesome in stick shift applications. Too much ahead and back action can create simple problems like poor shifting. Bigger (and more severe) symptoms like clutch chatter and even wasted clutch discs can be the result. Solid motor mounts help, but if the problems persist, you might want to consider a lateral engine limiter (almost mandatory in applications with motor plates).

265 AUTOMATIC TRANS PRIMER:
For initially filling and priming an automatic transmission: Jack the rear wheels of the car three inches off the ground. Then install four quarts of quality brand fluid in the transmission (red in color!). If possible, turn the engine with the starter only until the transmission has picked up the fluid and six to eight quarts of oil have been installed. Do not overfill! This method of filling primes the pump and is especially important on engines that idle over 1000 rpm. If the starter cannot turn the engine easily, start the engine at the lowest possible rpm and immediately complete filling the transmission as quickly as possible. Run the transmission through all ranges with light throttle and recheck the fluid level. The level should be one pint low with the transmission in Neutral or Park and the car on level ground.

266 DOWEL PINS:
After installing an automatic transmission to the block dowel pins, make certain the converter is free to move during and after the transmission is bolted to the block. Under no circumstances should the transmission be "drawn up" to the block. It should go flush to the back of the block with relative ease. Do not allow the weight of the transmission to hang on the block. It must be supported until at least two bolts are in place holding the transmission to the back of the block. When using a motor plate between the engine and the transmission, lengthen the dowel pins! They must be lengthened at least the thickness of the motor plate to ensure proper engine to transmission alignment.

267 ELIMINATE CLUTCH SLIP:

Tired of plastic clutch quadrant blues? An

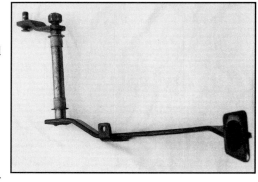

alternative is to replace your self-adjusting clutch pedal and quadrant with the manually adjusted pedal from the '79-'80 Mustang. Use the SVO clutch cable (part number D9ZZ-7K553-B) and fabricate a bracket to attach a spring to pull the clutch fork away from the pressure plate.

268 CLUTCH SPRINGS:

If the springs on your clutch disc are loose or missing in action, here's what the problem is: Typically, the hub springs are designed to take torque. After use, they will normally

become looser than they were when new. This doesn't create a problem unless the spring starts to wear the drive plate or back-plate of the disc. Unfortunately, some cheap discs have springs that are so weak, they will fly out of the disc—even though the facing material still looks good. If that's the case, it's time to think about spending a few more dollars on a disc. If you do, spend the extra money for a heavy-duty performance unit, such as this Ford SVO disc for late-model Mustangs.

269 CONVERTER RUNOUT:

Before you install a new converter, bolt the flexplate to the crank and then bolt the converter to the plate.

The idea is to check the runout on the pump drive neck. Set up a dial indicator so that it reads off the converter neck. Turn the engine over by hand and watch the dial indicator. If the converter runout is less than 0.006", everything is happy. More than 0.006" of runout is trouble. It could mean that the flexplate is goofy (or at least the bolt holes are out of whack). Try another flexplate. If it still has the same runout, then you could have a bum converter.

270 CONVERTER LOCK OR NOT:

If you're scrounging for used overdrive automatic transmission hardware, how can you tell the difference between a lock-up or conventional converter? Simple. Turn the converter over so that the flexplate side is facing up. A lock-up converter will have "flats" on the side. A conventional converter is round.

271 DISC BREAKAGE:

If the center of a clutch disc breaks out, there are two possible causes. If the hub and the two plates are still riveted together, but the plate the facings are riveted to is broken out, then there is a serious misalignment in the transmission. This can be due to a toasted pilot bushing or it can simply mean that there is an input shaft problem with the transmission. On the other hand, if the hub comes out and the two plates are not riveted together, then the clutch manufacturer did not install the rivets correctly.

272 CONVERTER PERFORMANCE:

Everyone knows that a high stall speed converter usually makes the car quicker and more responsive to throttle tip-in. But there is another reason why high stall converters influence performance, and that's weight. A 10-inch converter is quite a bit lighter than a 12- or 13-inch unit, and an 8-inch converter is lighter still. Not only that, the smaller converter holds less oil. As a result, it's like installing an aluminum flywheel in a car. Less mass means more throttle response, which means quicker launches off the line.

273 LOCATING STUDS:

In order to make manual transmission installation go a bit easier, try this: Buy some threaded rod and install it on the top pair of bolt holes in the bellhousing before the transmission is installed. Then slide the transmission over the rods. When the transmission is snuggled up to the bellhousing, replace the rods with bolts. Believe us, this saves plenty of aggravation.

274 CLUTCH CABLE:

If your Mustang clutch cable has given up the ghost, it probably looks more like a corn husk broom than a cable. But there is some good news on the horizon. Ford SVO offers a trick cable setup under part number M-7553-A302. This kit consists of a beefed-up clutch release fork and a heavy duty self-adjusting, Teflon-lined clutch cable. All 1984 and later cars have the HD cable as standard equipment. In addition, all 1986 and later cars have the HD clutch release fork as original equipment. To install the SVO kit on 1979-1980 Mustangs with manual adjustment clutch mechanisms, the 1981 and later self-adjusting quadrant must be purchased from Ford. Contact your local FoMoCo dealer for more info.

275 CLEANING FLYWHEEL:

When you've removed the flywheel from your car (or if you're installing a fresh flywheel) take some time to clean it and the pressure plate face (disc side on each component). Contact cleaner or any non-petroleum based cleaning agent will work. We can't stress this "cleanliness" aspect enough. And by the way, just remember that greasy hands and clutch discs don't mix. Also keep in mind the fact that many hand cleaners are petroleum based! Because of that, be extra careful when handling new clutch components!

276 INSTALLING PRESSURE PLATES:

Often a little thing like installing a pressure plate can become downright frustrating. You need three hands, and there's only room for two. To remedy this situation, try using three long set screws (in the thread size for your flywheel) and install them temporarily (instead of the correct pressure plate bolts). Slip the plate into place, then swap the set screws for the right hardware. You'll be amazed at how easy the plate installs—and you only need two hands.

277 MANUAL SHIFTERS:

How many of you have tried to install a manual transmission shifter with the transmission in the car? If you have, you know it's a real pain in the butt. In some cases (like a '63-'82 Corvette), it's far easier to pull the transmission than it is to simply install the shifter. If that's the case, why not install the shifter (without the handle) before the transmission goes in the car? It works. Besides, it makes shifter adjustment a whole bunch easier.

278 BUILT-IN TRANNY JACK:

When you're ready to install a transmission (automatic or standard) in a car, try moving the crossmember as far back as it will go on the frame. Then lift the transmission with a jack and use the crossmember as a rear support. Believe us, it saves plenty of cussing, sore backs and general aggravation.

279 SENSITIVE CLUTCH SPRINGS:

It is very important to loosen all of the clutch linkage components before the clutch pedal is depressed for the first time following a clutch R&R. Clutch springs (especially diaphragm models) are extremely sensitive to throwout travel. If the travel limit is exceeded just once, the diaphragm spring can be strained and permanently deformed. Loosen the linkage, then adjust the clutch before you ram the pedal to the floor.

280 CONVERTER DRAIN PLUGS:

Which way do FoMoCo performance converters go? ATI recommends that all C-4 and C-6 torque converters equipped with drain plugs should be installed so that drain plugs are aligned with the holes in the flexplate.

281 MOPAR CONVERTERS:

Mopar torque converters should be installed so that the small hole in the flexplate is opposite to the drain plug in the torque converter. There is only one correct alignment pattern for bolt holes in the converter and flexplate. If the converter does not have a drain plug, determine the correct pattern and mark the converter (and/or the flexplate) before attempting the installation.

282 WOBBLY STICKS:

Believe it or not, a shifter installation can be messed up with the installation of the ball (or T-handle) as well as the stick itself. Be absolutely positive that the stick is tightened to the max. You do not want any play in the stick or the ball! Having a loose ball or T-handle is fine for day to day driving, but when the urge for some powershifting overwhelms you, nothing is worse than a wobbly stick or shifter handle!

283 BURNOUT BANG UPS:

This might be old news to seasoned veterans of the quarter mile, but if you come out of the water box spinning the tires, then back off the throttle suddenly, you run the risk of wiping out the sprag in your converter. Back out of the gas slowly, so that the engine doesn't abruptly return to idle. Your converter will be much happier.

284 EASY VIEW DIPSTICKS:
Reading the level on automatic transmission dipsticks is a real pain—especially if the fluid is nice and clean (as it should be). To make viewing easier, drill one small hole just below the "add" line on the dipstick. Drill another just above the "full" line on the dipstick. You'll be surprised at how much easier it is to read.

285 CLUTCH LINKAGE THROW:
If your car has a diaphragm-style pressure plate, double check the amount of throw in the linkage. This is checked by pushing the pedal to the floor, then checking the actual clutch assembly to determine how far the assembly moves. In the vast majority of cases, a diaphragm clutch will not require maximum pedal travel (to the floor). In fact, many diaphragm clutch assemblies can go "over center" with too much pedal travel. The result is a pedal that sticks to the floor. If that's the case, try fabricating a simple pedal stop to limit the travel. Your engine and your nerves will be much calmer.

286 TH-350 CASE CRACKS:
Many a strong running car with a Turbo Hydra-matic 350 will eventually suffer from a cracked or broken case. The reason for this is that TH-350 cases tend to be weak on the cooling line side. A combination of solid motor mounts and a rubber transmission mount usually solves the problem. So does a good old-fashioned turnbuckle mounted from the left-hand side of the engine to the frame rail.

287 BASHED BUSHINGS:
When installing a new pilot bushing (or roller bearing) at the back of your crankshaft, keep this in mind: During shifts, or when the transmission is engaged and the clutch pedal is down, the rpm difference between the crankshaft and the transmission input shaft can be very high. Because of this, the bearing must be able to operate freely without any roughness. Installation is also important. It's a good practice to use Loctite to hold the bushing in place. Further to this, add a small amount of Lubriplate or molydisulphide to the inside of the bearing or bushing (where the tip of the transmission input shaft rides). The idea is to keep the bushing tight and lightly lubed. Believe it or not, this little bushing has a lot to do with shifting gears and clutch life.

288 MORE BUSHINGS:
Pilot bushings should be replaced on a regular basis (say every second or third clutch disc). Further to this, the clearance between the bushing ID and the OD of the transmission input shaft should not exceed 0.002-0.005". Any more and it's time for a new bushing. Loose bushings allow the tip of the input shaft to run out and can create clutch drag.

289 HOT RUNS:
If you're out testing your automatic-equipped race car, never make more than three quick consecutive runs (up/back, up/back, etc.). If you do, the transmission fluid will probably be heated severely (even with a healthy cooler). As a result, the ATF will

begin to break down, and the next thing to break down will be the transmission. Take the time to let the transmission cool (say 20 minutes) after three consecutive "hot laps."

290 CLUTCH MAINTENANCE:
How often should clutch assemblies be adjusted in a hi-po car? According to the experts, the answer is frequently. Freeplay decreases as clutch linings wear. If not adjusted, pressure plate release levers might contact the throwout bearing. This, in turn, can cause clutch slippage and early release bearing failure.

291 CUSTOM CROSSMEMBER BOLTS:
Owners of first-generation Camaros (along with '68-'74 Novas, Firebirds and other similar GM platforms) can ease some of their transmission crossmember R&R headaches with a set of specially shouldered bolts. Instead of having the bolt heads buried deep inside the frame rail, they're out in plain view. We use them all the time (probably because they're cheap). Nonetheless, they're readily available from B&B Performance, Moroso and other aftermarket manufacturers.

292 LONG-STYLE PLATES: Anytime a Long-style pressure plate refuses to release cleanly, the first thing to check are the pivot stands. Clean any clutch debris and very lightly lube the pins and eccentric bushings with high temperature molydisulphide. Be sure that there isn't too much lube. Otherwise, you'll soon be replacing the disk.

293 TORQUE CONVERTER BOLTS: Torque converter bolts should be periodically checked for tightness—even when Loctite is used on the bolts. This is especially critical on high-powered applications. When it comes to race cars, it's not a bad idea to include converter bolts in your regular maintenance schedule.

294 ATF MAINTENANCE: In a typical high performance application, automatic transmission fluid should be changed every 12,000 miles. In a severe duty application (where a small diameter converter is used), the ATF should be changed every 5,000 miles. If you don't follow this maintenance routine, you're only asking for the hassle and expense of an automatic trans rebuild or replacement.

295 HEADER HEAT: Headers and transmission cooler lines don't mix. When routing cooler lines, pay particular attention to the location of the lines. In many cases, the cooler lines are too close to the headers. If that's the case, then the heat from the headers can easily heat the ATF—even after it has been "cooled." One more thing to think about: Headers are hottest as they near the exhaust port.

296 USE ALL BOLTS: Don't be tempted to leave out a bolt or two on the bellhousing flange when you're installing a transmission (manual bellhousing or automatic). Sounds like common sense, but you'd be surprised how often this happens. The transmission (or bellhousing) needs all of the hardware in place to secure it firmly to the engine, and to ensure that it doesn't vibrate. Yes, there will be at least one bellhousing bolt that will be a bear to install, but take the time and do it right.

297 DOUBLE DETENTS: When installing a new shifter in your automatic-equipped ride (or re-installing a shifter—stock or aftermarket), keep this in mind: The detent in the shifter must correspond with the detent in the transmission. It's very easy to misalign these detents, which can result in a transmission operating "between" gears, even though the shifter says it is in gear. To get it right, have an assistant move the shifter through each gear while you check the transmission detents. By the way, detents are easily adjusted with the shifter cable (it's a length adjustment).

298 PRESSURE PLATES: As hard as it may be to swallow, the need for extreme pressures in a pressure plate aren't required. Although many people still believe that you need 3,000 pounds or more pressure in the plate, this is not so. All this does is bend (or

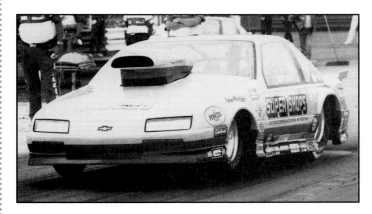

break) linkage and increase the amount of leg power you need to push the pedal. Modern pressure plates can live with 1800 pounds or less—even with a Pro Stock influenced fat block ahead of it. The key is in the clutch design. Check with McLeod for more information.

299 SWIFTER SHIFTERS: Many new manual transmission cars were (and still are) equipped with an inner and an outer shifter boot. These were installed so that interior noise levels would be reduced. Unfortunately, they also restrict the move-ment of the shifter. If you don't mind a bit of added road noise, remove the inner boot. Your shifter will be much quicker.

300 HAND RESTS: Many people have a habit of resting their hands on a manual shifter handle while driving. If that's you, break the habit! This practice places extra (and unnecessary) pressure on the shifting forks inside the transmission. In the end, that reduces the life of the forks—dramatically. Pick another place to rest your knuckles.

301 FRONT SEAL: If you have to remove and replace the front seal in an automatic transmission, try this: Use a set of drum brake spring pliers to remove the seal. It works, and the time saved could be considerable.

302 PLUGGING COOLER PORTS: There are few isolated situations where a transmission cooler isn't required for an automatic transmission (a good example are certain dragsters). If your race car falls into this category, do not plug the cooler ports in the transmission! The oiling circuit must be complete so that the transmission functions properly. To accomplish this, simply loop a section of cooler line from one cooler port to the other on the transmission case.

303 PRESSURIZED HOSE: Never use fuel line as a flexible vibration connection on automatic transmission cooler lines. The stuff just won't handle the heat and the pressure. As an example, a typical automatic transmission cooler line has to withstand as much as 75 psi. That type of pressure will kill a fuel hose in short order. If you're stuck for hose, try using power steering hose. It's more expensive than regular hose, but it's up to the task of handling hot and high pressure fluid.

304 DIPSTICK PLUG: When the time comes to remove the automatic transmission in your car, be prepared to stop the torrent of leaks. Aside from the cooler lines and tailshaft, one area that most people forget to plug is the dipstick tube hole. Oil will come pouring out if the hole isn't plugged after the dipstick tube is removed. Try plugging the hole with a wine bottle cork. Work quickly to install the cork after the tube is removed and you'll have a much smaller mess.

305 RELEASE BEARING NOISE: If the stick shift transmission in your car howls in neutral with the clutch out, try this: Depress the clutch pedal. If the noise goes away, then the culprit is a toasted release bearing. Replace the bearing and the noise will go away.

306 BALKY CLUTCHES: If the linkage in your clutch-equipped GM car feels sloppy and you've checked everything, there are two items that you may have overlooked: The ball studs that mount on the engine block and the frame. Typically, these ball-shaped studs will wear and go unnoticed. They're easy to replace and cheap too! By the way, the frame rail ball stud is GM PN 3898610 while Chevy engine ball studs were PN 3866568.

307 LENGTHY CABLES: When installing the cable for an automatic transmission, you'll almost always find that the thing is far too long. The reasons for this are many, but in any case, this can often lead to cables which touch hot exhaust components and live a very short life. To solve the problem, loop the cable over the top of the transmission to the passenger side. Then gently loop the cable back toward the transmission shifter arm(s). One or two strategically placed Adel clamps can be used to hold the cable in place.

308 CLUTCH CHATTER: If the clutch in your car chatters, there are a number of possible causes. Two things you should check before getting overly concerned are the linkage and the input shaft splines. Sometimes clutch chatter is created by linkage that is hanging up and then suddenly releasing. Chatter can also be caused by the disc binding on the input shaft (it can't move back and forth freely). In some cases, this is caused by dirt, rust and other corrosion on the input or disc splines. Check these two items carefully before you yank out the clutch.

309 MORE CHATTER: If the clutch passes the chatter test described in tip #308, then the next item to check is the clutch disc Marcel. According to McLeod, the Marcel is the wavy spring material that's found between the clutch disc surfaces. It is designed to allow the pressure plate to squeeze the disc to the flywheel and to allow the surfaces to move at the same speed when the disc is finally compressed flat by the pressure plate engagement. If the Marcel is flat, the pressure plate will attempt to squeeze the facing upon engagement, hit bottom and skip across the face of the disc. This causes chatter. In short, if the Marcel is flat, it's time for a new disc.

310 LIGHTWEIGHT FLYWHEELS:
Believe it or not, aluminum flywheels can be used in street cars. In fact, they're perfectly suited for certain applications (e.g., a car with big power and marginal tires). If you decide to try an aluminum flywheel on the street, be sure to purchase a model with a suitable heat shield. What's that? Essentially, it's a steel insert that is recessed in the flywheel. The insert saves the aluminum from being gouged by the clutch action.

311 CERAMIC DISC BUTTONS:
The only exceptions to previously mentioned air gap rules are clutches that have ceramic buttons in the disc. These clutch discs expand when hot. As a result, the air gap decreases. Because of this, the clutch air gap must be set when the clutch is heated (it's not fun).

312 BACKWARD DISCS:
Believe it or not, more than a few people have installed a clutch disc backwards. In most cases, it will fit, but don't expect it to live long and prosper. A disc installed backwards might not live to see 1,000 miles of light-duty street use. New discs almost always have a decal stating which side faces the flywheel. If not, then always install the hub assembly toward the transmission. You and your disc will be happier.

313 FLYWHEEL STOPPER:
When the time comes to torque down the bolts on your flywheel, you'll find that the big round wheel constantly turns. Sure you can have a pal hold the front of the engine via the crank snout bolt, but that isn't always possible. If that's the case, try this: Take a used valve and stuff it in your vise. Bend the stem at a 90° angle and slide the stem through one of the bellhousing bolts. Place the valve face on the ring gear teeth. The face holds the flywheel while you torque the fasteners.

314 SCATTERSHIELDS:
Don't scoff at the idea of installing a drag race style scattershield (safety bellhousing, "can," etc.) on your street car. We've seen more than a few clutch explosions, and they weren't pretty. In fact, they can cause damage so severe that some cars have been totalled due to the carnage. An SFI-approved "can" is a wise and inexpensive safety item. Of course, if you're competing in an NHRA or IHRA event, they are required by their rules, so you'll have no choice but to install one.

315 SAFETY PLATED:
When installing a scattershield, don't be tempted to leave out the block safety plate. Yes, we know it's a pain in the you-know where to install, but it does have a purpose. The safety plate is designed to save the block from the same carnage that can ravage the floorboards. Be sure to install the thing. Your engine will be glad you did.

316 BROKEN MOUNTS:
Never discount the fact that a broken (but invisible) motor mount could be creating serious clutch linkage problems. A mount that is torn or broken internally can cause an engine to rock severely (and you might not be able to see the fracture). When it rocks, it can easily throw the clutch linkage out of alignment.

317 DRILLING FLYWHEELS:
Never re-drill a flywheel to a different bolt pattern. A tiny error (say, 0.003") in drilling one single hole can cause a very noticeable and undesirable vibration caused by the dynamic unbalance of the clutch. Instead, do the right thing and buy the correct pressure plate for the flywheel.

318 NOT SO COOL:
There are a couple of automatic transmission oil pans available on today's market that offer "internal cooling." The concept behind these pans is to run a series of tubes through the bottom of the pan. Air flows through the tubes and cools the transmission fluid. It's a great concept, but not so perfect in the real world. The "holes" in the pan are very easily plugged with road debris, oil, grit and other junk. Before long, some (or all) of the holes are plugged and the cooling power goes away. Trouble is, you don't know that until the ATF begins to burn.

Further to this, the pans offer little, if any cooling effect when the vehicle is stopped. Most major hi-po transmission manufacturers do not recommend these integrated cooler pans.

319 **TOOL SCHOOL:** If you have to do a clutch job on a car that isn't common to your fleet, here's a cheap way to align the disc splines: Use one of the inexpensive wooden dummy input shafts that are available from most auto parts stores. Admittedly, they don't have splines and as a result, don't work as well as the special, expensive little tool that you will probably only use once or twice. To solve the problem, simply wrap the wooden dummy

shaft with a few layers of racer's duct tape. The tape conforms to the clutch splines and will provide a much more accurate alignment with the pilot bearing.

320 **PEDAL RETURN SPRING:** When you release the clutch pedal in a stick shift car, it requires spring pressure to return the pedal and the clutch linkage back to their normal locations. By adding an extra return spring, you can gain some assist for the throwout bearing. Cars with diaphragm-style pressure plates gain the most from this added return spring force. Also cars with an over-center spring on the pedal do not have "extra" return force!

REAR AXLE AND DRIVELINE

321 FROZEN YOKES: See this driveshaft yoke? It will spell death to the transmission tailshaft seal the moment it's installed. Any rust accumu-lation, small nicks and other damage should be removed be-fore installation. An easy way to clean it up is to dress it with sandpaper backed by a belt. Polish like you would a crankshaft journal.

322 LOCKED U-JOINT: If you're messing with late-model GM driveshafts (like those found in F-bodied Camaro/Firebird platforms), don't be too surprised if you can't remove the universal joints. GM included a special plastic seal that locks the U-joint in place. No amount of pounding will loosen the lock. To remove the universal joint, melt the plastic seal with a torch. It's easier than beating the universal joint to death with your biggest hammer.

323 RE-LOCKED: If your car does have one of the above plastic U-joint locks, it's a good idea to replace it with a conventional C-clip style of lock. Not only are they easier to service, they aren't as weak as the plastic parts.

324 MISSING NEEDLE BEARINGS: Recently, we've found that some new universal joints have needle bearings missing from the cap. Check inside the cap before installing them. Without the needle bearings, you'll be on a quick trip to nowhere when your U-joint seizes and your driveshaft goes south.

325 REAR END OIL: One of the biggest mistakes one can make when working on a rear end is to overfill the assembly. This creates foaming of the lubricant, air pockets and eventual component destruction. Filling is not accomplished with the cover removed! Instead, it is done by leveling the housing, pulling out the filler plug (on most GM rear axles, the plug is found at the passenger side of the housing, ahead of the inspection cover) and adding lube. Using a 12-bolt as an example, two quarts plus a small bottle of posi additive is about right. Any more and the lube will run out of the filler hole.

326 HI-PO COVER: You can substantially improve the life of your 8.8 axle assembly by installing a TA Performance cover girdle and bearing support studs. This cover is made from high grade alu-minum and incor-porates adjustable posts that butt against each carrier cap. This extra support greatly reduces housing distortion that occurs when the carrier is subjected to drag race launches.

327 CLUNKY POSITRACTION: Years ago, enthusiasts with positraction (limited slip) axles didn't think about noise. Soon cars with limited slip rear axles were banging and clanging as the clutches engaged. No, it doesn't mean that the rear will self-destruct. Instead, it's simply a sign that you should add some additive! Ford sells the stuff as "Hypoid Gear Friction Modifier" under PN C8AZ-19B546-A. GM sells similar goop. They both work.

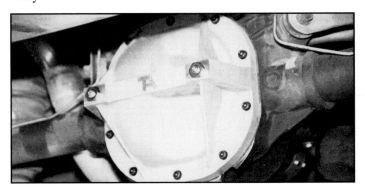

328 12-BOLT LEAKS: If you're familiar with Chevy's 12-bolt (the Dana 60 and other axles have similar setups), you probably know about the factory "system" of spot welding the axle tubes to the coconut with a couple of spot welds per side. In most instances, these welds are not sound and under close examination, pinholes in

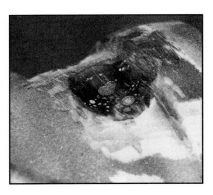

the respective welds will become evident. Now this doesn't affect the strength of the tubes on a modified housing (since the tubes have been totally welded to the coconut), but there is one small problem: The factory welds often leak or "weep" lubricant. Because of this problem, many a 12-bolt has had seals replaced, gaskets replaced and drain plugs swapped—only to find that the leak was in the area of a factory spot-weld. If you're modifying a housing, take the time to dig out the original spot welds and to fill the holes with a proper "rosette" or plug weld to stop the leaks.

329 NOISY DETROIT LOCKERS: If your street machine is equipped with a Detroit Locker and making loud growling noises, the first thing to check is the diameter of the rear tires. Don't just check the tire sizes. Remove them and measure the circumference. It's quite possible that two tires that have the same sidewall size are very different in circumference (and therefore shorter or taller in diameter). If that's the case, it will cause the Locker to ratchet and "work" even when you're driving in a straight line.

330 TWISTED STRIPES: If your driveshaft causes you grief from race weekend to race weekend (especially true on heavyweight race cars), you might consider painting a straight stripe down the center of the shaft. Once in place, you can quickly climb under the car and examine the stripe. If it is beginning to twist out of shape, then it might be time to swap the shaft before it decides to take an unwanted vacation. By the way, the same system works on axles. Just be sure to change the pieces before they decide to pack it in.

331 CHROME REAR COVERS: There's no question that chrome-plated rear end covers are popular, but before you purchase a cheapo chrome piece for your GM housing, give this some thought: The stock GM covers have a special "rib" which stretches from one side of the cover to the other. This isn't for strength

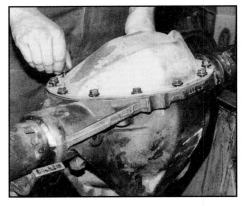

purposes. Instead, it directs gear lube from one axle tube to the other—supplying lubricant to the OEM wheel bear-ings. Unless you use a sealed after-market wheel bearing, this crossover is essential.
Unfortunately, some cheap aftermarket covers don't have this feature. In addition, you should be forewarned that chrome retains heat. Maybe the "look" isn't worth the trouble after all.

332 HEAVY-DUTY HOUSING RETENTION: Take a look at the bolts which hold the housing in place on leaf spring cars. Some of them are held in check with a lone 3/8-inch or 7/16-inch bolt per side. Under heavy loads, these bolts can either stretch or break. To solve the problem, replace the weak pieces with heavy-duty 1/2-inch U-bolts (available at most truck spring emporiums). The only other modification is to the spring perch. The hole size(s) will have to be enlarged to accept the new hardware.

333 PINION YOKE: One of the weak links in any rear end is the pinion yoke. Almost all yokes are designed for pedestrian applications—

they're cast iron and designed for long, dust-free life (most have an integral deflector flange which keeps mud away from the pinion seal), rather than ultimate strength. Aside from the construction tactics, these pieces are also engineered to accept rather small universal joints. In order to solve this problem, companies such as

Mark Williams Enterprises have come up with a group of heavy-duty 4140 steel yokes. Engineered for use with massive Spicer 1350 universal joints, these yokes are precision-machined on CNC equipment and as a result, feature extremely accurate dimensions. Better yet, they're almost indestructible.

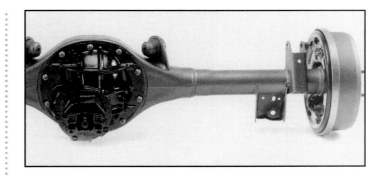

334 SPRING PERCH BRACES:
Although most manufacturers made use of a relatively heavy leaf spring perch, they still have a tendency to crack and work loose under severe loads. Some shops resort to

completely re-welding the perch, but here's another solution. Cut small plates of metal that brace the perch on both sides. The housing is cleaned and the plates are cut with a "V" shape to allow for total weld penetration. After they are tacked into place, MIG-weld them in place. The small brace plates are very effective, and combined with a proper weld job, look like factory parts. With this system of plates installed, the spring perch is heavily braced for fore and aft movement.

335 AXLE BOLT PATTERNS: When
selecting a bolt circle on custom axles, always try to use the largest possible bolt circle that "fits" the application. As an example, it is often possible to re-drill the brake drums so that axles with a larger-than-stock bolt pattern can be used. When the pattern size is increased, the unit load per stud is reduced. The larger the bolt pattern diameter, the lower the force imposed upon the lug stud. A lug stud on a 5.0" diameter bolt circle carries 11% less force than an identically sized stud on a 4-1/2" diameter bolt pattern. It is often possible (and relatively easy) to re-drill the brake drums so that axles with a larger-than-stock bolt pattern can be used. Obviously, if stock wheels are planned for your ride, this method of increasing the bolt circle is limited. Keep in mind that the Chevy pattern of 4-3/4" is larger than stock FoMoCo or Mopar passenger car patterns. Because of this, the unit load on each stud is less.

336 AWESOME 9-INCH: If you're
having problems with the 8.8" rear on your

late-model Mustang, a bolt-in 9-inch replacement from Currie Enterprises is the cure. The strength of the 9-inch Ford housing is legendary, and Currie Enterprises has made replacement relatively simple. Nine-inch units are also available from just about every axle manufacturer. But unless you have built out your 5.0 for 500-plus horsepower or swapped it for a 460 cid monster motor, the 9" is probably overkill.

337 REAR BEARING CAPS: The
rear bearing caps found on Dana 60 and 12-bolt rear axles are relatively fragile cast-iron pieces. Because of the nature of a ring and pinion, the torque forces of the powerplant will try to push the carrier outward—placing

additional strain on the driver's side bearing cap. Although this might at first be difficult to envision, think of the phenomenon like this: As the car accelerates, the ring gear attempts to climb out of the case or housing. To solve this problem, replace one or both of the factory caps with an aftermarket billet steel model (Summers, Mark Willams and others offer 'em). If installing a single cap, then the driver's side carrier bearing should be replaced. With the cap(s) in place, ring gear life is improved dramatically.

338 WELDING TUBES: When
reworking a rear axle housing such as a 12-bolt or Dana 60, the first order of business is to weld the tubes to the "coconut" or center section. The only reason the factory axle tubes stay in place is because of a pair of spot welds. Nothing else holds the tubes to the center section. In order to accomplish the job, the area should be ground down cleanly, then the factory axle tubes should be "stitched" to the coconut

REAR AXLE AND DRIVELINE

via a heli-arc weld. Of course, this process could be accomplished with another form of welder, but the aircraft style heli-arc weld proves much cleaner (no weld splatter or "spitting") and offers better penetration than other formats when properly

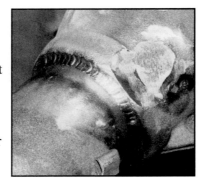

accomplished. In short, it's more labor intensive, but provides a better weld.

339 REPLACE WHEEL STUDS: It
might come as a surprise to you, but a stock GM intermediate/compact wheel stud size of 7/16 inch is not adequate for any vehicle destined for competition (even mild competition) or high performance use. All high-po

applications should have their studs replaced with a minimum 1/2-inch stud. Companies such as Summers Brothers do not offer axles in the 7/16-inch stud form and supply all axles drilled and tapped to accept 1/2-inch studs. Proper studs (or more correctly, bolts) are fashioned from Grade 8 materials and are threaded all the way to the head. Because of this feature, the bolt can be fully engaged in the backside of the axle.

340 SUPER STUDS: High horsepower,
heavy vehicles can benefit from the use of "drive studs." These are massive studs that are a full 11/16-inch (or larger) in diameter. Designed to fit the holes in aluminum race type wheels (e. g. Centerline, Cragar, Weld, etc.), the studs make use of a positively huge 3/4-inch axle thread (the portion of the stud that screws into the axle). Consider these components overkill if you like, but if bent or broken axle studs are plaguing your car, give 'em some consideration! By the way, "drive studs" are available from Summers Brothers, Mark Williams and other high quality axle parts companies.

341 TOUGH GEARS: Believe it or not,
there's more to selecting a ring and pinion

than choosing the gear ratio. For example, Richmond gear offers "street gears" (49 and 69 series) and "pro gears" (79 series). The Richmond 49 and 69 series gears are actually softer than OE-issue ring and pinions while the 79 series are softer still. Rockwell hardness tests of OE production line gears reveal a minimum Rock-well "C" specification of approximately 59-60 with a maximum figure of 65. The Richmond "street" gears register approximately 58-59 on the Rockwell scale with a maximum of 62. "Pro gears" (series 79) will register approximately 52-56 on the Rockwell "C" scale. Aftermarket gears such as the Richmond examples are manufactured from high nickel content steel (SAE 8620), but OE gears have very little nickel alloy content. Why a "soft"

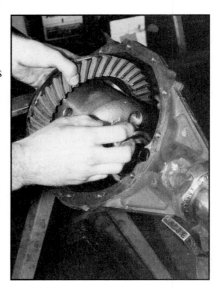

construction for high performance gears? The reason is impact loading. When a relatively high amount of shock loading is introduced into a conventional "hard" ring and pinion, the gears can shatter. Softer construction allows for a certain amount of tooth "bending," but this is certainly preferred over shattered teeth! Because of the differences in Rockwell hardness, gears destined for drag race use only ("Pro" or 79 series) are not appropriate for street or street-strip use. The gears wear rapidly because of the softness. Due to this fact, all cars destined to see some amount of street use should make use of street gears (Richmond 49-69 series).

342 SPLINES EQUAL STRENGTH:
One of the keys to rear axle (and total rear end) strength is the actual spline count. Axles endure two types of loads—torsional loads (twisting) and bending loads. The larger the diameter of the axle, the greater its ability to withstand these forces. If the axle diameter is doubled from 1.0-inch to 2.0-inch the torsional strength is increased eight times. More (and larger) splines on the axle means more ultimate strength. Unfortunately, in the past, the only way to increase the actual numbers of splines was to use a spool in the rear axle. And of course, spools don't work that well in some

applications or under certain conditions (e. g., in the rain). Happily, that's all behind us. Thanks to the folks at US Gear, a new 33-spline 12-bolt positraction unit is readily available. This assembly allows the axle spline count to be

increased from a stock 30 splines to a 33-spline configuration. While this might not seem like a major improvement, the resulting strength improvement is close to 33% over a stock axle spline. The increase in spline count, in turn, strengthens the axle by increasing the axle's "minor" diameter. And for anyone using the FoMoCo 9-inch, Lenco has recently introduced a new 35-spline "locker" for that application. Like the US Gear 12-bolt, it too increases strength dramatically. Check 'em out. There's more to axle strength than meets the eye.

343 US GEAR FEATURES: With the US Gear positraction setup (mentioned in #342), you'll also find that a thicker, webbed flange is used on the case (which is also reinforced)—effectively reducing ring gear deflection. Spider gears are forged from tool steel which makes them approximately 50% stronger than Chevrolet "service package" assemblies. Four more friction discs are

included (totalling 22 discs) and this allows for more even distribution of shock loads to the side gears as well as improving the torque split ratio significantly. Spring plate size as well as the springs themselves are considerably larger than a stock Chevrolet differential. This modification provides for an even bias ratio between the rear wheels. The result? Improved straightline traction. As indicated previously, the US Gear piece is designed for use with huge 33-spline axles—a marked improvement over the factory 30-spline arrangement. While custom axles are

required for this positraction unit, it is virtually bulletproof. It should also be noted that heavy-duty US Gear positraction units are designed for use with ring and pinions ranging from 4.10:1 to 6.14:1.

344 AXLE RING: An innovation you'll immediately see on a Summers Brothers' axle is the "gold ring." This special ring significantly improves axle life by strengthening the high stress area on the axle shaft, which locates the axle bearing. On a conventional axle, this

area features a shoulder which joins the shaft with a corner radius of approximately .078 inch. High stress loads can cause cracking and axle fractures at this point. The Summers Brothers' gold ring installs between the wheel flange and the axle bearing. It allows

the axle to be machined with a radius of .188 inch, which is twice as large as the original. The end result is a radius that reduces the concentration of stress, which in turn produces a much stronger, more durable axle assembly.

345 STREET OR STRIP AXLES? When selecting axles for a specific application, keep this in mind: Street-driven vehicles cannot use the same axle as their drag race-only counterparts. Drag race cars are subjected to the same types of forces and environment at all times. Street cars must endure side loads and of course the "unexpected." Cornering forces, minor encounters with curbs and other "environmental hazards" all produce side loading. In a worst case scenario, assume that your street/strip car is involved in an accident and another vehicle hits the rear wheel. A drag racing axle would sheer immediately, but due to the special heat-treatment of a dual-purpose street/strip axle (a slightly softer heat treatment process), the axle will bend rather than break.

346 CLEAN AXLE HOUSING: Before commencing work on the rear axle housing, try this on for size: An excellent method of cleaning the housing is to have it dipped in your local chrome shop's cleaning vat. All lubricant is removed in the process and as a

result, the housing proves easier to work on.

347 **PONY GEARS:** What type of gear ratio is best for your 5.0 Mustang? Ford sends it to the streets with a limp 2.73 final drive ratio—good for high fuel economy numbers but not good for much at the strip. According to William Mathis, author of HPBooks' *Mustang Performance Handbook*, you should switch to 3.55 gears for a mildly modified street car driven on the highway occasionally. However, the 3.73 ratio is by far the best choice for a hot street setup. Gear ratios beyond this are better suited for drag-race-only applications. Generally, a normally aspirated car set up for drag racing can use a 4.10 or 4.30 ratio to put the car at 6000 rpm at the finish line.

348 **WRAP CAPS:** Whenever you pull the driveshaft out of your car, you always run the risk of having the caps fall out of the universal joints. And no matter how careful you are, it seems at least one of these babies will drop to the floor, littering it with dozens of tiny needle bearings. Once the bearings are on the floor, good luck gathering 'em all up. To solve the dilemma, simply wrap the U-joint caps with masking tape every time the driveshaft comes out. It saves a bunch of headaches.

349 **PINION ANGLE:** Pinion angle is extremely important. And if you have swapped a rear end into your car, or raised or lowered the ride height, you must check the relationship between the rear yoke and the driveshaft. In lowered applications, you might find that the pinion points up—which is the worst possible angle. This throws the driveline out of phase. Worse yet, it yanks the driveshaft back (away from the transmission) as the car accelerates. Generally speaking, the more angles you have in your driveline, the more power it takes to turn the works. So what's the best pinion angle? As a rule of thumb, the pinion should point down 4-5 degrees when the car is stationary and on a level surface.

350 **BRACING DRIVESHAFT:** If you have to pull the rear end out of your car, you don't necessarily have to take the driveshaft out. An alternative is to place a 2 x 2-inch piece of wood over the exhaust pipes so that they support the driveshaft. This way, you don't have to worry about the transmission leaking at the yoke seal, and best of all, you don't have to worry about getting bonked by a loose driveshaft, which can be pretty painful.

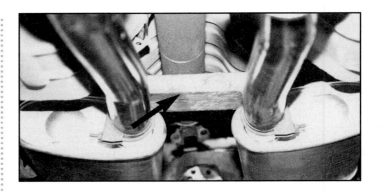

351 **C-CLIP ELIMINATOR:** Not only are the factory C-clips a pain in the you know where, they're also illegal in most drag race classes. In a stock Chevrolet application the splined end of the axle is machined with a special small diameter groove to accept a C-clip. This groove not only weakens the axle by a significant margin, it can prove very troublesome to remove and to replace (no matter what anyone says). With a C-clip system in place, the axle is retained from the inside rather than the outside. If an axle breaks anywhere the wheel can (and will) quickly depart

from the vehicle. The use of a C-clip eliminator kit makes it possible to remove the axles from the automobile without draining the lube. Finally, the old drill of grinding off the ring gear teeth to clear the spider gear shaft simply is not required with a C-clip eliminator kit. Mark Williams, Summers Brothers, Strange and others manufacture a variety of NHRA/IHRA-legal C-clip eliminator kits. Most replace the stock axle bearings with sealed, press-on bearings (many are Olds/Pontiac types) and do not require welding for installation. In most cases, all necessary bearings and hardware are included in the respective kits.

352 **SPOOLS:** The vast majority of drag race cars use a "spool" instead of a differential. The spool is a simple piece of equipment that provides a solid link between the ring gear and the axles. Because of this, both wheels receive an equal amount of torque all of the time. If you decide to run a spool on the street, remember that the car could be a handful when the streets are slippery (e.g. it rains). Also, the spool places a considerable load on the axles. Don't be tempted to run a spool without proper aftermarket axles!

353 SPEED DIFFERENTIAL: If a
"spool" locks the rear axles together, how does a differential work? Internally, a differential is connected to the axle via a series of splines. In essence, the axles are connected via the splines to the axle gears or "side gears" inside the differential case. The side gears are engaged by the pinion gears or "spider gears" which are mounted on a common shaft assembly. Moving in a straight line, the pinion gears are stationary— there is no turning action on the pinion shaft. The side gears are driven equally but when the vehicle turns, the pinion gears turn on the shaft. One half or side of the

carrier then speeds up while the other slows down. The result? A smooth turn without one tire spinning. The purpose of the positraction unit is to maintain additional force so that the pinion gears remain stationary unless absolutely necessary. When engine torque and power is supplied in a straight line, the clutches lock and drive both sides of the carrier equally, but when the vehicle is turning, the clutches become "unlocked," allowing for the previously described "smooth turn."

354 DRIVESHAFT VIBRATION: If
you have a vibration in your car and you can't find it, don't overlook the driveshaft. Driveshafts should be balanced. If they aren't, the shaft will vibrate and in some cases, the harmonic frequencies will be so violent that U-joints will die quickly along with transmission and rear axle yoke seals. Another, often overlooked problem when it comes to vibration is dirt (and even small stones) jammed between the driveshaft and the universal joints. Believe it or not, dirt in general is a common cause of driveshaft woes. It can wreak havoc with the balance and universal joint operation. Just keep an eye on the shaft—especially if your car develops an odd vibration.

355 FORD GEARSETS: Ford
Motorsport offers replacement high-performance ring and pinion gearsets with ratios from 3.27 to 4.56 for late-model 5.0-liter Mustangs (shown) and for other Ford products as well. BBK Per-formance and other Mustang

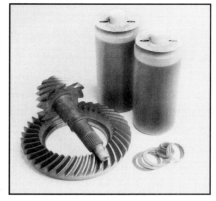

vendors sell these complete sets along with all necessary shims and gear oil. (Photo courtesy BBK Performance)

356 CARRIER BEARING: When
setting up a 12-bolt Chevy rear axle, be careful when setting the carrier bearing preload. Too much bearing preload will kill the bearings almost instantly. Too little preload will cause the carrier to move back and forth. In order to check the preload, install an inch-pound torque wrench on the pinion nut and measure the preload without the carrier installed in the housing. Then repeat the process with the carrier installed. Installed, the pinion nut will require between 7-1/2 to 10 inch pounds more force to turn than when the carrier was empty. By the way, preload is adjusted by adding or subtracting equal thickness shims to both sides of the carrier. Adding shims increases the preload. Removing shims decreases it.

357 QUALITY U-JOINTS: When
shopping for universal joints, don't bother with the generic replacements. Buy high quality U-joints from Spicer or Lakewood. The cost differential between good universal joints and junk is minimal. Further to this, Lakewood offers a wide range of "conversion" universal joints. These assemblies have various sized caps which allow swapping of rear axles and driveshafts (such as installing a Dana 60 where a 12-bolt once lived).

358 POSITRACTION TEST:
Remember the old method of determining if a car had positraction? You know, lift it off the ground, turn one wheel and watching the relationship of the other wheel. Well, that "system" isn't always foolproof. The best method (and the only accurate one) is to remove the rear cover and inspect the works. A positraction axle will have clutches visible inside the carrier (carriers have large openings where the clutches and differential gears reside). An open axle will not have clutch packs. By the way, Auburn style differentials use special cones

REAR AXLE AND DRIVELINE

instead of clutches in their posi assemblies.

359 JUNKYARD SHOPPING TIPS:
When scouring the swap meets or salvage yards for GM gears or complete axle assemblies, keep this in mind: Most factory GM gearsets have the ratio stamped onto the edge of the ring gear. This stamping will most often show up in the following sequence: "39/10". Translated, this is 39 divided by 10 or 3.90:1. If the numbers aren't stamped, you'll have to count the ring gear teeth, and divide it by the pinion tooth count.

360 TIGHTENING U-BOLTS:
After you install a driveshaft, you have to tighten the U-joint bolts. If the joint is held in place with U-bolts (the preferred system), don't get carried away during the tightening process. Too much torque can literally crush the universal joint caps. If they're crushed, you can plan on replacing the U-joints in short order.

361 GEAR COMPOUND:
You might have heard the tip about using machinist's blue or dye instead of standard gear marking compound when setting the gear pattern in a rear end. Well, forget about it, it doesn't work! The best stuff to use is the correct gear marking compound, an icky, gooey sludge designed specifically for this purpose. Quality installation kits include the correct yellow marking compound, or you should be able to pick it up at most auto supply stores. You may have to hunt around a bit, though.

362 PINION BEARINGS:
When setting up a rear end, the pinion bearings have to be installed and removed several times. Although it's probably more convenient to hammer the bearing on and off the pinion gear, don't do it! Use a press rather than a hammer to install the bearings. Although most home workshops don't have a hydraulic press, almost everyone can find a shop with a press to "borrow"—it makes life much easier on the bearings—even though it will take longer to set up the gears.

363 CHEAP(ER) 12-BOLTS:
It's no secret that some 12-bolt housings are becoming hard to find and because of their popularity, they can be expensive. The 12-bolt that was originally destined for use with Camaros, Chevy II's and Chevelles differs in length, axle size and rear bearing size when compared to the easily located (and cheap) Impala housing. Better yet, the Impala rear axle features 1.617" diameter axle shafts while the Camaro/Chevy II/Chevelle housing uses 1.399" axles. The Impala brakes are substantially larger and because of the size difference, they make use of a larger axle flange bolt pattern. Due to the availability, price and strength factors, you might consider using the Impala housing and narrowing it to Camaro, Chevy II or Chevelle width.

364 CRUSH SLEEVES:
Many rear axle assemblies incorporate crush sleeves. A crush sleeve or collar is a round metal tube with a "kink" in the center. As the name implies, it is designed to "crush" as torque is applied. The purpose of this component is to preload the bearings. Once installed, it is difficult, if not impossible, to re-use it. Because of this fact, it should not be installed during the initial stages of ring and pinion setup.

365 BALANCED GEAR PATTERN:
When working with ring and pinions, you'll often hear the term "balanced pattern." What does it mean? It's one where the "wipe" of the pinion gear against the ring gear is equal on both sides of the ring gear tooth. Having a balanced

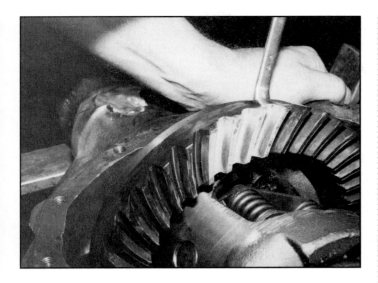

367 **PATTERN PAINTING:** Believe it or not, there's a right and a wrong way to paint the ring gear teeth with marking compound. Always coat the entire tooth (from the very top to the very bottom). This painting format allows you to obtain the most accurate pattern on the first check.

368 **STRAIGHTENING AXLES:** Before an axle can be checked for straightness, it must be allowed to cool "naturally" (following any welding). When an axle housing does require straightening, some shops prefer to straighten a housing using a press or a come-a-long. There is another answer when it comes to straightening, and one which many professional

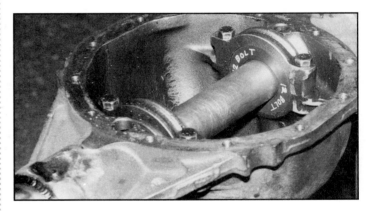

pattern simply means improved gear life, but a side benefit is less noise. In addition, a proper pattern will look like a relatively long, smooth-shaped oval, and it should slightly favor the toe or inside of the ring gear. Why should the pattern favor the toe side of the ring gear? In a typical hi-po situation, the pattern will "stretch" under loads (which can be quite high—especially if there is some heat under the hood and some hook at the back end of the car). In essence, this pattern reaches from one end of the gear tooth to the other (from the toe to the heel). If the pattern favored the "heel" or outside portion of the ring gear, then there's a good chance that the "pattern" or true contact area will go right off the end of the ring gear. It should be noted that a pattern that favors the toe or inside of the gear tooth will be noisier than a heel pattern, but in this case, that is a small price to pay for reliability.

chassis shops use (we should point out that this method works extremely well). Applying a small amount of heat in the right places can easily straighten a wayward housing. It's less work and much more accurate than other methods of straightening. Because of the finesse required, it's a good idea to leave the "heat" straightening to the pros.

366 **TRACTION-LOK MODS:** If your budget doesn't have the room for the purchase of a new Detroit Locker or a high-performance Auburn differential, you can improve the lockup of your Ford Traction-Lok by replacing a driven disc with a drive plate and stacking them in series as shown here.

369 **RING & PINION PRE-ASSEMBLY:** When setting up a ring and pinion, part of the pre-assembly ritual includes a thorough parts cleanup, but also included is the installation of the ring gear to the carrier (differential) assembly. All of the threaded holes in the ring gear should first be cleaned with a tap prior to installation. Loctite should be used on all

bolts (which, if you make use of a proper installation kit, are of the grade eight variety). Only then can all the ring gear bolts be torqued to factory specifications. Also, you should deburr the mating surfaces of the carrier and the ring gear, making sure they are absolutely clean and burr-free. The best way to do this is to use a high-speed sander with a Scotchbrite® pad to deburr the surfaces. After that, smooth both surfaces with a surfacing stone.

370 CHECKING BACKLASH: In order to check backlash on a rear end, you have to set up a dial indicator against the ring gear teeth. Install the dial indicator in a plane which is perpend-icular to a tooth,

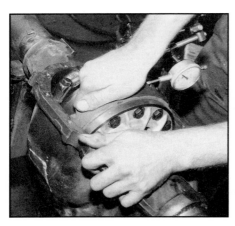

then wrap a rag around the pinion yoke. With a careful hand, gently move the yoke with a back and forth movement. According to Chev-rolet, the ideal gear backlash dimension is between .005 inch and .008 inch for a 12-bolt rear axle.

Drag strip-only 12-bolts can be as tight as zero in the backlash department. In order to increase the backlash, shim material is removed from the right side of the carrier and added to the left-hand side.

371 REAR END RUNOUT: Runout is seldom a problem with a good quality gearset and a similar, high quality carrier. Nevertheless, runout should not exceed .002-inch. If it does, then the mounting face of the positraction (or other differential) unit along with the mounting face of the ring gear should be surfaced.

372 CARRIER CONFUSION: When shopping for 12-bolt differential parts at a swap meet, keep this in mind: Chevrolet generally used three different types of differentials for the 12-bolt—the two series carrier, the three series carrier and the four series carrier. The "two series" has little use in a hi-po application and should be avoided if at all possible. The three series carrier accepted ring and pinions that ranged from 3.08:1 to 3.73:1 while the four series carrier accepted ring and pinions ranging from 3.90:1 to

6.14:1. While there are a number of subtle variations between the three types of carriers, a major difference is the thickness of the gear flange. Two series carriers are the thinnest while three series flanges are thinner than four series flanges. Because of the size of the flange, the carriers cannot be randomly used with ring and pinion sets from the trio of "families" (unless of course special gears with custom ring gear mounting surfaces are used. These special gears are readily available from Richmond Gear and U.S. Gear). Additionally, the two series carriers do not have any webs on the top of the carrier. Three and four series carriers do have webs.

373 PINION SUPPORT: It's no secret that in order to improve upon the strength of a Ford 9-inch rear axle, a system of supporting the pinion is mandatory. There are a number of different pinion supports available in the aftermarket—almost all of which rely upon a system of tapered roller bearings. Naturally, the tapered roller bearing design is extremely strong, but it also adds a significant amount of parasitic drag to the rotating assembly. In order to overcome this frictional loss problem, the folks from Mark Williams have recently released a new "extra low friction angular contact ball bearing" pinion support. Of course, it wasn't as easy as simply changing bearing designs. First, a suitable bearing had to be located. M-W found the perfect example in the angular contact format and designed an all-new pinion support around it. Included in the new pinion support is a profile-milled aluminum pinion housing, all necessary seals, O-rings and, of course, the ball bearing support. The new design fits virtually all 9-inch carriers—including the special aluminum and magnesium M-W models. Further to this, a large pinion model (for supercharged applications) is also available from Mark Williams.

374 LIGHTWEIGHT GEARS: Racers being racers, they're always concerned about weight. One piece that has recently caught our attention is the special lightened ring and pinion assembly from Mark Williams. The backside of the ring gear has been carefully machined. Depending upon the ratio (the ratio actually determines the thickness of the ring gear), the weight loss can amount to anywhere from two to four pounds! In short, more horsepower-sapping rotating weight is removed but there isn't any sacrifice in ultimate ring gear strength. We should point out that M-W will lighten any 9-inch ring gear set they sell. The option cost is $75.00 per set. At least from a racer

perspective, three to four pounds less rotating mass for less than a hundred bucks is a good buy.

375 TORQUE TIPS: When torquing main caps on rear end housings, don't get carried away with "tricks." Follow the OE manufacturer specs. While some individuals have their own preferences with regard to torque specifications, most rear axle specialists (along with most of the major aftermarket axle manufacturers) prefer to follow the factory recommendations.

376 BEEFY AXLE BEARINGS: Most aftermarket axle manufactures offer a number of different techniques to both increase axle strength and to provide for a secure method of retaining the axles. The best bet (and one we've successfully used on 12-bolt Chevys) features new housing ends that accept massive 45mm wheel bearings (available from Summers Brothers, Mark Williams and others). An axle machined for special 45mm wheel bearings (1.771" inside diameter) is substantially stiffer than standard axles. The outside diameter of these special bearings is identical to those used on the standard Olds/Pontiac housing end or the large Ford wheel bearing. As an example, the Summers housing end can be ordered with a Chevy backing plate pattern. As a result, the stock Camaro (Chevy II, Chevelle or Impala) brakes can be reinstalled. The

only major modification required for the swap is to enlarge the diameter of the axle shaft hole in the backing plate—something that can be easily accomplished by a local machine shop.

377 HOUSING STAND: When working on a rear end housing when it's out of the car, you'll probably find that the thing is bulky and hard to maneuver. If that's the case, try this: Peel off the cover (if it's a Salisbury) or remove the center section (if it's a Hotchkiss) and line it up with your engine stand. It should bolt right on, provided that you use the appropriate bolts. Now, you'll be able to rotate and manuever the bulky housing in the same manner as an engine while working on it.

378 U-JOINT FITTINGS: Universal joints that are equipped with a grease fitting should be installed with the fitting compressed. In other words, they should be installed so that they are ahead of the driveshaft in the direction of rotation. Installing them opposite to this will cause the grease fitting hole to open which will eventually lead to universal joint failure.

379 FORD 8.8 AXLE UPGRADE: Big slicks and high horsepower spell disaster for the skinny Ford 28-spline factory axles. This is particularly true during drag race launches and if the engine is putting out more than 400 horsepower. Upgrade your 8.8 with a set of 9-inch axles and bearing carriers. A kit is available from Greg Moser Engineering and several others. Although beefier 28-spline replacement axles are available (good for high performance street), go with the 31-spline units for racing.

380 U-JOINT PRESS: When installing a new universal joint in a driveshaft, try using a large C-clamp as a press. Use a socket between the jaws of the C-clamp and the U-joint cups to press the works into the flange. Be sure to press 'em in far enough so that the retaining clips can be installed.

381 REAR END BREAK-IN: When you've finished rebuilding a rear axle assembly, it's best to break it in before you go out and do burnouts. Here's a quick break-in routine: Drive the car forward and in reverse several times. Then drive the car around in either direction (circles). Listen for any unusual noises and watch for unusual vibrations. It's also a good idea to jack the wheels off the ground and "warm" the rear lube prior to using the fresh rear end. Once this is done, the rear end should be ready for use and abuse.

382 SEAL DEAL: Believe it or not, there is no need for a special seal puller when working with 12-bolt axles. Old axle seals can easily be removed in a 12-bolt housing by prying them out with the end of the axle. And if you're real good, you can remove the axle and "pull" the seal in one easy step!

383 SHOULDER BOLTS: When purchasing aftermarket ring gear bolts, think of this: Bolts that are fully threaded (to the head) are not as strong as bolts with shoulders.

384 NUT CASE: Pinion nuts should never be re-used. This is because nuts that have been subjected to torque can back off. As you might have guessed, the back-off routine can occur at the worst possible moment, such as right in the middle of a launch during the final round of the biggest race of your career. And, you know what happens next if the nuts back off. New pinion nuts are cheap insurance.

385 12-BOLT PINION DEPTH: Pinion depth on 12-bolt Chevys is critical, but even more so when you are working with ratios deeper than 4.10:1. When the ratio is numerically lower (such as a 3.55:1 and lower), the correct pinion depth is not quite as critical for overall gear life.

386 AXLE HOUSING DETAIL: If you're sweating for the last thousandth of a second of performance from your car, it might be a good idea to prep the inside of the rear axle housing. Just pretend that it's an engine block: Grind the interior smooth with a die grinder, clean it and then paint it with several coats of GE Glyptal or Rustoleum. The smooth surface allows the lube to flow smoothly and besides, it makes draining less of a chore since the lube literally falls from the cast internal surfaces.

387 DANA PRELOAD: Dana 60 rear ends used in production applications (hi-po Mopars and many pickup trucks) are equipped with tapered roller axle bearings. Although this is a superior bearing, it does require preload adjustment to function properly. The proper end play is 0.005 inch for "off road" use and between 0.008-0.012 inch for street applications. By the way, if you tire of the tedious preload adjustment, Lakewood offers a replacement ball bearing that requires none of the monkey business.

388 GIRDLE COVERS: Like the Ford 8.8 (see tip #326) the Dana 60 and 12-bolt Chevy axle housings can benefit from the installation of a girdle-style rear end cover from T/A Performance. The girdle replaces the rear end cover and includes a pair of preloaded bolt inserts (accessible from the outside). The idea behind the preloaded bolts is to eliminate, or at least minimize, the amount of distortion experienced by the main caps under load. They work and when all is said and done, you can expect added ring gear life.

389 RING & PINION NUMBERS: If you carefully examine an aftermarket ring and pinion, you'll find that the pinion gears are etched with

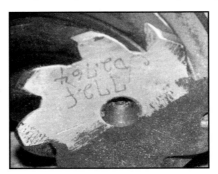

gearset numbers. You'll also find that the pinion depth is also etched next to the set number. Generally speaking, this is the distance from the rear of the pinion to the centerline of the carrier. Similarly, the ring gear will also be etched with the set number. The ring gear will also carry a backlash specification. These figures can save countless time when setting up the rear end.

390 MAXIMUM U-BOLTS: Universal joint "girdles" have been available for some time. They replace the U-bolt or strap with a billet "girdle." Companies such as Moroso offer 'em. But there is one thing to remember with U-joint girdles: They can interfere with the pinion (or transmission) yoke under certain conditions. If you install them on your car, be positive to check the relationship

between the yoke and the girdle through a complete range of suspension movement. You might be surprised at how close they come in certain applications.

391 DRIVESHAFT LOOPS: Driveshaft

loops are very good sources of protection for any car. But if and when a driveshaft does break, the loop can be a lifesaver. Contrary to what you might read in some publications, the loop should be placed within six inches of the front universal joint (not in the center of the driveshaft span). The idea is to stop a wayward shaft from literally pole-vaulting a car into the air. If the driveshaft breaks near the rear joint, it might cause some sheet metal damage, but it won't "launch" the vehicle. By the way, adjustable loops should be set so that they are round rather than oval. This saves a bunch of carnage should the shaft break.

392 TORQUE SPECS: If you take the

time to torque wheel lug nuts in place (and you should, especially if you are racing), here are some recommended numbers: If you have a 1/2-inch wheel stud, torque to 65-70 ft-lbs. If it's a 7/16-inch wheel stud, torque to 50-55 ft-lbs.

393 CHECKING GEAR RATIO: If

you're not sure of the axle ratio in your car, follow these steps: Jack up the rear of the car and slip a set of axle stands under it. Mark one tire with chalk on the inner sidewall so that you can count revolutions while you're under the car. Mark the driveshaft in an area near the pinion. With the car in neutral, rotate the driveshaft and count the revolutions it takes to get the tire back to the starting point. The number of driveshaft revolutions required is the approximate rear axle ratio. As an example, if you turned the driveshaft 3-3/4 turns for every revolution of the tire, then the axle ratio is probably a 3.70 or 3.73:1 assembly.

394 NINE-INCH MODS: One problem

with Ford 9-inch housings that people tend to forget is the fore-and-aft movement of the center section. You see, the hypoid action of every ring and pinion (Ford or otherwise) will always try to force the ring gear out the back of the housing or carrier. The more power available and the better the traction, the more aggressive the fore-aft action. Compounding the problem is the fact that all 9-inch housing "banjos" are stamped 2-piece assemblies. In short, the stamped construction doesn't cut it. In order to solve the problem, Mike

Pustelny of MPR welds a series of tubular supports around the respective bolt holes inside the housing (linking the face of the housing to the back side). MPR calls this "caging" the housing. A similar process developed by George Cathy of Pro Designs uses a series of gussets which link the face of the housing (where the carrier bolts) to the backside. Copy the idea. It can lead to significant improvements in ring gear life (how about five times the life?).

395 PRESS PILOT: When pressing axle

bearings on an axle shaft, be sure to support the axle on the pilot that centers the brake drum. Do not support the axle on the wheel lug flange. You're only flirting with disaster.

396 CHECKING FOR AXLE WEAR: If a set of original equipment

axles are to be re-used, they should be inspected for wear. One of the places where wear can cause grief is next to the flange. The axles can wear heavily in the seal and bearing area. If that's the case, then the axle will have to be replaced.

397 PINION TOOL: To

set the pinion depth correctly and with accuracy on a Ford 8.8-inch axle, pick up a special tool designed just for this task. Although there are a lot of shadetree mechanics that install new gearsets without one, doing so is a big gamble. If the pinion depth is set wrong, the ring gear will howl and you'll probably ruin it in the process.

398 WIDE TRACKING: When shopping

for an OEM Mopar Dana 60 housing or complete rear axle assembly, keep this in mind: The Dana used under 1966-1970 Coronets and Belvederes is narrower than the axle assembly installed on 1970-'71 Barracudas and Challengers. Additionally, the "wide track" E-body jobs all featured a 35-tooth axle spline. Old design models (pre-1970 Dana 60 axles) had 23-spline axles.

399 BUSTED DIFFERENTIAL:

Smoke from the inside tire is a clear

indication that your differential has gone south. If it is an Auburn, as is the case in the photo, you may be able to sand the glaze from the cones and seats for a small revival. If you have driven it hard with the cones slipping, you may not be able to revive it.

400 BEARING & SEAL SWAP: New style (1970 and later) Dana 60 rear assemblies (with 35-spline axles) are equipped with seals and axle bearings that interchange with conventional 8-3/4 axle assemblies.

401 DANA DIFFERENCES: The Dana 60 is one heavy-duty piece. But the actual differential used in 1970 and newer models (called a "Traction Lok") isn't as strong as the older "Powr-Lok" which saw service between 1966 and 1969. Keep in mind that axle splines are different between the years. On the other hand, Chrysler did service replacement 35 spline Powr-Lok differentials. The folks from Mopar offered the 8-3/4-inch rear axle in three distinct models (the series began way back when in 1957). The small pinion jobs (with a 1.625" pinion diameter) are the least desirable. They can be identified by an "X" cast into the third member. The middle sized, 1.75" pinion job was offered from 1957-1968. It can be identified by a straight pinion. Finally, the last model had a large 1.875" pinion. It can be identified by a tapered pinion. The best carriers for these rear ends have a "42" or an "85" casting number (they are manufactured from the strongest material).

402 TOUGHEST REAR END: Need deep wheel tubs and fender-to-fender slicks for your Pro Street Mustang? You'll be going nowhere fast if you don't beef up the rear end. Zander Action Products of

Houston, Texas, can fix you up. They offer housings utilizing the Ford 9-inch carrier, built on a jig. The units could handle the torque of a bulldozer, or just about any horsepower level, provided it is below 5,000.

403 LOW BUCK POSITRACTION: If your budget has run out and you have a car without a limited slip rear axle, try adding an air bag (Air Lift Company) to the right rear spring. Experiment with the air pressure in the bag. Once you get the pressure set correctly, the air bag will help to equalize the load between both wheels. It won't be a true limited slip, but it will certainly be better than an open differential.

404 STOP SHOP: When you swap a rear end from another vehicle in your car, don't forget about the brake balance. When stock front brakes are included in the vehicle "package" and the "new" rear end has

larger-than-stock brakes, the relationship of the front braking force to the rear braking force (brake bias or balance) changes. If this change is significant, the chances of locking up the rear brakes under panic situations becomes magnified. In this case, an adjustable proportioning valve will be required.

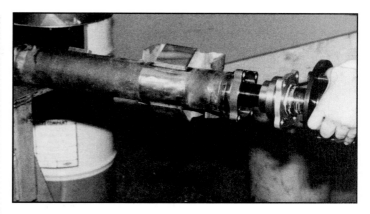

405 STUD TORQUE: According to the folks at Summers Brothers, wheel studs must be installed using Loctite or an equivalent thread cleaner along with "most severe service" thread locking compound. The bolt head on the backside of the stud must be torqued to 65 ft-lbs. If this isn't done, there is a chance that the lug bolt head(s) could interfere with the rear brake cylinders. Finally, the installed torque of the wheel studs should be checked periodically.

406 SPLINE SERVICE: Axle splines must have a minimum of one inch of full depth spline engagement in the spool or differential gears. Any amount of engagement less than one-inch could result in spline failure. If the axles are of different lengths, they should be marked for driver's side and/or passenger's side of the vehicle so that incorrect installation is prevented. If the axles are swapped from side to side, you can expect "early" axle failure. This, of course, can be most disconcerting in the middle of a 200 mph pass down the quarter-mile, or while leading the field during a road race or circle track event.

CHASSIS, SUSPENSION AND BRAKES

407 HOSE CONNECTORS: Hidden inside Earl's Performance catalog are a line of fittings called "tube mates." And what they do is amazing. They allow you to mate hard line to AN hose without any flaring, welding or any other monkey business. The Tube Mate package includes the hose end, a special nut, a small proprietary aluminum washer and a rubber-type crush sleeve. Joined together properly the pieces form a leak-free "mate" between hard line and braided hose. Best of all, the number of parts is small and no bulky adapters are needed. Excellent stuff for oil and fuel lines.

408 TORSIONAL TWISTING: Maximum traction is something every street or strip enthusiast searches for. But if maximum traction is available, then something can break or at the least bend. In order to solve the torsional twisting, Pro Designs (5817 #2 East Berry, Fort Worth, Texas, 76119, PH # 817-457-7365) suggests that all rear axles (stock or modified) be fortified with a simple performance type anti-sway or stabilizer bar. Aside from improving handling, the traditional Detroit-style of swaybar helps to spread and transmit the torque loads more equally. The end result is a rear suspension/rear axle assembly that isn't bending, twisting or breaking. Instead, it maintains rigidity and yes, a "built-for cornering" component can actually help your car go quicker and faster in the quarter-mile!

409 CHASSIS PAINT: When painting the undercarriage of your street machine or racer, think about using eggshell black. It's not shiny and it's not flat, but it is extremely easy to clean and easy to look after. It doesn't look bad either! Of course, trying to find the right shade of black that isn't shiny and isn't flat for the frame can be a real chore. Most paint shops will give you a real strange look when you ask for "eggshell" paint. The following is the correct formula:
PPG Delstar or Dupont Centari
•Three quarts mixing black (sometimes called "strong black")
•One quart flattening agent

•Use PPG DTR601 quick dry reducer. Enamel is used on the frame and suspension pieces since it is more durable than lacquer and will quickly wipe down for a "wet" look.

410 ACORN NUTS: There are a lot of places where you can use trick acorn nuts on cars. They're neat looking and provide a finished appearance to the installation. Beware of shiny acorn nuts that are nothing more than a regular nut with a plated tin top. They can twist off if they are over-tightened. Instead, shop at a local marine store and buy some solid stainless-steel jobs.

411 BRAKE LINES: If you are competing in a road racing class, substitute steel-braided Teflon lines for the factory brake hoses to improve pedal feel and feedback. Often times the driver will complain of a long or spongy pedal, especially in a fast autocross event. Everyone scrambles to bleed the air that somehow managed to get in the system at the last second only to find the sponge gremlin returns again toward the end of the next run. Many times the problem is caused by expansion of the stock brake hoses under intense braking pressure after being softened by hot brake fluid. The average Mustang will lock up ordinary tires with about 600 lbs-in. of line pressure on the street. However, it is not uncommon to see brake pressures upwards of 1,600 lbs-in. under severe racing conditions. With these kinds of pressures the stock hoses will not function properly. The steel-braided Teflon pieces are the only way to go. Always use #3 lines. Using incorrect I.D. lines screws up the hydraulics and the differential braking.

412 CONTROL ARM BUSHINGS: There are a many different control arm bushings available from the automotive aftermarket. When the time comes to replace your versions, don't be tempted to use the special "non-serrated" bushings (designed for drag racing) on a street car. These bushings have the internal serrations removed for ease of suspension travel. The loose action created by the non-serrated bushings will make the vehicle totally undriveable on the street (believe us, we've tried it).

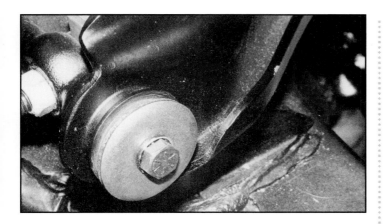

forget to re-torque them after a few miles. More than one set of wheels has been ruined (elongated stud holes, wheels that fell off) simply because the new owner didn't take the time to check the lug nuts. Re-torque the wheels after 25, 100 and 250 miles. After that, they should have taken a set. We should point out that this is not restricted to aluminum wheels (although it is more common). Check all wheels after installation!

Instead, use bushings designed for street use if that's where you'll be driving most of the time.

413 USE LOCK NUTS: When installing equipment on your car, forget about lock washers. They don't work that well and they're outdated. Instead, use "elastic stop nuts," or more commonly, lock nuts with nylon inserts. They do the job better, and unless they are subjected to high heat loads, they never back off.

414 STEERING DISASSEMBLY: When disassembling front steering and suspension components, mark and label all shims with regard to their location (passenger control arm—upper, bolt at nose of car: 3 shims). In addition, count all of the threads remaining in various pieces, such as the tie-rod ends, before you disassemble them. When it comes time to reassemble the front end parts, the alignment will not be completely out of synch and driveable until you can get it to the alignment shop, which should be as soon as possible.

415 WOBBLY WHEELS: If you've just installed new wheels on your ride, don't

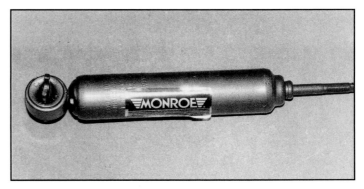

416 SHOCK TALK: According to the drag race suspension gurus at Tri City Competition, a great dual-purpose street/strip shock doesn't have to be exotic. Instead, Tri City Competition suggests you try a set of very conventional, very mundane 50/50 hydraulic assemblies on the nose of your car. After extensive testing, Tri City Competition determined that most vehicles respond favorably to a set of inexpensive front hydraulic shocks. In other words, no high-tech, gas-charged, multi-adjustable shock absorbers. Just down-to-earth Monroe-Matic specials. Expect elapsed times to come down but without the hassle of lengthy shock tuning or adjustment procedures.

417 REAR SHOCKS: Although you might find it difficult to believe, high-dollar, multi-adjustable shock absorbers aren't always required on the back of the vehicle either. Many applications work exceptionally well with a conventional 50/50 ratio gas-filled street shock. Which gas-filled shock is right for you? Past experience has shown that an inexpensive shock such as the KYB models work well in this application. Air shocks shouldn't be considered for a hi-po street-strip application. These components are designed for load compensation and have little or no value in a street/strip automobile. Generally speaking, the same applies to the many "helper" spring equipped shock absorbers.

418 BRAKING POINT: When working on drum brakes, you'll invariably encounter several springs and clips that are a pain to remove and re-install. Instead of fighting the hardware, buy the right tools. Brake pliers look like water pump pliers, but their long handles are designed to install and remove stiff brake return springs. The brake shoe tool (it looks like a screwdriver with a goofy head) is designed to compress the springs and twist the metal cups which hold the linings to the brake backing plates. Get the right stuff, it avoids launching a spring across the garage.

419 FUEL FILTER LOCATION: You might be shocked at the amount of garbage that is actually floating around in the fuel you use in your car. Past experience has shown that even specialized aircraft fuels (such as 110-130 and 115-145) are loaded with crud and junk. Because of this problem, a filter is an absolute necessity. Unfortunately, the arguments regarding the best fuel filter location will probably never end. Should it be mounted before the fuel pump or should it be mounted after the fuel pump? Given the amount of debris in today's fuel (and in the interests of saving any electric pump from carnage), the best location for a fuel filter is before the fuel enters the pump.

420 LOOSE WHEEL STUDS: Sometimes heavy-duty drag race (or circle track/road race) applications make life tough on wheel studs. Some (especially those with aluminum brake hats mating to aluminum wheels) actually loosen up during use. The stud isn't actually loosen-ing, but the distance between the wheel and the hat or backing plate is increasing slightly. Because of this, the

wheel moves back and forth on the studs, eventually wearing out the lug holes. To stop the problem, try adding a small amount of valve lapping compound to the backside of the wheel (on the mounting surface) before snugging the

wheel to the axle. The coarse nature of the lapping compound actually creates friction between the wheel and the hat or drum flange. The result? No more "loose" wheels.

421 WEIGHT WATCHERS: Looking for some inexpensive weight reduction on your mid-sized GM ride (and that includes vintage Camaros, Novas, Venturas, etc.)? Check this out: 1978-and-later Malibu (and other GM A-bodies) uses a rear brake drum backing plate that weighs only 1.5 pounds. The aluminum drum with a steel liner weighs only 9-1/4 pounds. Compared to steel hardware, these things are absolutely scrawny. A mid-size GM brake steel brake drum tips the scales at 17-1/2 pounds, while the backing plates typically weigh 5 pounds. As you can see, there's some serious weight reduction available with a swap to later drum brake hardware.

422 U-BOLTS: We've mentioned the U-bolts which loop over the axle housing and attach to the lower spring pad on leaf spring cars before. But there's something else to check out: Many vehicles only use one of these bolts per side. The other location is sometimes fitted with a pair of small T-shaped bolts. Unfortunately, these T-bolts are quite fragile and under load can easily bend or break. To

fortify the package, swap the T-bolt for an extra U-bolt. While you're at it, specify the heavy thick nuts (which are about twice as thick as a conventional nut)—they provide twice the thread area in comparison to a standard nut. Drill out the lower spring mount pad to accept the larger U-bolts and install the new hardware. Just be careful during installation so that the rear brake line is over the U-bolt, not under it, if your car is designed as such.

423 AN FITTINGS: AN hose end fittings are trick, but you should check your assembly very carefully after the hose ends have been installed. Once the hose is assembled (hose ends installed), pour solvent through the line. If it pours through normally (doesn't dribble out), then the line is sound. A second check (only possible when both hose ends are of the straight variety) is to lay the completed

hose end on a flat surface. Dim the lights in the shop and shine a small flashlight through one end of the hose. Carefully done, you can actually see your handiwork inside the hose. Any obstructions will be clearly visible.

424 BIG WHEEL DEAL: New wheels are cool. They look trick and we all know which wheels are right for our own cars. When you buy new wheels, mount them on the car before you mount the tires— even if you're sure that the backspace is right. This ensures that there won't be any clearance or fit problems. Besides, they're far easier to exchange before they've been mounted!

425 TIRE GAUGES: Optimum tire pressures are critical not only for fuel economy and tire life, but for maximum performance as well. It is also critical to make sure the suspension is correctly aligned. The easiest way to fine tune your suspension for cornering is with a pyrometer. By reading the temperature of the tire's contact area at the inside, middle and outside you can determine if the tire pressure is correct and how your suspension is working. The Longacre digital pyrometers shown are the best direct reading units available. Only extensive testing will help you determine optimum tire pressures (such as on a skidpad or drag strip). But once you

determine the optimum psi, either from testing or as recommended by the manufacturer, understand that it is when the tires are hot. Tire pressure increases as the tire heats up, so you should set

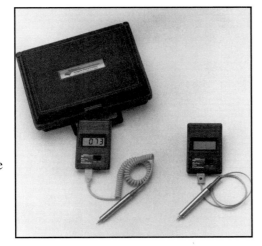

the pressure "cold" a few pounds less than the optimum pressure. Check pressures after the tire is hot. If you're above or below your optimum pressure, adjust your cold setting accordingly. This way, when you set your cold tire pressures, they'll reach peak pressure for maximum performance once the tire heats up.

426 DISAPPEARING BRAKE FLUID: If you check your master cylinder level occasionally, don't be too alarmed to find that the brake fluid is "disappearing." It's normal, but where does it go? You've checked all the lines and fittings for leaks, and everything is locked up tight. What happens sometimes is that

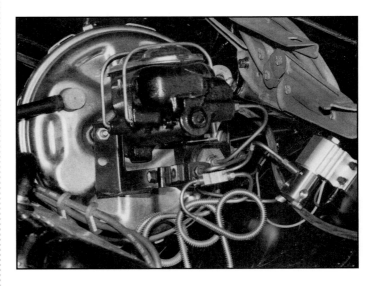

as the brake pads wear, the caliper pistons automatically move closer to the rotors. As a result, some space is taken up and the fluid level goes down. It's an automatic compensation, but it also means that you've got to keep checking the fluid and keep it topped off.

427 PICKLE FORK: You know the old trick about adding a nut to the tie rod threads and pounding off the rod? Forget about using a nut on suspension parts and pounding it out. Well, it works sometimes, but it does ruin nuts (and sometimes fingers). Instead, do it right! Use a pickle fork. They're not costly and they save a bunch of wear and tear on nuts, suspension components and in many cases, your fingers.

428 MR. CLEAN: Don't you hate cleaning disc brake dust from your wheels? It's especially acute on the front wheels of most cars. You could add those disc brake "covers" that have recently become available, but there is a chance that these covers partially block air flow to the brakes, reducing cooling. This is normally not a problem for everyday street driving, but turn up the wick a bit and brakes can fade and overheat. So, instead of the covers, try using a product called S100 Motorcycle Cleaner. It cuts right through the brake dust.

429 BAD LUG NUTS: Beware of replacement lug nuts. Some aren't right in shape or thread engagement. You can tell when the nuts are replaced. They physically move fore and aft (by a considerable margin) on the stud. We've found that this problem is especially acute when it comes to standard nuts for OEM type wheels. Typically, the hardware has been purchased from auto parts jobbers (some from a big chain). Do yourself a favor and buy replacement nuts from a new car dealer or from a reputable aftermarket manufacturer.

430 QUICK STEERING RATIOS: Don't bother using a quick ratio steering box for cars that will see drag strip duty. Drag cars "feel" better with slower steering. Besides, the tall skinny front tires that are common on 1320 cars have little steering resistance, and

require very little steering input to turn even the slightest amount. As you're going straight anyway (or trying too), quick steering response is not necessary; in fact, the opposite is true. You're better off with a slower steering ratio.

431 GLASS BEADING PARTS: I once had a perfectly good steering box. It didn't leak and it only had 29,000 miles on it. Trouble was, it was once painted metalflake silver, then repainted a sort of glossy black. In order to remove the paint, we had it glass beaded. This removed the paint, but it sprung a leak. Apparently, the high pressure glass beads damaged a seal. Now we have to take it apart and install new seals. The moral of the story is simple: Don't glass bead "assemblies" like the steering box. Take them apart first.

432 UNDERCARRIAGE DETAILING: The top show cars always have nice, clean undercarriages. And to tell you the truth, getting the undercarriage clean is tedious, dirty and time-consuming work. In order to strip your chassis, you'll need a heat gun for the easy stuff, a propane powered torch for the difficult goop, a putty scraper, a couple of big wire brushes and

a good supply of Scotchbrite® pads. Begin with the heat gun and the putty scraper and remove the big chunks. The wire brushes and propane torch do wonders for the difficult areas. When you're done, clean the area with solvent and Scotchbrite. Just be careful with the heat. Remember, solvent can burn, and so can gasoline. A week's worth of evenings will probably clean your entire undercarriage. Once it's painted, you'll understand how rewarding this job can be.

433 EXHAUST CLEARANCE: Do you have a problem with exhaust system clearance? It can be especially troublesome with late-model cars. If your car falls into this group, try using oval section exhaust tubing. Most stock car racing companies offer the stuff, and some shops have kits with various bends and adapters (back to round). Not only is the oval tubing low profile, but one of our engineering pals at GM has tested the tubing and found that it is just as efficient as conventional round exhaust tubing, so horsepower doesn't suffer.

434 MASTER CYLINDER BLEEDING: Always bench bleed the master cylinder before installing it on the car. This is done by running brake lines from the outlets on the master cylinder to the fluid chambers on top. These lines should be well into the chambers so they will remain below the fluid level at all times. Clamp the master cylinder in a vise and fill the chambers with fluid. Slowly pump and release the piston with a long punch until air no longer exits the lines as you pump. This will ensure there is no air trapped between the pistons that could make it impossible to bleed properly.

435 DRUM CLIPS: Buried at the back of the wheel studs on many drum brake-equipped cars is a clip which retains the brake drum. Some types of aftermarket wheels might rub the clip and interfere with the wheel. You won't notice anything until the car is driven. Then, the wheel will wobble. And don't worry about not having the clips in place.

The drum won't fall off 'cause the wheel will hold it in place.

436 BALANCING WHEELS:

Occasionally, you'll come across a wheel/tire combination that refuses to balance well. Or, the combination requires a bunch of weights. Before you add a pound of weight to one side of the wheel, try breaking the bead and rotating the tire on the rim. This allows the heavy side of the tire to counter the heavy side of the wheel. In the end, you'll need less weight on the combination.

437 BRAKE HOSE CLIPS: A part that

often is removed, misplaced or missing on many street machines (or race cars) is the little clip that holds the brake hose to the control arm. This little clip is more

important than you might
think, because it protects
the hose by securing it to
the control arm. If it's
missing, then the hose
will rub as the suspension
goes through its travel.
Worse yet, the hose can
become pinched under
certain
turning/suspension
movements. Check to
make sure that these are
in place as part of your
routine maintenance.

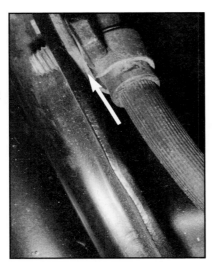

438 WHEEL VS. TREAD WIDTH:

When selecting your wheel/tire combination,

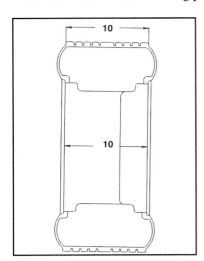

remember that for
maximum corner
performance, the wheel
width should be at least as
wide as the tire's tread. In
the example shown here,
the tire, a 275-50/16, has a
tread width of
approximately 10 inches.
The wheel, at 16 x 10
inches, provides excellent
sidewall stabilization by
matching the width of the
tread.

439 SECURING WHEEL WEIGHTS:

Tape-on wheel weights are used in a wide variety of applications, and they are especially convenient if you're changing tires all the time, such as between rounds or passes through the cones. We've used tape weights in the past—even on 14-inch-wide drag slicks. Trouble is, they often depart when you need them the most, such as in the middle of a road or circle track race. Depending on the level of imbalance, the wheels will vibrate, possibly leading to an increase in tire wear and a decrease in handling ability and effectiveness (remember, in racing, tire compounds are extremely soft). In short, the two-sided, sticky tape on the weight isn't always reliable. To solve the problem, simply cover the weight with a strip or two of racer (duct) tape.

440 ROLL-OUT: Every racer knows the

importance of roll-out, but do you know how to vary your race car's integral roll-out? Simply play with the front tire pressure. Adding air pressure to the front tires decreases rollout. How? The increase in psi decreases the

amount of rubber "seen" by the stage beam. On the other hand, you can decrease the air pressure and increase the roll-out. In essence, the tire "flattens" out in the beam, fooling the beam into thinking that there is more rubber on the road. Of course, this little game has its limits. Don't get carried away with tire pressure. The car can become a real handful on the big end if the tire pressure is too low.

441 NARROW DRAG TIRES: Do

you need a narrow 15-inch wheel for your GM racer or weekend warrior, but you don't have the funds to buy a set of pricey aftermarket units? Try your local junkyard. Chevy Impalas circa 1967 came optionally equipped with

narrow 15 x 5.00-inch Rally wheels. These wheels accept narrow race tires and have almost zero offset. This means that you can tuck 'em up under the nose of a race car without fear of the rubber meeting the inner fender. Besides, the wheels can usually be found with a price tag that is less than half the price of a standard narrow aftermarket steel wheel.

442 VANISHING VALVE STEMS:

Big old wrinkle-wall drag slicks have done wonders for quarter-mile elapsed times. Trouble is, to work properly, they have to run at low pressures. When a tube is involved, the low pressure has a way of moving the tube around inside the tire. When that happens, the tube valve stem gets swallowed up and the next thing that happens is a flat tire. To solve the disappearing valve stem dilemma, simply install a hose clamp around the valve stem (at a point that is very close to the wheel rim). Earl's Performance sells slick, small-diameter, stainless-steel pieces.

443 REAR SHOCK LENGTH: Have

you ever considered the length of the rear shock absorbers on your car? Very few racers or enthusiasts do, but there is a good chance that they are too short. Many leaf spring drag cars that aren't quite hooking properly have shocks that are of the improper length. To check the shocks' length, jack the rear of the car and install some axle stands on the frame so that the rear end can drop freely. Remove the lower shock mount bolt and allow the rear axle to drop to its lowest point. Pull the shock absorbers down as far as they will go. If they don't meet the axle shock mount, they are likely too short. In most cases, the solution is just as simple. Run over to your local speed emporium and pick up a set of shock extensions—Mr. Gasket makes them for almost every application and also stocks several different lengths. In most cases, a two-inch extension will do the trick. Add the extensions to your package and check your 60-foot times—you might be pleasantly surprised!

444 TIRE SPIN: This is another tip that

most of you already know about. In order to verify the fact that a car isn't spinning as it leaves the line, you'll have to mark one or both of the slicks and have an observer or two watch the rear rubber. Use a piece of racer tape or simply paint a fat white line on the tire sidewall with shoe polish. If the observer(s) easily sees the mark as the car launches, the tires probably aren't spinning. On the other hand, if the mark is a blur, the car is spinning—and therefore wasting precious time in the first 60 feet. If that's the case, it's time to go back to the chassis setup drawing board.

445 FRONT SUSPENSION TRAVEL:

This is a tip taken directly from the old Junior Stock drag racer notebook. Most GM cars (and some other Detroit marques) feature a system of limiting the downward movement of the front control arms. In a race car (especially a low horsepower race car), you need as much front end travel as

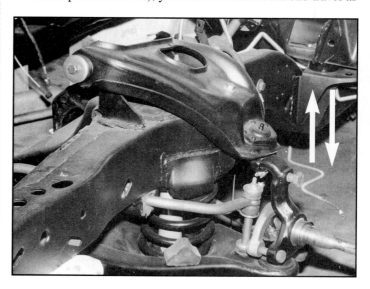

possible. Short of adding some ball joint extensions, there is a way to increase front end travel in these vehicles. GM used a rubber snubber mounted to the upper control arm to limit A-arm travel. This snubber is very similar to a conventional slapper bar snubber. If the snubber is trimmed, the front end of the car will have more travel, helping to keep the front tires planted to the pavement as weight transfers to the rear during a launch. But don't trim too much of the snubber away. If you trim and suddenly the 60 foot times increase, you've cut too much. Also, you don't want front end travel to increase so much that the brake lines become stretched. If you've cut too much, then swap the snubber for one used on a snubber bar.

446
REAR RUBBER: Just how much rear tire is really required to go fast down the quarter-mile? According to the experts, less than you might imagine. Although the tire companies seldom agree on what tire is best for a given application, all concur that the smallest tire possible is best suited for drag racing. Race cars go quicker and faster if you play the tire game correctly. The best

tire is the one that allows the car to hook without spinning, but if too large a tire is used, both the elapsed time and the mph numbers will suffer. In short, the wider and larger the tire, the more rolling resistance it has, and the more power it takes to turn it. The best thing is to test different tire sizes until you get one that allows a hard launch, but don't use the tires as a crutch for an inadequate suspension setup!

447
FUEL LINE SIZES: Many race cars have fuel line sizes that are far too small—especially if they are running the latest high tech fuel pumps from SuperFlow, Barry Grant, Mallory, Holley and others.

According-ing to SuperFlow, a high flow system should use a main fuel line that checks out at number 10 AN size. The line between the fuel tank and the filter should be number

12 while the line from the filter to the pump should revert to number 10. The bypass or return line from the pump should be number 8. SuperFlow has wet-flowed a variety of line combinations, checking the fluid dynamic properties of each and every size of line. When using gasoline, the ideal sizes just happen to be those mentioned above.

448
ROUTING FUEL & BRAKE LINES: When routing fuel and brake lines, you must be careful where you locate them. Even though braided stainless-steel lines are nearly bullet-proof, they are still vulnerable to failure if mounted in the wrong location. The ideal spot for fuel lines is on the inside of the frame rail—tucked up on the undercarriage side, not the curb side. Keep the lines away from any moving suspension components to keep them from shearing and by all means keep them away from the exhaust system. Aside from the fire hazard, exhaust heat will heat the fuel, increasing the

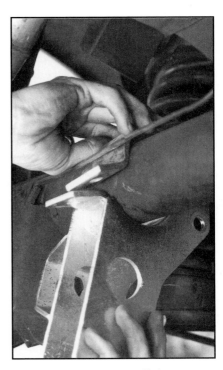

chance for vapor lock and reducing combustion efficiency. Braking fluid does not respond well to heat either. Also, make every effort to keep the fuel line away from the clutch bellhousing or the transmission converter housing. In the event of a clutch or converter explosion (highly unlikely, but it does happen), the last thing you need is a ruptured fuel or brake line!

449
DUAL TIRES: If you have a street/strip car that pounds the pavement at the local drag strip occasionally, you might consider using M&H Racemaster tires. Available in a variety of sizes and types, these D.O.T.-approved, treaded tires feature a soft compound and work almost as well as full-tilt drag slicks. If your racer is a dual-purpose ride or if you like to drive your car to the nearest Super Chevy show and run in the shootout event, then these

are for you. M&H has a wide range of sizes, from minuscule to massive. They even have some 16-inch rubber designed especially for late-model Camaros and Firebirds. Don't expect the tires to hook quite as well as a set of all-out drag slicks, but they sure work better than anything else on the market. If a stock-appearing car can do a wheelie at launch, then you know the tires are hooking up. If you decide to use the above M&H Racemaster "cheater" tires on the street, be careful when it rains. These tires aren't designed for foul weather use. The tread isn't designed to channel out water (say, like a modern radial). In short, save these tires for dry sunny weather.

450 ASPECT RATIO: Ever wonder what
this is? Aspect ratio is basically the relationship between a tire's section height and section width. The section height is the straight distance from the rim to the

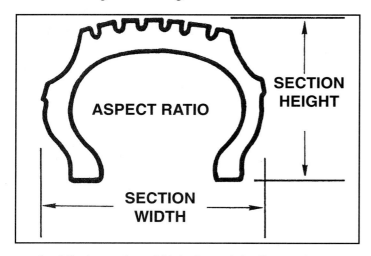

tread, while the section width is the straight distance from the outside of one sidewall to the outside of the other. Dividing the section height by the section width provides the aspect ratio.

451 DRAG RACE ALIGNMENT:
Before you can align the front suspension, you must first prepare it ahead of time. First, place weight in the driver's seat that is equal to the driver's weight. Shot bags and/or weightlifting equipment will work. Next, be sure to top the fuel tank or cell with the appropriate level of gasoline. Set the tire pressures to your race "norm." With the car on the rack, jack the nose up to duplicate the normal race attitude (an inch or two seems to be the norm). Finally, you're ready for the adjustments. Keep in mind that every car will be different, but here are the alignment targets:

•Camber should be set at zero; you should try to keep the front wheels straight up and down.

•Toe should be zero; toe-in change should be kept to an absolute minimum and be positive that the car does not exhibit any toe-out while the nose is in the air.

•Caster should be between three degrees and six degrees.

•Bump steer must be eliminated at all costs.

452 TIRE NOMENCLATURE: What
do those numbers and letters on the sidewall really mean? In the example, P designates the tire for passenger use. LT would mean light truck. The next three numbers, in this case 275, define the section width of the tire in millimeters. To convert to inches, divide by 25.4 (in this case the section width is just about 11 inches). The next two numbers, in this case 60, express the percentage that the height of the tire is of the section width. In this case, 60%, which is an average profile (40% would be a serious cornering tire).

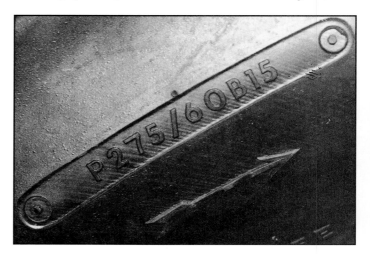

The next letter, "B," indicates the tire is bias-belted, as opposed to radial (R). New tires will have a speed rating before this letter, such as Z or H. The last two numbers, in this case 15, specify the diameter of the wheel that must be used with the tire, which is 15 inches here. The arrow is characteristic of Firestone and M&H Racemaster street tires that points in the direction of rotation. Goodyear's aren't quite as easy. These tires don't have an arrow, but they do have an eight digit code (not the same as outlined above) on the sidewall. This code appears on but one side of the tire and according to the Goodyear doctrine, the code must always face the right hand side of the car. When mounted, the driver's side code will be against the tub and the passenger side slick will have the code facing the "curb."

453 BUSHINGS: Street cars need nice
compliant suspension components. Those bits

and pieces of rubber help to isolate road noise from the cockpit, and soften the ride for the comfort of the passengers. But high performance cars are more interested in flat cornering without suspension deflection. The rubber bushings on most suspension components, such as swaybars, strut mounts, end

links, steering racks, trailing arms, control arms, etc., are made of soft rubber and allow for considerable movement when cornering. Replace them where possible with a set of urethane bushings, such as these sold by Energy Suspension. Your handling will improve immediately.

454 SPRING RATES: Spring rates are defined based on the number, diameter and spacing of the coils in conjunction with the wire thickness. Shown here are two front springs manufactured by Eibach for the 5.0 liter Mustang. The spring on the left is an 850 to 1000 lbs-in. variable rate while the one on the right is a specific 700 lbs-in. rate spring. The differences in wire diameter and coil spacing provide a graphic example of why one spring is stiffer than the other.

455 HOT SLICKS: When it comes to drag slicks (or any tire for that matter), heat means increased air pressure. If you are stranded in what seems to be a mile of cars in the staging lanes and the sun is beating down on you and your car, try covering the slicks with some white towels. The white material reflects the heat and keeps the tire pressures from rising excessively. To be on the safe side, drag your tire pressure gauge along. Just before it's your turn to play, check and reset the tire pressure. We can guarantee that the air pressure didn't go down while the car sat in the sun (unless you have a flat)!

456 SWAY BARS: The best way to increase roll stiffness is to increase the size or effectiveness of the sway bars, which are sometimes called

anti-roll or *stabilizer* bars. Sway bars limit the roll angle of a car by using their torsional stiffness to resist the movement of one wheel up and one wheel down. If a car is to roll, one wheel will be up in com-pression and one wheel will be in

drooping down. Connecting both wheels to each end of a sway bar causes this motion to twist the bar. The stiffer the bar, the more resistance to body roll it can provide. Since the forces that cause the car to roll are being absorbed by the swaybar, and these forces are fed into each lower control arm, the outside tire loadings will increase as the sway bar twists. The stiffness of a sway bar increases very quickly as its diameter is increased. The stiffness is a function of the diameter to the 4th power, or: Stiffness = D4. This means that a 1-1/4-inch diameter stabilizer bar is 2.44 times as stiff as a 1.00-inch diameter stabilizer bar. The length of the arms that feed the stabilizer bar loads into the chassis also have a dramatic effect on how much roll stiffness a given bar can produce on the chassis. The longer the bar, the less effective it will be. For example, 6.00-inch long sway bar arms will produce twice as much roll stiffness as 12.00-inch long arms. Also, the total roll stiffness of a given swaybar is dependent on the stiffness of the frame mounting, the stiffness of the arms, the stiffness of the drop links, and where the drop links connect to the lower control arms.

457 **VENT GAS CAPS:** Some cars featured totally vented gas caps while others did not. Be sure that your cap is correct for the application. If you don't, you could create a major pressure build up within the tank. The result is, of course, the smell of gasoline vapors inside the car along with surging performance—especially on warm days. Better still, the cost of a new vented cap is cheap insurance—even if your old version looks fine.

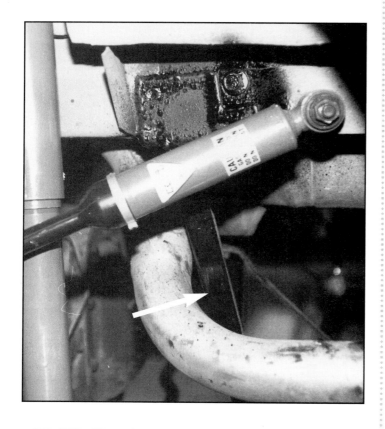

458 **FOX MUSTANG PANHARD BAR:** The Fox-chassied Mustangs built from 1979-1993 definitely need help in the handling department. Installing a Panhard bar can improve the rear axle compliance and lower the rear roll center. There are numerous bolt-in bars available, and if you decide to install one for your street-driven 5.0-liter Mustang, make sure you provide adequate clearance around the exhaust pipes. This installation had very little room for movement of the tailpipe, and resulted in a very irritating rattle. Leave at least 1/2" of clearance or you will suffer the same fate.

459 **WHEEL OFFSET AND BACKSPACING:** At the risk of over-simplifying, here's the basic definition behind these two wheel measurements. Backspacing is the distance from the axle mounting face to the tire mounting lip of the wheel. In this example, a 16 x 10" wheel, the backspacing is 6-3/4". Offset, on the other hand, is the distance from the axle mounting face to the centerline of the wheel. The offset of the wheel is further defined by the direction of the offset. When the centerline of the wheel is offset toward the exterior

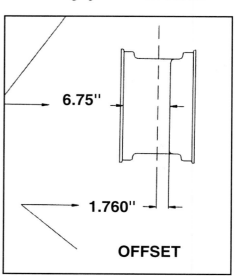

of the car, it is positive. Offsets toward the center of the car are negative. The example shown here has a 1-3/4 negative offset. For how to measure backspacing, see tip #504.

460 **SLOPPY STEERING:** Do you have a mysterious steering malady? Everything checks out and you've replaced virtually every component on the front end—rebuilt the steering box, checked the steering column. And the car still feels a bit "loose." Our guess is that you never gave the rag joint a second thought! These rag joints are just that—flexible couplings that can become contaminated over the years, saturated with oil, baked from the exhaust and yes, abused. The replacement process is relatively simple, but the results are far from it! Give it a try—it might prove to be the answer for a sloppy steering syndrome.

461 **BRAKE BOOSTERS:** Delco power brake boosters are plated in a special gold irridite plating. When new, this gold plating has a neat rainbow effect—something that cannot be duplicated with a spray bomb. Additionally, the boosters do wear out with age. We have

successfully used boosters prepared by several different restoration companies in the past. The results have been well worth the minimal costs of a pro restoration. The better booster resto companies completely rebuild the boosters and unless you have the necessary specialty tools required for disassembly and reassembly, it's far easier to send out your booster for a total rebuild.

462 BENDING BRAKE LINES:
Forming small diameter brake lines or gas

lines can be a pain in the you know where—unless, of course, you use the proper tool. Imperial Eastman offers this inexpensive tubing bender that allows you to bend angles from 90 degrees on down. The tool is indexed (for degrees of bend) and is capable of bending lines cleanly without any kinks. It is just the ticket for redoing the formed brake lines found on your hot rod.

463 GRUMPY TRIM RINGS: While
this tip generally applies to the Chevy-set, other cars can also benefit from it. If your rally wheels are equipped with genuine Chevy trim rings (complete with a minimal four clips), you might find it difficult to snap the rings into place—especially on the smaller five- and six-inch wide examples. To ease the suffering, simply deflate the tire partially. This makes the sidewall much more pliable which then allows the clip to easily slide behind the wheel lip. When installed, simply pump the tire to the correct operating temperature. It sure beats installing the trim rings with a 10-lb. sledge hammer.

464 TIRE PSI: According to the experts,
maintaining adequate tire service life from street tires isn't really that tough—you just keep the wheels aligned, have the tires balanced, rotate them once in a while and keep the pressure correct. Here are some other tips:

•Tires on the same axle should always be inflated to identical pressures. Check pressures every two weeks and always check tire pressure prior to taking any long trips.

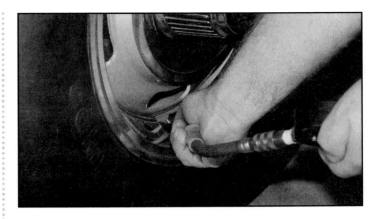

•Tire pressure should be checked when the tire temperature is cool. The best time to check pressure is after the car has been stationary overnight or after it has not been driven for several hours.

•Seasonal temperature changes will affect tire inflation pressure. For example, for every 10 degree F change in ambient temperature, the tire pressure will change 1 pound per square inch. Normal bi-weekly tire pressure adjustment should take this into account.

•Tire pressure should never be bled-down while the tires are hot. Pressures will normally rise during highway driving and then return to normal when the tire cools.

•Cold inflation pressure should never exceed the maximum pressure presented on the tire sidewall and should never be less than the vehicle manufacturer's recommended specification.

What can you gain by properly monitoring the tire pressure? As you are probably well aware, fuel economy will suffer if inflation pressures are below the manufacturer's suggested figure. In addition, tire pressure is a critical component of tire wear. Goodyear claims that a four PSI decrease in inflation pressure below the recommended limit can result in a 10% loss in tread wear. On the steering axle, this underinflation can create very rapid and accelerated shoulder wear.

465 LARGER BRAKE
PEDAL: Installing an SVO Mustang brake pedal in place of the stock unit (top), is one of the simplest and least expensive improvements you can make to

your Mustang's stock braking system. This pedal is manufactured using the larger automatic transmission foot pad. If you are into high performance driving, this will help you hit the brakes more securely.

466 BYPASS SURGERY: If you take a close look at many of today's hi-po fuel pumps (e.g. SuperFlow, Barry Grant, etc.), you'll find that they include a pump bypass system. Why use a bypass? Unknown to most enthusiasts is the fact that virtually all electric fuel pumps make use of an internal return system. The problem

with these setups lies in the fact that they simply return the excess air and fuel to the inlet side of the pump. The result of this phenomenon is a relatively large amount of air being allowed into the system which in turn displaces fuel in both pressure and volume. False pressure gauge readings result and if you haven't guessed by now, this can easily lead to tuning problems and destroyed engine components. In order to counter the problem, today's sophisticated pumps incorporate an external bypass system which allows the pump to dispel all of the unneeded air—primarily pumping fuel to the carburetor. Because of this special design consideration, the new style pumps can actually pull a prime from virtually any fuel pickup location (which, incidentally, makes a hidden street pickup location viable).

467 LIGHT WHEELS: When looking at drag race wheels, unsprung weight must be taken into consideration. Think of the wheel/tire combo as a

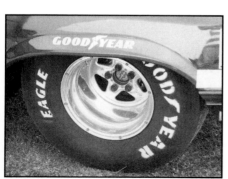

massive flywheel. It's easy to see that a big, heavy flywheel is hard to get rolling and just as hard to stop, especially when it's up to speed. Getting this set of rolling "flywheels" up to speed requires a

lot of power, and conversely, slowing them down takes a fair amount of braking power. If the weight of these flywheels is reduced, more horsepower is available so that quarter-mile times can be reduced. At the same time, you should consider the aero influences. As far as aerodynamics are concerned, there really isn't much you can do with regard to the rear wheels and tires. If they are hanging out in the breeze, you can bet that they are dragging. On the other hand, a pair of fat rear tires tucked up inside the wheelwells are about as aero as you can get with a conventional drag race chassis.

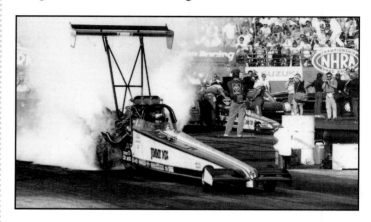

468 BAD BURNOUT: We've all seen this goof at one time or another: Someone pulls into the bleach box at the drag strip and remains there until the starting line, timing tower and most of the grandstand are filled with smoke. Now that might look neat, but according to the Goodyear engineers, it's a bunch of wasted time and money. In the good old days, drag slicks were made of harder rubber compounds, and as a result hard burnouts were required to get 'em up to operating temperature. Today's slicks are just the opposite. The compounds are much softer and require less time in the bleach box to get up to effective operating temperature. Not only are the shorter burnouts easier on the tires, they keep the entire powertrain much happier! Just remember, when those little wear holes in the slick face are gone, so are the tires.

469 SHOCK VALVING: If your car rides rough, don't be too quick to place the blame on the springs. In the vast majority of "bucking bronco" rides, the culprit is the shock absorber valving—not the springs. Shock absorbers are critical when it comes to tuning the ride quality of your ride. In fact, a very stiffly sprung car can be made to ride nicely, but the shocks cannot be overly stiff.

470 REMOVE TUBES: If you check around at major drag races, you might find something missing on many sportsman race cars—the drag slick tubes. In the search of lower unsprung weights, many racers have taken to eliminating the slick tubes entirely. Due to recent advances in lightweight wheel technology, the rear wheels don't leak like they did in the past. Sure there's some minor air leakage from the slicks (those wrinkled

sidewalls are still thin), but it isn't something that creates major aggravation. By the way, the installation of wheel/tire screws is unchanged, except you should be positive that a bit of silicone is added to each screw during the install process. Some racers claim minor improvements in both short (60-foot) and quarter-mile times, but like the old saying goes, "it's just one less part to go wrong."

471 REAR PONY DISCS: With all of the aftermarket goodies for 5.0-liter Mustangs available, it's easy to double the horsepower. But if you do, remember to upgrade the brakes accordingly, especially the rears. Most all Mustangs (except for special models) built from 1979-1993 were equipped with rear. One of the better conversion kits available is this rear disc setup from Stainless Steel Brakes. The kit bolts in pretty quickly. If you can't afford them, then at least check out SVO's five lug rotors and axle/drum kits, which add strength and increase your choice of wheels. The kit uses the stock brakes and installs with no special tools.

472 PONY SLICKS: The largest slick you can generally run under the rear fender of your Mustang without modifying the wheelwell opening is a 26 x 10-15 tire. This size slick will require a 10" wide wheel with a 6" backspacing. Any bigger than this and you'll have to enlarge the wheelwell or install tubs.

473 STUD ENGAGEMENT: The National Hot Rod Association rule book states that the stud thread must extend into the "hex portion of the lug nut by a distance that is at least equal to the diameter of the stud." Translated, that means that if the studs are 7/16 inch in diameter, then 7/16 inch of thread must be inside the hex portion of the lug nut. Why are we mentioning this? The above rule of thumb is applicable to all cars—not only race cars. And it can become critical if thick center aftermarket wheels are installed on your car.

474 PADS: If you're running triple digit speeds, especially on a road race or oval track, your stock brake pads will vaporize quickly. Make sure you upgrade to high quality pads. They can dramatically improve the braking efficiency of your stock rotors. Before installing them, it is important to heat temper them. You can do this in an old toaster oven (don't use your wife's current toaster unless you like sleeping on the couch). Put the pads in face up and leave them for at least 30 minutes, preferably

one hour, then let cool. Then, the pads should be bedded in with the rotors by making a series of hard stops from high speed until the brakes begin to fade. After cooling they should be ready for competition.

475 SHOCK DAMPENING: Extra firm shocks actually can have a negative effect on ride and handling. The tires cannot follow the road's irregularities unless they are free to move in relation to the chassis. The relative motion must be as free as possible, but it also

must be controlled. If the shocks are too firm, the suspension will be over-dampened, and the tires will not be able to keep contact with the road. What is needed is critical dampening, which is just enough control to keep the suspension from cycling. Basically, run your shocks as soft as possible—enough so the car doesn't wallow over bumps.

476 CORNERING SPRINGS: The
purpose of suspension springs, at least for high performance cornering, is to hold the car steady while allowing the wheels to follow road irregularities. In general, the softest possible springs will do this job best. Softer springs will allow each individual wheel to move in relation to the

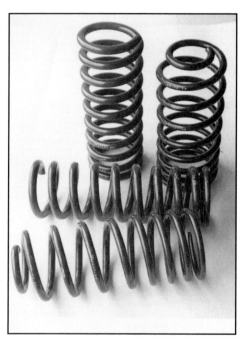

chassis while having the minimum effect on the driver's compartment. This translates into a soft ride, noise isolation and good handling. All stiffer springs do is make the car have a stiff ride. They have no ability to make a big improvement in handling. As long as the springs on a car are stiff enough to keep the

car from bottoming out, they are adequate. If a car is lowered, a slight increase in spring rate can be used to compensate for the reduced ride travel. Some car enthusiasts have the mistaken belief that if 300 lbs-in. coil springs are good, then 600 lbs-in. springs have to be better. They're wrong. Optimum road-holding demands that the tires be in contact with the pavement; a soft spring lets the wheels follow road irregularities so that the tires can generate maximum adhesion. Our recommendation for front springs on a street-driven car is to use the standard factory coils. For street use, you can trim 1/2 coil off the top of the spring with an acetylene torch to lower the car slightly. Most front spring rates range between 300 and 350 lbs-in. Trimming the coils as we've recommended will increase the rate approximately 10%. But the true purpose of trimming the front springs is to lower the car for improved

aerodynamics and better handling, not to increase the spring rate. Several cars, like the Corvette with F-41 suspension, the WS-6 Trans Am and the later model Camaro Z-28's, are equipped with very high rate springs. We have found that the ride can be greatly improved by installing softer springs, with no effect on the handling capabilities of these cars. Many enthusiasts buy the standard rate soft springs from their dealer for these cars and cut 1/2 coil for the proper ride height.

477 BRAKE CALIPERS: After you've
pulled the brake calipers off your car and then

reinstalled them, be sure you have the calipers on the correct side of the car. Unfortunately, both sides look similar. Which side is "right"? The brake bleeder should point up instead of down. If it points down, then bleeding will be difficult, if not impossible.

478 HOMEMADE LOCK NUTS:
Every car has at least one location where you can't use a locknut, lock washer or Loctite. And it always seems that the lock-less location is the one that always features a "self-loosening" bolt. To solve the dilemma, try slipping a short piece of nylon fishing line into the nut before screwing down the bolt. The fishing line "locknut" works every time.

479 CALIPER PISTON PUSHER:
If you're in the middle of a pad change on disc brakes, it's frustrating to find a piston that refuses to release (it's stuck "out"). The result, of course, is a brake job that can't be completed since there isn't enough room to install the new pads. Now, there is a solution, but it can become pricey. Most tool companies offer dedicated caliper piston presses that do the deed. Trouble is, they're expensive. A cheap replacement for a custom tool is a run-of-the-mill C-clamp. Affix it over the caliper body and tighten the clamp. Magically, the piston(s) will retract and you can install the new pads.

480 SHOCK EASE: Removing and
replacing front shocks on vintage Mopars with torsion bar suspension systems can quickly turn into an aggravating experience. To make the R 'n R go smoothly, try removing the rebound bumper (found on the underside of the

upper control arm). Removal allows for more suspension travel, which in turn provides more room for shock installation.

481 SOFTNESS TEST: How do you know if your shock absorbers are too soft or too firm? Find some O-rings that will fit around the shock shafts (you'll have to split the O-ring. Just be sure it remains tight). Install the O-ring in the center of the shaft and take the car for a spin. If the O-ring is shoved to the top of the shock, it's too soft. If the O-ring hasn't moved, chances are the shock is too stiff. What you really want is an O-ring that's about 2/3 of the way up on the shaft. On a similar note, this tip can be used to check rear shock travel in a drag racing machine. If the O-ring is moved all the way to the end of the shock, the car needs more shock absorber length.

482 SPIN BALANCED: Tires that are spin balanced on the car must always be mounted in the same position on the car (if they have been removed). If they aren't, then the balance will be gone. To solve the problem, dab some paint on one wheel stud and add a dab of paint to the corresponding lug hole on the wheel. If you don't follow this process or something like it, then you can expect to pay for re-balancing the combination.

483 STRATEGIC CLAMPS: Years ago, Chrysler Corporation spent a considerable amount of resources on drag race "Super Stock" leaf springs. A strong front "bias" existed and so did a series of heavy duty spring clamps strategically placed on the front spring bias. One method the Mopar bunch used to stop the spring "snake factor" was to heavily clamp the front of the leaf spring pack, while at the same time removing the segment clamps from the rear of the spring. Coupled with the biased spring, this allows the car to hook as well (or better than) a car fitted with traction bars. When working with spring clamps, try using a set constructed from heavy flat stock such as the Tri-City Competition versions shown in the photograph. Each of the clamp

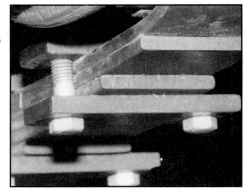

"flats" is threaded, accepting a grade 8 bolt without the use of a nut. Although each application will require a different mix of clamps (different location, different number of clamps), the idea of clamping the forward segment of the spring pack and leaving the rear segment "open" still applies. This system allows the rear of the spring to separate under acceleration. If you subscribe to the above clamping theory, you might consider adding another leaf to the right-hand spring package. When a drag car launches, it will tend to plant the right spring into the pavement with more force than the left spring. An extra leaf on the right-hand side will tend to even out the launch.

484 BOLT-IN ROLL CAGE: Whether you're running your pumped up 5.0 Mustang on the street, strip or through the cones, it's best to think safety first. If you don't want to tear apart the interior and start welding (i.e., your car is dual-purpose, driven on the street) then look at bolting in a prefabricated roll cage. For late-model Mustangs (1979-1994), it's hard to beat the Super Street

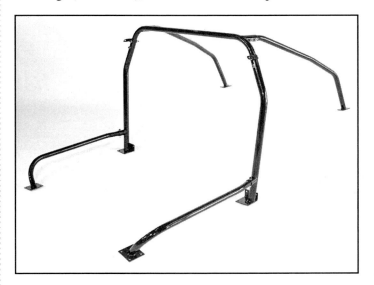

Cage™ from Kenny Brown Performance Products. This cage will provide some measure of rollover protection (no cage is absolutely safe) and add some rigidity to the chassis.

485 STRAP IN: No race car is complete without an approved safety harness. This popular Simpson harness provides excellent 5-point support with shoulder, lap and submarine belts to contain and protect the driver. Before you install belts, check your sanctioning body rule book to find out what's required. Then, make sure the belts are installed with welded brace plates and through-

CHASSIS, SUSPENSION AND BRAKES

bolts, or according to the manufacturer's directions.

486 CHASSIS WELDING: If you're going to be welding in chassis braces, or welding up body seams, gussets and roll cages, you should use 3M's Weld-Thru Coating. It's an excellent product to spray on bare metal before welding. This stuff forms a tough zinc coating when welded through, providing a strong barrier to rust. It also works great on the back side of areas that are hard to reach for painting afterwards.

487 BRAKE SWITCH: Some people have been led to believe that the special "brake pipe distribution and switch assembly" found on many vintage GM cars is an adjustable proportioning valve. Not so! The distribution switch assembly is located under the master cylinder. The front and rear hydraulic brake lines are routed from the master cylinder through the brake pipe distribution and switch assembly. It is from this point the brake lines to the front and rear of the vehicle are routed. The switch is wired electrically to the brake lamp "alarm" in the instrument cluster. It is not an adjustable proportioning valve! The purpose is to house the brake warning system and to distribute the brake fluid to the respective "corners" of the vehicle.

488 BODY MOUNTS: Swapping the soft body mounts on certain cars with aluminum ones is a good performance move. Why use solid body mount bushings rather than factory rubber insulated units? The original mounts are a compromise between ride, road noise and handling. When pushed to the limit, the rubber mounts deflect. While deflecting or moving under load (such as in cornering or in the case of a drag car accelerating), a considerable amount of energy is wasted compressing or stretching the body mount. The suspension has to work harder to keep up with the deflection, and starting line capabilities are

compromised. When you buy a solid body mount kit, don't use the supplied aluminum mounts under a radiator support—especially if your car sees street duty. Often, the aluminum mounts will be too harsh for the radiator. The result? Mysterious radiator leaks.

489 SOFT DRAG SPRINGS: One area where drag race technology becomes a real asset for hi-po street/strip performance is front springs. Although marked "for drag race use only," aftermarket springs such as the Moroso assemblies can find a home in specialized, limited use street/strip applications. These springs feature

added coils, a longer overall length and slightly smaller-than-stock wire diameter. This configuration allows the spring to "store energy." While stationary, the car remains level (or in some cases, has a slight forward rake), but when the throttle pedal is mashed to the floor, the nose of the car will rise rapidly. While accelerating in the upper gears, the springs settle down quickly, dropping the nose of the car to a much more aerodynamic profile. Moroso front springs are available in a wide array of configurations to fit a number of varied applications. A spring of this sort is not intended for heavily stressed street work such as cornering. Be forewarned that the nose will rise rapidly and the car will have a tendency to dive hard under braking. As a result, weight is quickly transferred to the rear of the car where it will do the most good for quarter-mile elapsed times.

490 PONY BRAKE UPGRADE: If you want to improve the braking of your

modified 5.0 Fox-chassied Mustang but are short on funds, step up to the larger 73mm calipers from the SVO Lincoln LSC brakes. Kenny Brown Performance Parts has made the job easy by offering a Club/Sport Brake Kit which includes the larger calipers, correct master cylinder, heavy-duty pads and an adjustable proportioning valve.

491 SILICONE BRAKE FLUID:

Unless you have the mega-dollars to flush the system completely every time the car goes to the track, do not use silicone brake fluid, and definitely do not use it on the street. This stuff sucks moisture like regular fluid but does not keep it suspended. Instead, moisture in silicone brake fluid pools and vaporizes into a large spongy steam pocket as the temperature of the fluid passes water's boiling point. Brake pedal feel becomes spongy and the differential braking gets weird. Then, when the race car sits for a couple of weeks until the next race, that pooled water creates a nice rusty pit inside the brake line, caliper or master cylinder where it happens to settle. Again a most uncool situation. Unfortunately, silicone fluid is also altitude sensitive. As the atmospheric pressure decreases (as altitude increases), the silicone fluid will exhibit signs of a spongy pedal. Finally, silicone will cause some of the rubber parts (like seals) to swell. Stay with the conventional heavy duty brake fluid.

492 LINE LOCKS: "Line-locks," "roll

controls," "stage-locks" are all names for the

same type of device. This aftermarket brake component provides a method of isolating the front or rear brakes and controlling them with a simple electrical micro-switch. In function, the roll control consists of a electric valve which is plumbed into the brake line(s), a micro switch to operate the system and a red "on" warning lamp. The most common application is in drag racing where the roll control is used during burnouts and staging. In operation, the brake pedal is pumped several times (to engage the brakes) and the roll control button is depressed. The brake pedal is then released.

Pressure to the front brakes is maintained, but rear pressure is released. The result is a set of locked front wheels which enables the car to perform a burnout or to inch slowly into the drag strip pre-stage and stage beams. A warning lamp indicates the roll control is in operation. When the burnout is complete or when the drag strip "Christmas tree" comes down, the button is released, allowing the brakes to revert to their normal method of operation. They are a great addition to any car that will see even occasional drag strip duty.

493 MORE ON LINE LOCKS: Hurst

advises that roll controls are primarily designed for use on race cars. The roll control should never be used on vehicles larger than a 3/4-ton pickup truck. It is not intended as a replacement for park brakes and is designed for momentary use only (approximately sixty seconds maximum engagement). Vehicles equipped with anti-lock brakes and spit diagonal brake systems cannot be easily adapted for use with the roll control!

494 TRACTION BARS: Did you know

that bolt-on traction bars can be tuned? One of the first things to tune is the snubber air gap. The air gap between the front bar snubber and the leaf spring eye determines how much spring windup is possible before the traction bars become effective. While novice builders will often tighten up the snubbers against the leaf spring eye, they are actually hurting the vehicle "launch." An air gap will also allow the snubbers to "smack" the spring eye with more violence. This in turn helps to shock the tires—effectively making

them "bite" harder. To a certain degree, the larger the air gap, the more violent the suspension reaction. The ideal situation would have both the right hand air gap and the left hand air gap identical, but when reality comes into play, there will likely be a difference between the two air gaps. Why? If the car consistently "pulls" to one side under power, you should increase the gap on the opposite side snubber. It's a trial and error process, and one that can easily be affected by exact vehicle weight with the driver on board. In other words, if the car is setup to run a specific way with the driver weight only, it will react differently if a passenger is riding shotgun.

495 TRACTION TUNE-UP: The location of a bolt-on traction bar snubber is also critical. Early versions have a snubber location that is much too far rearward. The ideal location for the snubber is directly underneath the spring eye—not on the main leaf. Should the snubber contact the spring leaf, it will soon bend the spring out of shape—rendering the spring useless while destroying the effectiveness of the traction bar. If your bars do not meet this criteria, they will have to be lengthened. This might involve adding as much as two to three inches to the overall length via welding. Nonetheless, the work is worth it. Correct snubber location translates directly into increased traction.

496 TIRE PATCH: Did you know that the overall diameter of a tire plays just as important a role as the tread width when selecting a size? If you examine a mounted tire from the "curb" side, you will note that a good portion of the foot print is spread out from front to back as well as the common side to side measurement. In other words, the tread contact patch is like a square or a rectangle—supported on the sides via the tread width. The length of this contact patch is determined by the overall diameter or circumference of the tire. The larger the O.D. (or tire height), the larger the contact patch. It's some food for thought—especially if your car doesn't have enough room for "wide" rubber. By the way, McCreary Road Star tires are some of the most popular tires for the stoplight to stoplight crowd. They are D.O.T. approved, have a treadwear rating of 000, are very reasonably priced and have enough tread to allow driving in wet conditions.

497 CASTER/CAMBER PLATES: The Fox-chassied Mustangs need help with handling, and one great addition is this Caster Plus Kit™ from Kenny Brown Performance. These bolt-in units provide improved caster and strut compliance without the road noise typically transmitted through the more serious camber

plates. This is an excellent kit similar to the SVO "onion head" upper strut mount, except with more positive caster. If you're into high performance and autocross racing, these are a must.

498 REPLACING BUSHINGS: When working with front control arm bushings, it's a good idea to have the bushings replaced by an alignment shop prior to painting any component. The press-off, press-on process will easily chip and scratch the control arms. After the bushings have been installed, simply take the time to mask off the various non-painted areas and then squirt the paint. By the way, these are polyurethane bushings sold by Energy Suspension.

499 J-BOLTS: The special bolts on the Competition Engineering traction bars (a very popular brand) are called "J-bolts." They're designed to wrap around the rear axle tubes. What are they for? These bolts absorb the stress that would normally be directed at the spring "U" bolts as well as the leaf spring perches, but they must be properly installed! During installation, tighten all four J-bolts equally. If necessary, count the number of threads remaining on the hardware, but be absolutely certain that both the right and the left hand slapper bar J-bolts are equal in terms of thread count figure. The J-bolts should not be used to tighten down the front of the bar or the snubber against the spring. This only leads to spring distortion and accomplishes nothing else.

500 FRONTAL BOLTS: Now that you know what the J-bolts accomplish on a traction bar, what's the purpose of the front U-bolt? It only has one purpose. It acts as a safety precaution in the unlikely event that the traction bar breaks. Of course, it also keeps the bar from taking a nose dive during panic braking situations. The U-bolt should not be used to compensate for snubber height! Like the J-bolts, the front U-bolts should be tightened equally.

501 MOUNTING FUEL PUMPS: Believe it or not, electric fuel pump mounting

is critical (with any electric pump). In order to fit an electric fuel pump in cramped quarters, many enthusiasts resort to awkward mounting positions—sideways, tilted and even upside down. While most pumps will function properly in this mode, it is only an accident waiting to happen. A fuel leak can easily contaminate the electric motor. It certainly doesn't require a rocket scientist to determine that gasoline and electricity can only mean one thing! To guard against this problem, be sure that your pump is properly oriented: Up means UP!

502 FUELISH FILTERS:

When adding an inline fuel filter to your car, don't waste your time and dollars on a plastic filter. They can restrict fuel flow, they are easily plugged and almost all examples have an inlet/outlet port that is too small for high performance use. Furthermore, the vast majority of disposable filters are constructed without AN ends. The only solution is to use worm gear clamps to hold them in place. If you're still not convinced, then consider that the pressure of an ultra-high-performance electric pump can collapse the internal filament of the filter. If you're going high performance, go all the way and upgrade your filters too.

503 SUPER FUEL PUMPS:

While it might sound impossible, a single four-barrel street-strip car is perhaps the most difficult to set up when it

comes time to plan and lay out a fuel delivery system. In a typical multiple carb drag race or Pro Street app-lication, there are four rather large bowls available to feed the engine. Additionally, an all-out race system doesn't need amenities such as a fuel level gauge, an easily accessed fuel tank filler neck, quiet operation, sufficient fuel capacity for sustained cruising and at least another dozen variables. Basically, a street fuel system centers around compromises. But there is a solution, and that's the new professional pumps from SuperFlow and Barry Grant. These

are incredible pieces of pumping machinery. As an example, a single SuperFlow pump can manage in excess of 400 gallons per hour and will also pull a vacuum reading due to its incredibly close internal tolerances. Best of all, these "super pumps" are relatively quiet and yes, very well suited for street use. It could solve your fuel handling needs.

504 CHECKING BACKSPACING:

Tip 459 described what backspacing is, now let's talk about how you find it. Checking backspace begins by

flipping the wheel over so that the wheel flange (where the wheel center meets the brake drum or hub) is visible. The first step in measuring the backspace involves laying a straight edge over the wheel rim. Anything that's straight will work—even a household level such as the one shown in the photo. Measure down from the straight edge to the wheel flange. The number that you come up with is the wheel backspace. Compare this number to the OEM wheel. The idea is to use a wheel with a backspace dimension that places the center of the tire contact patch in a location that is close to the factory specification. Obviously, a wheel with little backspace (and a bunch of "reverse" offset) will move the tire contact patch away from the normal location. That can spell trouble. And if the wheel has too much backspace, then it might contact the inner fender or suspension and steering components. That's the reason backspace numbers are so critical!

505 SQUEAKY BUSHINGS:

We've been recommending all through this section to replace your soft rubber bushings with stiff polyurethane pieces. Although they do wonders for handling, they do tend to squeak once the graphite lube works its

way out of the shell. And, removing them every 3,000 miles or so to relube them isn't very practical. One solution is to drill a hole, tap it, and install a zerk fitting so the bushings can be lubed along with the rest of the chassis during periodic maintenance. Although it is hard to see in this photo, there is a fitting at the rear of this swaybar bushing.

506 **DUST BUSTERS:** If you've been scouring the parts stores for a new set of tie rod end dust boots, you're probably resigned to the fact that they just aren't available—unless of course you're willing to buy a complete set of tie rod ends. Fortunately, Energy Suspension has solved that problem. They have recently released a complete range of replacement boots. The boots are manufactured from a rugged polyurethane material and feature special three-point seal for extra protection. Not only are they available in two different styles, they also come in a full complement of colors. Best of all, you don't have to buy the tie rod ends just to get a set of boots!

507 **HANGERS:** When working on the front suspension and brakes of your car, and you have to remove the brake caliper, do not allow it to simply hang by the brake hose! This can stretch the hose. Eventually the hose will crack and you know what happens next. Instead, always tie the caliper to the control arm or frame when it's temporarily removed. You and your brakes will be much happier.

508 **CABLE COUPLERS:** If you've ever had the pleasure of removing or re-installing a set of parking brake cables through the backside of a drum brake backing plate, this tip is for you: The shielded park brake cable features a set of fingers that encircle the shield. In order to remove or to install the cable, all of the fingers have to be depressed. Unfortunately, that's not so easy. To make the job much easier, wrap the locks with a small hose clamp and tighten it. Slide the "compressed" end into (or out of) the hole in the backing plate. Remove the hose clamp and you can then slip the works all the way in. This tip can probably save 20 minutes of frustration.

509 **CONTROL ARM TORQUE:** Once you've installed a new set of control arm or leaf spring bushings, don't be tempted to torque the hardware in place while the car is suspended on axle stands. If you do, then the bushings will be preloaded when the car is returned to mother earth. The correct method is to drop the car to the ground first, then tighten the bushings to specs. Not only does this provide for superior handling, it also improves the life of the bushing.

510 **COIL SHORT CUTS:** Never use a torch to cut coil springs! While it's been done time and time again, the use of a torch can radically lower the tensile strength of the spring. It might be easy, but in the long run, you'll simply kill the spring. The right way to shorten springs is with a cut-off saw or cutting wheel.

511 **HUB HOLES:** When shopping for aftermarket wheels, one thing most people forget is the actual size of the center wheel hole. Believe it or not, the center hub holes in wheels are not all the same. In fact, certain vehicles have significantly smaller hub holes than others. A good example is the late-model Corvette. A wheel designed for the 'Vette often has a much smaller hub hole than a similar wheel designed for use on a new Camaro. Check first before you buy.

POWER TUNING

512 WIRE SLEEVES: There are many types of wire sleeves available in today's market. They're good insurance against inductive crossfire. Unfortunately, many racers and enthusiasts have discovered that certain types of sleeves retain moisture between the sleeve and the wire. The result is wire deterioration and even shorts since the moisture is a pretty decent conductor. To solve the problem, try using sleeves that can have the ability to allow air to escape through the material so moisture doesn't collect underneath.

513 HEADER COLLECTOR: Hooker has come up with a new "merged" collector for adjustable headers. Designed as an offshoot of the standard 4-into-1 system, they are available in all popular primary tube and collector sizes. In terms of weight, a pair of 1-7/8" x 3-1/2" collectors weigh only 5 pounds, 4 ounces. These collectors are constructed with the primary tubes joining as

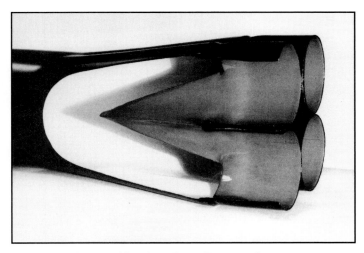

they make the transition into the collector to form a spear. Eliminating sharp edges and voids reduces turbulence. In turn, the reduced turbulence provides for improved aerodynamic exhaust flow, but it also allows more precise management of the header sound pressure waves.

514 SENSOR PROTECTION: If you're running long-tube headers on your 5.0 GT Mustang, it is important to wrap the oxygen sensor wires with heat deflector tape and secure them up out of harm's way, especially if you're running a racing exhaust system. The

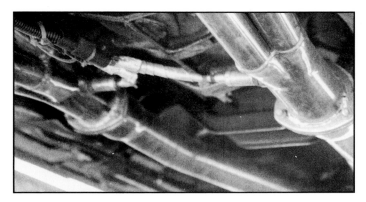

extreme heat generated by a racing exhaust system can bake the wires and cause the insulation to exfoliate.

515 CARB FLOW: See this hole in a Holley metering block gasket? If you compare it to the metering block, you'll find that the gasket hole is considerably smaller. It may not seem like such a big

deal, but if you open the gasket hole up to 3/8 inch (a punch or a leather awl will work), you'll remove a major restriction in the carburetor main jet circuit (according to most carb experts, it's worth about two jet numbers).

516 IGNITION POINTS: There is a difference between high performance and replacement ignition points. High performance points are of much higher quality than OEM or jobber type parts. As an example, Accel point sets are manufactured from stainless steel rather than carbon steel, have laminated phenolic rubbing blocks rather than molded plastic, use a screw rather than a clip for condenser retention, feature riveted brackets rather

87

than clipped components, include larger than stock diameter, self aligning point surfaces, include locking compound on the adjustment screw threads and more! Be sure to use the 32-oz. street points rather than the ultra-heavy 42-oz. race points—the street points live much longer.

517 MSD RUN-ON: Run-on is a condition where the engine continues to run even though the ignition key has been turned OFF. Two things can cause the run on—dieseling or a charging system that is leaking back to the ignition system. If your MSD-equipped car has this problem, the Autotronic Controls Corporation engineering staff offers this solution: Since the MSD is connected directly to the battery by a heavy red wire, only a very small current is required to keep the ignition energized. If the engine continues to run smoothly after the key is turned OFF, then the MSD may be receiving a small current through the charging system. It is easily cured by installing a diode to block the reverse leakage current. The diode should be installed on the voltage regulator terminal marked #4 on early GM's and on terminal #1 (or "indicator lights") on Ford regulators. Late GM's with integral regulators should have the diode connected to the wire that leads from the alternator to the dash indicator light (usually the smallest wire on the alternator). In any case, use a 1A-100V diode.

518 POWER PLUG GAPS: On most cars equipped with high-powered aftermarket ignition systems, the spark plug gap is usually .050 inch. Unless of course the car is turbocharged or supercharged. In this case, the engine will need smaller gaps (.035-inch or less) because of higher cylinder pressure. Greater pressure means more resistance—hence the tighter gap.

519 AV-GAS: For years, racers have been running higher octane aviation gasoline (Av-Gas) in their hi-po engines, because it was superior to pump and racing fuels in the past. The problem is, real high-octane aviation gasoline (115-145) is becoming impossible to find (some antique helicopters still use the stuff). And, even if you do find it, it isn't as good as today's race car gasoline blends. Av-Gas also has a different knock rating that is conducted under different engine test conditions. 115-145 Av-Gas does not have 115 RON and 145 MON. Instead, it works out to a RON of approximately 107 and a MON of about 105 (average of 106). You're better off using today's made for racing high-octane racing blends, usually available at the track you're competing at, rather than hunting down, storing and transporting your own Av-Gas.

520 STAGGERING JETS: Some engines (such as the big-block Chevy fitted with an open plenum dual-plane intake manifold) require *stagger jetting*. This means a separate jet is used in each corner

of the carburetor. An engine like the Chevy rat operates like a pair of big old V4's. Because of this, some cylinders run richer than others and as a result, the carburetor jetting compensates for the peculiar breathing arrangement. When rejetting a stagger combination, always use the original number as a baseline. For example, assume that the carburetor has a jet setup like this: Left front #80, Right front #76, Left rear #76, Right rear #78. If you want to enrich or lean the mixture, change all the jets up or down in size, but do it proportionally. That would mean that a two-step richer mixture would have a left front number of 82, a right front number of 78, a left rear number of 78 and a right rear number of 80. The same thinking applies when you lean the combination.

521 PLUG ANTI-SEIZE: Aluminum heads and steel spark plugs do not mix well. Besides the natural electrolysis deterioration that occurs, overtorquing can cause the plugs to seize in the threads. The next time the plugs are removed, the threads in the head come with them, seriously damaging the head. Always use a good anti-seize compound on the plug threads to reduce the potential for damage if you're using aluminum heads.

522 HI-PO DISTRIBUTOR CAP: Most OEM distributor caps and rotors are manufactured of thin plastic with aluminum terminals. They are prone to oxidation corrosion on the aluminum terminals. No doubt you've seen the chalky white buildup that forms on the inside of your

distributor cap's terminals. This stuff kills your ignition spark. Even a very thin layer of oxidation significantly increases the resistance to current flow. Resistance produces a voltage drop that converts the electrical charge into heat energy. In plain language, your spark begins to change from a strong blue to a weaker yellow. You should definitely upgrade the cap rotor with high performance units from name-brand manufacturers such as Accel, MSD or Mallory. Once you upgrade, it is very important to regularly (before every race) service the terminals. If there are signs of blue–green corrosion on the terminals, scrape or sand them to clean brass, then polish with a red Scotchbrite® pad. Even if you do not see any corrosion, polish the terminals with the Scotchbrite pad. Often times you will notice a black tint to the terminals. This is oxidation tarnishing that happens to brass. Like the white corrosion on the aluminum, the black residue resists current flow and reduces the voltage necessary to deliver a hot spark. Polish it clean before racing.

523 TUNE-UP ORDER: When tuning
the engine combination in your ride, don't go about it in a helter-skelter fashion. Instead, follow this path: 1. Compression & no vacuum leaks. 2. Valve lash. 3. Ignition. 4. Carburetor. When you're done, go back and check the ignition and then go back to fine tune the carburetor. The result is a very crisp, professional tune-up.

524 GRUNGY WIRES: After several
months of use, ignition wires become dirty. As the dirt (usually a combination of oil, grease and dirt) builds, the wires deteriorate. Because of this, it's a good idea to keep the wires squeaky clean. Two methods of cleaning 'em include a bit of Gumout® Carburetor Cleaner sprayed on a rag. Just wipe down the wires and the dirt disappears. If the

Gumout seems too powerful for your precious wires, use good old-fashioned 409® cleaner. It works as well as Gumout, but takes more elbow grease. When you're done, wipe the wires again, this time with Armor All. The wires remain soft, clean and pliable. Best of all, you can nearly double the life span of your wires.

525 CRISS-CROSS TORQUING:
You know the pattern that you use to tighten

wheel nuts? It works on other bolts or screws too. When tightening up components such as Holley bowl screws, use a criss-cross pattern to provide equal torque to the fasteners.

526 REPLACING PLUG WIRES:
How do you tell when it's time to replace plug wires? Use the following as a general rule of thumb: 1. If your plug wires have more than 30,000 miles on them, replace them. 2. If you can hear or see spark arcing, replace the wires. 3. If, in a pitch-black environment (moonless night without light), you can see a blue corona glow on any of the wires, replace them. 4. If, in a pitch-black environment, you touch the wires and you see a blue corona form around your finger tips, replace the wires. 5. If you hook an ohmmeter to each end of a plug wire and find the resistance changes as you draw the wire through your hand, replace the wires. 6. If your car is equipped with the factory wires and you are making more than 350 horsepower, replace them with a name-brand set of spiral-wound racing wires.

527 CHEVY'S K66 DISTRIBUTOR:
One of the finest Chevy distributors ever

offered was the magnetic impulse, tach drive, ball bearing unit offered as a service component. It featured a cast-iron body and in all aspects, it was a truly amazing hi-po piece. In fact

this part was so good that it was picked up as the "only" distributor for NASCAR Winston Cup competition. Fortunately for street racers, Chevy offered a similar line of distributors on "K66" electronic ignition Corvettes. These distributors have almost the same attributes as the over-the-counter piece, except they aren't ball bearing units. And

because they aren't overly rare, you won't have to re-mortgage the farm to buy one. They can easily be converted to operate with current electronic buzz boxes and with that conversion, they prove to be remarkably reliable. This distributor does have one shortcoming but it too could be a blessing in disguise for weekend warriors—it has a built-in automatic retard. After full mechanical advance has been reached, the distributor will retard approximately 1 degree per 1000 rpm.

528 ELECTRICAL SHORTS: Virtually all cars are equipped with several small

braided ground straps. And believe it or not, they're important from a tune-up perspective. More than one engine electrical gremlin has been traced to a poor chassis ground. Available as reproductions, you might be able to salvage your existing examples by cleaning them with carburetor cleaner and a stiff wire brush. If they are frayed beyond salvation, swap them for new items.

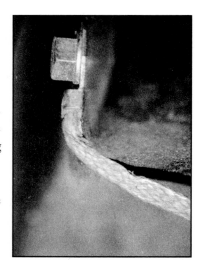

529 NITRO GAS: So, you figure that a dash of nitromethane in your gas tank will really wake up your combination? After all, Top Fuelers and Floppers use the stuff and they fly (literally). But this is wrong. Nitromethane is not effective when mixed with gasoline. Why? It has a low-octane quality and reduces the octane number of the gasoline it is blended with. Fuel racers use the stuff almost straight up with a dash of alcohol.

530 FULL POWER: It's no secret that high performance ignition systems need fully charged batteries to operate correctly. But what is the definition of fully charged? According to the folks at MSD, a fully charged battery will read 13.6 volts on a voltmeter and will not drop below 8 volts when cranking the engine. A fully charged battery will read 1.260 on a hydrometer in each cell.

531 STICKING GASKETS: Perhaps you've read the tip about using ChapStick® on Holley gasket surfaces to keep the gaskets from sticking. We've used it before and so have many other guys. It works, but so does PAM® (the spray-on cooking oil). If you're all out of lip balm, try the spray-on cooking stuff. It is as effective as ChapStick and because of its size, you'll spend less time hunting for it.

532 BATTERY CHARGER CAUTION: Here's a tip from the MSD staff: Never start or run an engine while a battery charger is connected. Potentially damaging high voltage spikes are produced by some chargers. The result of this voltage spike could be a fried ignition control box.

533 REO KITS: Many automatic transmission cars respond favorably to the large Holley 50cc (or REO) pump kit. When installing an REO kit, check the clearance between the pump and the intake manifold. In many cases, there isn't sufficient clearance—you'll need a small carb spacer or you'll have to grind down the intake.

534 LEAK DETECTOR: Vacuum leaks
rank right up there with sick valve springs as the curse of the internal combustion engine. If it "leaks," then it won't run. Two places that are seldom checked are the PCV hose and the power brake booster hose. Check them if you've encountered an impossible-to-find leak.

535 HEADER HARDWARE: Before
installing a set of headers, place a header bolt into each hole at the flange. Some holes are obstructed by tubes, or the hole isn't drilled correctly. It's a bunch easier to re-drill holes (enlarge them) or to bend tubing before the headers are buried inside the engine compartment.

536 CARB BASE PLATES: Are you
plagued with broken carburetor base plates? Many times, the base plate breaks because someone tightened the carb stud nuts much too tight. A good rule of thumb is to snug the nuts, then go 1/2 turn past that (even better, check a factory manual for proper torque settings). If that's not the case, then look at the carburetor base plate gasket. A base plate gasket that is too thick can fool you into thinking that the carb wasn't tightened correctly.

537 TERMINAL ILLNESS: In some
applications, header tubes and spark plug wires are just too darned close to each other. If that's the case try routing the plug wires under the headers and use 90° boots on all of the spark plug terminals. Add wire dividers as you normally do. Not only do the wires stay away from the headers, they're also hidden.

538 CARB CATCH CAN: Changing jets
on a Holley carburetor is often a messy (and occasionally hazardous) job—especially if the engine is hot. Rather than allowing the gasoline to run all over your flawless intake manifold (staining it permanently), try placing a plastic spray paint can lid under the corner of the bowl when you loosen the appropriate screws. Once the majority of the fuel has dripped into the lid, slide a shop towel under the bowl. No spilled gas, no messy intake manifold, and you reduce the risk

of header fires.

539 CARB DRAIN PAN: Can't find a
spray can lid? Want the trick setup? Designed by carburetor wizard Gary Williams, this plastic fuel cup makes use of a channel to catch dripping fuel and direct it into the cup as you remove the bowl screws in a Holley carbur-etor. The cup is large enough to catch a bowl's worth of fuel and it's manufactured from a fuel resistant polyethylene plastic (it's

mounted backward in the photo, but you get the idea). Moroso sells it.

540 JET TOOLS: Not really, but jet tools for
Holley carburetors have been around for awhile. This one is neat since it's short, which allows removing jets while the carb is still mounted on the car (especially handy on the secondary side). If you have a close look at the jet tool, you'll see that it uses a collar config-uration. This ensures the driver doesn't slip off the jet. In the end, that makes it easier on the jets and saves the skin on top of your knuckles. It's also available from Moroso.

541 MOUNTING BALANCE PIPES:
Balance tubes or pipes have been around for a long time. Essentially, they join a pair of exhaust pipes aft of the header collector with the result (supposedly) being improved horsepower and torque. A side benefit of these tubes is the "quiet effect" they have on the exhaust note. That's great, except, how do you know where to install the balance tube for your combination? It might prove easier than you think. Simply draw a thick line down the length of each exhaust pipe (after the collector) using a crayon or grease marking pen.

Make a normal hard run 'round the block with the car and examine your crayon mark. The temperature of the exhaust gasses within the pipe will cause the mark to discolor or burn at a specific location on each exhaust pipe. The point of discoloring is where the balance tube should be mounted.

542 CROSS-OVER CONFUSION:

Here's something to get you thinking: Jere Stahl (noted and well-respected owner of Stahl Headers & Cams) ran through 330+ gallons of fuel dyno-testing a pair of street small-block Chevys (a 350 and a big 400 cubic-inch rat). The dyno tests were primarily run at part throttle—2550 and 3050 rpm. In every manifold/header combination tested, an exhaust balance tube hurt fuel distribution. It never helped part or full throttle horsepower either. The tests were done with a full-length vehicle exhaust system and tailpipes, which makes the results even more impressive.

543 PLUG READINGS:

Fine-tuning the ignition and fuel pressure requires you take a plug reading or "plug chop." It is best to install a fresh set of spark plugs before attempting to take a plug reading. It is just too difficult to analyze a spark plug once it has been run under other conditions. Reading a spark plug is something learned

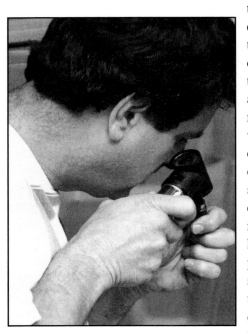

through years of experience. Since the average racer does not have this to draw from, here are a few simple rules to follow when doing a plug chop on a new set of plugs: 1. If you see specks on the electrode or plug rim, you probably have a detonation problem. Those specks are typically small bits of the piston. 2. If the cement around the metal electrode has bulged out "cement boil," you probably have a detonation problem. 3. If the electrode is cracked or broken, or the grounding tip has burned away, you definitely have a detonation problem.

544 JET EXTENSIONS:

Everyone loves a hard-launching car. Trouble is, a car that "hooks" can also uncover the jets in the secondary side of a Holley carburetor. What this means is that the fuel is being pushed away from the rear jets under acceleration. Holley, Moroso and others offer kits that extend the jet. These jet extensions are actually little pieces of metal or high-tech plastic

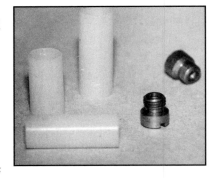

that slip over the jet body and extend to the rear of the fuel bowl.

545 HOLLEY POWER VALVES:

Over the years, Holley has produced several different types of power valves. The most common have holes drilled around the body. The next most common are the window type (large rectangular holes in the body). Performance isn't much different between the two, but the gaskets they require are. The window-type power valves use

round gaskets. The drilled-type have round gaskets with three internal tabs. If you mix them up, then you could be asking for an internal fuel leak in the carburetor.

546 PLUG BOOTS:

When installing spark plug boots on new ignition wire sets, the boots will often freeze on the silicone wire covering. To speed up the process, most people recommend the use of dielectric grease on the wire. That's cool, but a good shot of WD-40 inside the boot and over the wire will do the same thing. Besides, it smells better.

547 BUMP STARTER SWITCH:

Setting the valve lash on a performance car can get old in a hurry, especially if you have to jump inside the car, tap the ignition switch and run around to the engine and verify the balancer location. Temporary remote starter leads are one answer, but who wants to burn their hands every time you hook it up? The solution is a permanent bump starter switch. Moroso, Mr. Gasket and others offer trick weatherproof switches that can be mounted in a convenient location (like this Camaro radiator support). Wiring is simple—one lead goes to a power source such as the battery cable lead on the starter while the other lead is wired to the

switched "Starter" or "S" terminal on the starter. In operation, the ignition switch remains untouched. Simply press the bump starter and let electricity spin the engine over to the appropriate balancer location.

548 TIMING MARKS: Eyeballing the
timing marks in a dark engine compartment is no fun, and to make matters worse, the timing marks are sometimes harder to read when the engine compartment is lit up. Even the addition of a degreed balancer or timing tape can still make for some serious squinting. In many cases, the problem isn't the balancer. Instead, it's the timing pointer. Try trimming your stock full width pointer to a sharp "V" shape at the zero mark. The pointer is now easier to read and there is no confusion over the mark location.

549 SEIZED DISTRIBUTOR: Do you
have a GM-powered car with a pre-computer HEI distributor? Does the car seem doggy, even after a tune up? If so, there's a good chance that the advance weights have "frozen." For some reason, these distributors seem more prone to corrosion on the advance mechanism than their earlier counterparts. If your car has these symptoms, spray the weights with WD-40 or even heat riser valve lube. The weights should move freely after the lube job, but remember to keep an eye on them when you do normal maintenance.

550 COLLECTOR LENGTH: As you
are probably aware, header collector length can be varied. And by varying the length of the header collector, you can also adjust the powerband of the engine. Basically, if you want to improve low-end torque, you should increase the header collector length. On the flipside, if you want to decrease low-end torque, shorten the collector. That's

great, except how do you know what length is just right for your combination? By using the same method as in Tip #541. Draw a thick line down the length of the collector using a crayon or grease-marking pen. Make a normal hard pass with the car and examine your crayon mark. The temperature of the exhaust gases within the collector will cause the mark to

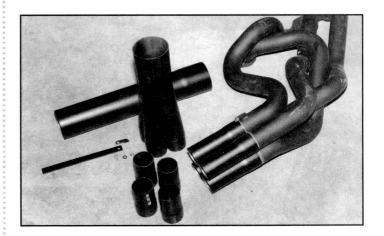

discolor or burn at a specific location on each collector. You can shorten the collector at this point. Just be certain to leave an inch or two of added material for further fine tuning. It's tough to add material to the collector once it has been cut!

551 NOTCHING FLOATS: Jet
extensions have a number of benefits when installed in the rear bowls of Holley carburetors. The only problem with the extensions is the fact that only short ones can be used—unless you notch the floats. Now, that can be a messy job (especially if your notch-job results in floats with pinholes). Fortunately, the folks from Moroso have come to the rescue with a line of pre-notched floats.

552 RECURVING DISTRIBUTOR:
Performance cars equipped with automatic transmissions are without question the most popular in drag race circles. Unfortunately, autobox racers are also the most critical when it comes time to recurve the distributor. If the distributor curve is setup for a stick shift ride, the automatic car will almost always prove to be a curse to drive. The answer is a special "automatic-only" recurve. An automatic will become more responsive when initial timing is increased (somewhere between 20-28 degrees initial). But with this much initial, the centrifugal advance has to be shortened as well. Shoot for a total advance number that works best in your application (most cars work well with something in the area of

38-44 degrees). Generally speaking, an automatic car will also like the curve "all in" by 2400-2600 rpm. Needless to say, these are just guidelines, but if you play with the curve using these guidelines, the car will not only become more driveable—it will also run quicker and faster.

553 OPEN SECONDARIES: If your
car has a common vacuum secondary Holley carburetor, keep this in mind: Many Holley vacuum carbs include a heavy spring in the secondary side (black or brown). Believe it or not, the secondaries might not be opening, even at very high rpm. A typical street-driven small block will not open a black secondary spring-equipped carb at an engine speed of 8500 rpm. That means that the engine is running on the primary side of the carburetor at all times. To solve the dilemma, simply install a very soft secondary spring (vacuum secondary spring kits are available from Holley) and then work your way back to a point where the car is both driveable and responsive. We should point out that vacuum secondaries should not hammer open. The ideal situation is a gentle and even opening rate.

554 LABEL YOUR CAP: Have you ever
noticed that when you're in a hurry, things always seem to get fouled up? And it's the little things like pulling the distributor cap and/or the wires. Number one cylinder on the distributor always seems to disappear—you can't remember where it was or which direction the rotor was pointing. Instead of fumbling your way around the firing order, simply take a felt marker and plant a big number "1" on the distributor post that holds the number one spark plug wire.

From there, you'll easily find your way to number one cylinder— each and every time the wires are removed.

555 CARB VENT EXTENSIONS:
Many drag racing or high performance cars fitted with Holley carburetors launch extremely hard. Unfortunately, these two factors don't always mix—especially when the fuel bowl vents are considered. When a Holley-equipped car launches, raw fuel can pour out of the bowl vents and spill directly into the venturi area. As you can well imagine, this does nothing for the fuel mixture or the launch. In order to solve the problem, try extending the vents with 5/16-inch neoprene hose. The extensions should be approximately three to four inches in overall length and can be fastened to the air cleaner stud. Just be sure that you keep 'em away from a high pressure area (such as a direct path to the hood scoop). Large amounts of airflow over the vent opening

may cause fuel to actually siphon out of the vents. This in turn can create a lean condition at high rpm —and you know what happens to high dollar internal engine parts when that happens.

556 FILTERING FUEL: It's no secret that
every fast car runs a high capacity fuel filter, but have you ever thought about filtering the fuel before it ever hits the gas tank or cell? Try adding a DuPont paint strainer to your fuel funnel as you pour the race gas into the tank. You just might be astonished at the amount of crud and garbage that turns up in the paint strainer. Besides, this tip makes life a lot easier for your standard fuel filter. Leave it in place, but as a second line of defense against dirty fuel.

557 COIL CROSSOVER: Do you have a
sour running combination—one that starts poorly, but idles OK and has decent power up to a point? And at that point, it becomes a dog. You've tried everything: Vacuum leaks, cap ionization, carb problems, points, condenser, dwell, timing, etc. Did you check the coil wires? In this case, we don't mean the power lead to the distributor cap. Instead, have a look at the wires. A coil will function, even if

the positive and negative wires are reversed. Trouble is, it won't run all that well, especially at higher rpm levels or during initial starting. The reason for this is the fact that it takes 60% more voltage to fire the plugs when the wires are crossed. The right wiring

scheme includes the distributor wired to the negative terminal on the coil while the positive terminal is the hot or power lead. Install the wires correctly and your sour running blues should be over.

558 CHECK W.O.T.: Many performance cars don't open to full throttle even with the pedal at wide open throttle (W.O.T.). In fact, many stock, unmodified cars don't open their throttles all the way either. Have an assistant jump behind the wheel of your car and with the engine shut off, get your helper to mash the pedal all the way to the floor. Check to see if the linkage is opening the carburetor completely. Things like carpet, insulation and improper linkage adjustment can be the culprits. Just be sure that you don't adjust the linkage too far. An over-center

condition can lead to a stuck throttle. Our personal big-block plaything was opening the Holley to about 7/8 throttle and no more. A full hour was spent readjusting the linkage to make up for the deficiency. Your car could be doing the same, so check it out.

559 IONIZATION: High-powered ignition systems, such as the MSD units, do wonders for performance. Unfortunately, the nature of the beasts sometimes creates a phenomenon called *ionization*. This is basically a bunch of electrically charged ions jammed inside

the distributor cap. Once they develop and build, they have no place to go. The result is normally a high speed miss that refuses to go away. When you pull over to find the problem, you'll likely lift off the distributor cap. What you have done is given those little ions a place to escape—but you haven't solved the

problem. The gremlins will appear the next time you wring out the car. Rather than chucking the ignition system, try drilling a series of holes around the cap (between the posts). The ionized air can escape and the miss will be gone—permanently. By the way, MSD sells pre-drilled or "vented" caps for most Delco or Chevy applications.

560 CHASING THE LASH: There are different methods for setting valve lash. Some are quick and not-so-accurate while others are time-consuming ordeals that take forever. The following system for Chevys might take a bit longer than normal but it's positively foolproof:

1. Warm the engine to operating temperature. Spin the engine over until the Zero mark on the balancer and the timing pointer "Zero" line up. Check the valves as you crank over the engine. If the number one cylinder valves do not move as the engine approaches the zero location, the powerplant is in the number 1 firing position. If the valves move, the engine is in the number 6 firing position. If that's the case, spin the crank over one more revolution to reach the number 1 firing position.

2. With the engine in the number 1 firing position, adjust the valve lash on: Exhaust #4, #8/Intake #2, #7.

3. Rotate the crankshaft 180 degrees (1/2 turn) clockwise, adjust the lash on: Exhaust #3, #6/Intake #1, #8.

4. Rotate crankshaft 180 degrees (1/2 turn) clockwise. The timing marks will return to zero (number 6 firing position). Adjust the valve lash on: Exhaust #5, #7/Intake #3, #4.

5. Rotate crankshaft 180 degrees (1/2 turn) clockwise, adjust the lash on: Exhaust #1, #2/Intake #5, #6.

561 TUNING POWER VALVES:

Many hi-po Holley carburetors are equipped with a power valve system. It adds a specific amount of fuel to the power system during acceleration. If your carburetor uses a power valve system (on the primaries or primaries and secondaries), here's a tuning tip that will provide a clean idle as

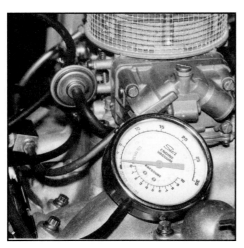

well as crisp throttle response: Holley brand power valves are numbered in reference to their opening point. As an example, a number 65 power valve will open at 6.5 inches of manifold vacuum. In order to determine which

valve is right for your combo, check the powerplant manifold vacuum at idle. The correct power valve is one that opens between 1" and 1.5" below the manifold vacuum at idle. In simple terms, if your engine has an idle vacuum reading of 5", then you should install a number 35 power valve (which opens at 3.5" of manifold vacuum).

562 CAP ADAPTER: Most standard and aftermarket distributor caps were designed

around 7mm spark plug wire. In some cases, you might (and it's a pretty big "might") be able to stuff an 8mm spark plug wire into the cap. Rather than risking a poor connection or damage to the cap (and wires), consider adding a set of MSD "Power Towers." These units

adapt a conventional distributor cap to a spark plug type lead. This means that you can use 90-degree spark plug boots and clips on the distributor cap. The wires are then easily installed or removed without fear of damage. Additionally, the spark plug configuration terminal ensures a positive connection at all times. Besides, the price for these bits and pieces is right.

563 TIMING LIGHTS: Guess what? All timing lights were not created equal. As hard as it might be to believe, your old faithful timing light just might be out of synch by a bunch. A few years back, the folks at MSD tested almost every unit on the market. They found that many of the lights (and some of them were high buck units) were designed for use under 2000 rpm. Some lights were equipped with a trigger delay—something that has little effect on light performance—at very low engine speeds. But when the engine was brought up to hi-po levels for timing verification, the timing appeared to retard. Additionally, some lights were affected by radio frequency noise—and that's a common thing if your car is equipped with solid-core wires. The results of their test indicated that many timing lights were simply inaccurate and because of this inaccuracy, enthusiasts were (and are) setting their timing erroneously. The solution is to compare your light against something like a fresh Sears Craftsman lamp (part number A-2134). MSD found that this was one of the few accurate lights and it doesn't cost an arm and two legs. If your light is out of whack, swap it for either the previously mentioned Sears piece or step up and buy one of the new MSD timing lights (part number 8990).

564 JET SET STANDARD: Have you ever wondered what type of criteria is used to calibrate a Holley carb? The folks at Holley advise that their carburetors are

calibrated at sea level at 70° F. The factory offers the following jetting recommendations: For every 2,000-ft. increase in altitude or for every 35° increase in air temperature, the jet size should be decreased by one jet number. If the

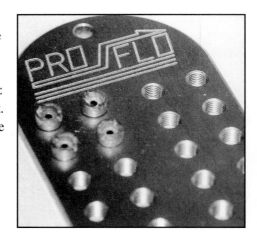

temperature drops 35° F, then increase the jet size by one number. Naturally there are other variables present like headers, actual inlet air temperature and the like. You certainly can't beat a good spark plug read to determine the proper air/fuel ratio, but at least the Holley numbers will put you in the ballpark.

565 ALTITUDE & POWER VALVES:
Altitude plays a very important role in the selection of power valves. The circuit must be "readjusted" to compensate for the decreased intake vacuum. Power valve timing or size should be reduced 1.5 inches for every 3,000-ft. increase in altitude above sea level. This adjustment is done simply to compensate for the lack of available "air." Keep this tip in mind whenever the altimeter soars—even if you live near the ocean!

566 SPIRAL CORE WIRES:
Most Pro Stock drag racers have switched to spiral-core suppression ignition wires. And it's not because they like to

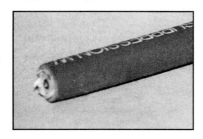

listen to radios in their racers. With onboard computer data systems on the cars, the old solid-core wires sometimes create false readings, but not so with the spiral wound wires. But there was (and is) another benefit—and one that suits most low buck car nuts. In some instances, the spiral wire sets actually improve performance. This is confirmed by a series of dyno tests conducted by a leading engine builder. A measurable amount of horsepower was found with the swap to the high tech ignition wires. Just about every leading ignition wire manufacturer offers such components.

567 SCREW GASKETS:
Holley carburetors are normally equipped with a small gasket behind each bowl screw. There is nothing wrong with these components, but the bowls are constantly coming off and going back on again throughout the tuning process.

Sometimes, the little round gaskets will stick to the bowl, stick to the bowl screw or worse yet, tear. And they always seem to tear just after the local speed shop closes. Moroso offers a neat nylon type bowl screw

gasket (part number 65225) that stops the problem. It should be noted that several other manufacturers offer similar non-stick bowl screw gaskets as well.

568 CHECKING SPARK:
The current crop of sophisticated, high powered electronic ignition systems do wonders with regard to firing the spark. In fact they are so good that most speed freaks install and then forget them. Unfortunately, they are not infallible. They can be damaged and one of the quickest ways to hurt some of the high-powered units is to

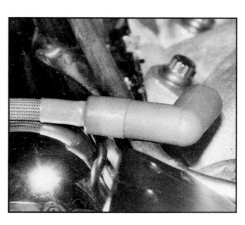

check for spark without completing the circuit. In simple terms: Don't check for spark using an empty plug lead. While this might be fine with an old-fashioned "Kettering" system, it doesn't cut it with the new electronics. When checking such an ignition system for spark, install a spark plug in the boot and be sure that the plug is properly clipped inside the socket. Lay the spark plug body on a good metal ground and then check for spark. This ensures that the circuit is complete. By the way—don't be tempted to grab the plug and check for spark using the "human ground" method. Your hair will probably be straight for a week.

569 STORING JETS:
Some people store carb jets by stringing them through a piece of wire and tossing them into the tool box. But jets are precision machined to a very specific diameter. If you store them on a piece of wire,

the constant movement of the jet on the wire can change the internal dimensions of the jet, eventually rendering the jet useless. To properly store your jets in an organized, safe manner, try Holley's "Jet Set" or a similar aluminum jet plate. The jets either pop in (Holley) or screw in (some aluminum brands). Your jets will be handy, in order and will not take a beating from the wire.

570 INDEXING PLUGS: To index
plugs, mark the spark plug insulator body with a felt pen—on the side where the ground electrode

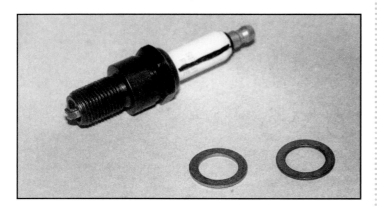

attaches to the spark plug body. The idea is to position the plug so that the gap is facing the center of the cylinder toward the exhaust valve (at least that's the most common arrangement—some engines "like" other gap locations). Instead of tearing through boxes of spark plugs to locate the elusive combination of perfect plug threads that match the respective cylinder head threads, use aftermarket indexing washers. These soft copper washers are available from Moroso under part number 71900 for 14mm taper seat spark plugs and 71910 for 14mm flat seat spark plugs. The washer kits are supplied in .060", .080" and .100" thicknesses. Because of the copper's soft nature (as well as the varied washer thicknesses), you can easily thread the spark plug into the cylinder and tighten it to a point that your index mark is situated correctly—relative to the combustion chamber. Just be certain that you do not double up on the washers! They're not meant to be used in pairs.

571 UNDERDRIVE HORSEPOWER:
Underdrive pulleys significantly reduce the horsepower that is consumed by the alternator and water pump. If your car is run on the street, stick with the sets that offer moderate crank pulley reduction, such as the Auto Specialties CNC-machined pieces shown here.

The racing set with the small diameter crank pulley will not provide adequate operation of the alternator or water pump below 2000 rpm. These are for a 5.0-liter Mustang.

572 COOL FUEL: This is an oldie but a
goodie. Everyone knows that cool is right for fuel. Because of this, fuel lines that run in the engine compartment or in the area of heat should be insulated. Cheap insulation is available at your nearest air conditioning/refrigeration supply company. Simply slice the stuff open and slip it over your fuel line. The internal gasoline temperatures will decrease, creating a denser air/fuel intake charge, which rapidly translates into more horsepower. Keep your fuel cool!

573 IDLE MIXTURE: Setting the
carburetor idle mixture screws is often a "guesstimate" at the best of times. Radical camshaft profiles, massive intake manifolds and lots of carburetion make it difficult to fine tune the idle mixture. And that spells trouble during staging. Try installing a hand-held vacuum gauge on the engine (reading manifold vacuum). Set the first idle

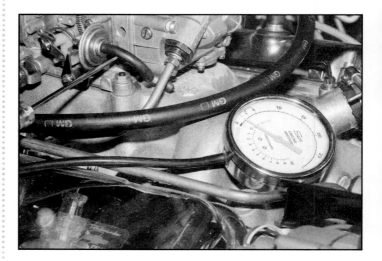

mixture screw to read the highest reading and then move to the second idle mixture screw. Do the same thing and then repeat the process once more—going from one side to the other. If your carb is equipped with a four-corner idle system, you will have to repeat the whole process one more time. In most cases, you'll find that this method of setting the idle will result in a significantly higher idle speed. Once you have the carburetor idle mixture "balanced," set the carb idle speed down to a sane level. The throttle response will now be much cleaner and so will the car's driveability. If the carburetor on your car has just been rebuilt and the engine won't start, try this: The idle mixture setting can be "approximated" by turning both screws all the way in (be careful not to over-tighten the screws against the internal seats). Back the screws out approximately 1-1/2 turns. The engine should start, but always reset the mixture with a vacuum gauge in place.

574 FUEL PRESSURE: Regulating fuel pressure is a key ingredient to developing horsepower in an EFI engine. Unlike a carbureted engine that depends on the pressure differential in the carburetor's venturi to draw fuel into the air stream, the EFI engine must have a constant supply of fuel at a high pressure level. The 5.0 H.O. Mustang engine typically has fuel pressure fixed at 38 to 39

psi from the factory. Since the factory fuel pressure regulator can not be adjusted, you must install an adjustable fuel regulator. This is not an option. Proper fuel pressure is critical to performance on an EFI engine. There are numerous companies that sell an adjustable fuel pressure

regulator. If you have a Ford dealership nearby, an adjustable regulator can be purchased under the Motorcraft part number E0SY–9C968–A. This is an excellent regulator that has a rear exit for the vacuum line. Fuel pressure is easily adjusted by inserting an Allen wrench into the top of the regulator and rotating it to the desired pressure.

575 STRAY SPARKS: Some dark cold night, try firing up your car and then take a peek under the hood. With the lights off, you might be surprised at the lightning show around the ignition system. A natural phenomenon is the "halo" effect that surrounds the electricals, but scattered sparks scurrying to the closest ground isn't. Those stray sparks are a sure sign that you have an ignition system leak. One way to solve the problem is to use some "dielectric grease" on the inside of the plug boots as well as the inside of the distributor terminals. MSD sells the goop under the name "Spark Guard." It's cheap, works wonders and is extremely easy to use.

576 ACCELERATOR PUMP SHOT: Some hi-po cars are plagued with an off-idle stumble in their Holley carburetors, especially those equipped with automatic transmissions. Initially, the problem is often diagnosed as way too much carburetor—it seems right because the car goes "waaahhhhhh" and then falls flat. Unfortunately, the most common diagnosis is often incorrect. What your car is experiencing is a "hole" in the fuel curve. The throttle is wide open, the automatic is placing a major load on the engine and it is running out of

fuel. The solution is rather simple. Increase the accelerator pump shot. This can be accomplished several ways, but always use the Holley "system"—a larger pump shooter as well as tuning the pump cams. If the stumble still appears, you might have to resort to larger pump volumes. You can increase the pump volume by taking a standard accelerator pump diaphragm and cutting away the center. Stack the cut diaphragm in conjunction with the standard diaphragm and you'll pick up some volume easily. If that isn't enough, your only choice will be the installation of a 50cc pump kit (commonly called a "REO" kit, see Tip #533)—readily available from your local Holley distributor.

577 DISTRIBUTOR ROTORS: Distributor rotors aren't identical. In fact, many late-model and jobber rotors are not designed for performance—they hinder it. Hi-po rotors are available from Accel, MSD and other companies. So what makes them better than the corner parts store variety? The performance units are

commonly constructed from an alkyd material which is much more resistant to carbon tracking. The arc ribs that surround the rotor blade and beside the rotor screw holes are larger. The rotor blade is constructed from brass (often riveted rather than bonded to the rotor body) and the length of this blade is longer than the late-model OEM components. Finally, most of the high quality hi-po parts feature a stainless-steel spring along with a larger than stock contact button. When all of these improvements are combined you can easily see that the rotor is more efficient in terms of dishing out the spark to the respective cylinder.

578 NEEDLE & SEATS: Holley manufactures an endless variety of needle and seat assemblies. Now, the good folks at Holley carburetor didn't do this because they had nothing else to do. Each and every needle and seat assembly has a specific purpose. Most of the store-bought Holleys feature a Viton tipped needle and seat. The Viton material is a perfect marriage within the confines of the carburetor—except if your fuel is laced with alcohol, benzene or acetone. For these applications, you must utilize a steel needle and seat assembly. But that's not all there is to know about these critical little parts. There just happen to be four steel needle and seat assemblies applicable to hi-po carbs and a full half  dozen of their Viton tipped counterparts. Holley offers the following size guidelines for needle and seat hardware: Small cfm carburetors—up to .097" N&S. Carburetors up to 715cfm—.110" N&S. 750cfm & larger carburetors—.120" and .130" N&S

579 5.0 THROTTLE BODY: One of the simplest ways to improve performance on your 5.0 Mustang engine is to install a larger throttle body and EGR plate. The best buy on the market is the Ford Motorsport 65mm unit shown here (M9926-A302). This SVO component has been used on engines producing over 600 horsepower. The factory unit has a 60mm throat (except '86 which was 58mm). The options available that will fit the factory intake vary from 65mm to 90mm. The 65mm unit works fairly well up to the 400 horsepower range and close to 500 horsepower on a turbo or supercharged engine. Beyond this level, the stock block can not handle the horsepower that a larger throttle body can make,

so anything larger is a waste. Engines running high boost (10 to 12 psi), can benefit from 75mm throttle bodies when equipped with the Pro–M mass airflow meter. Because a blown engine (which forces compressed air into the intake), is not dependent on vacuum to generate airflow, the larger throat provides less restriction to airflow.

580 OVER THE GAP: If your spark plugs have too much gap, the combination won't run up to its maximum potential. How do you tell if the gap is excessive? Pull off a spark plug boot and look at the outside of the spark plug ceramic insulator. It will look like someone took a lead pencil and drew lines on it (lengthwise). The solution? Tighten the gap.

581 DISTRIBUTOR SHIMMY: Most Delco distributors suffer from too much end play. Big deal you say? Too much end play can cause erratic ignition timing, not to mention the damage that can occur to the distributor. Believe it or not, some sparkers have in excess of .100-inch end play. The factory specs call for a mere .015-inch end play. To solve the problem, yank the gear and install shims between the drive gear and the housing. Moroso offers shim packs and so does Chevrolet. The Bow Tie part number is #1927529.

582 IDLE FEED MODS: Although this tip was initially developed for use with Dominator carburetors (4500 series), it also works well for the more common 4150 Holley carburetors: Engines with "healthy" long duration camshafts create idle screw needles that lack sensitivity. Instead of playing with external bleed passages, you can improve the idle quality by increasing the size of the idle feed restrictions. This is accomplished by installing a wire of approximately 0.010 to 0.015-inch diameter in the idle feed restriction channels of the primary metering block. The wire is cut and then bent into a "V" shape prior to installation. When the gasket is added, the wire cannot fall out. The result of this easy surgery is increased idle sensitivity (it works very, very well on applications with very low manifold vacuum).

583 SEPARATING PLUG WIRES:
Carefully separating ignition wires is important, but when you add a super high-powered electronic buzz box, carefully divided wires become critical. Street rodders tend to make them pretty and tight, but that's not the ticket to high performance. Real racers keep their wires well separated and use plenty of nylon or plastic wire dividers. The trick is to eliminate any chance of spark crossfire between the

respective wires and the use of metal dividers is only an accident waiting to happen. So what if the wires are too close? In a typical firing order, two adjacent cylinders normally follow one another.

Using a Chevy as an example, the firing order is 1-8-4-3-6-5-7-2. Cylinders #5 and #7 are right beside each other on the bank. If a high-powered spark leaks to #7 from #5, it's like running a wicked initial advance. #7 will fire too early. That alone can reduce performance, but if it happens too often, it can also split a cylinder wall.

584 CARB FILTERS: Have you ever tried
to chase down a lean out condition or a shortage of fuel problem and met with nothing but dead ends? Sometimes it is the fault of the filter. Holley uses these special bronze filters in several of their carburetors. The filters are tucked away behind the fuel inlet in the bowl and if you

haven't removed the original bowl fittings, there is no way of knowing that they are installed. The filters do an admirable job of filtering but they can also become a major source of restriction if they become plugged.

The answer? Install a high quality in-line filter and throw away the bronze babies buried in your carburetor.

585 KEEP PLUGS CLEAN: Believe it
or not, the outside of a spark plug (as well as the inside) has to be clean in order to function correctly. Marks made on the insulator to index the plug or oil and dirt provide a potential path for spark energy to jump the insulator. This is particularly important with high-powered ignition systems. Keep the plugs clean. Otherwise, you're throwing away performance.

586 ELECTRONIC BOX LOCATION:
There are two things that are very hard on electronic modules—heat and vibration. When mounting an ignition add-on module, such as the MSD 6AL, it is important to place it so there is a cooling airflow across it. Heat is deadly for electronic components, so always mount them away from hot exhaust manifolds. The best approach is to locate them in

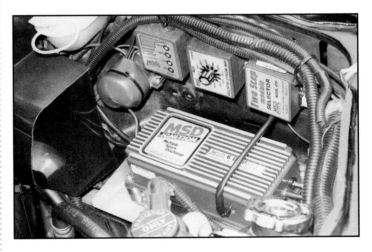

an airstream or duct air to them. The footings on the module should be insulated from the attaching structure with rubber to reduce vibration. If your module did not come with rubber mounting insulators, use the mounting insulators for a factory airbox.

587 MANIFOLD ICING: For many
weekend warriors, it's common practice to ice down the intake manifold between rounds at the drag strip. You know the routine: Run down to the corner store and buy three or four bags of their coldest. Then when you get to the track, make a pass and return, you go through the old "ice down the intake" process. Everything gets wet—even your shoes. Is there a better way? We thought you'd never ask!

POWER TUNING

Instead of constantly buying ice, make a stop at the local camping or outdoor supply store. They sell these neat self-contained ice packs. Pop 'em in the freezer a day or so before you hit the strip and when it's time to depart, store them in a cooler. Arrange them around the intake—just like the ice, except they don't leak! If you are worried about the intake heat melting the plastic bodies, simply use your favorite "ice" towels and wrap them up. No mess, no aggravation and better still, your shoes don't get wet.

588 CRIMP TESTER: How do you know if crimps made on custom spark plug wires are sound? Use an ohmmeter to check for continuity between the distributor post and the spark plug. If no continuity is found, a problem exists with the wire or the terminals. And if you are using a state-of-the-art spiral core wire, expect to see a reading of 150 ohms per foot of wire.

589 HI-PO FORD COILS: The Ford 5.0-liter factory EFI coil produces a spark with about 30,000 volts of pressure behind it. This is over 150% of the output of a pre–electronic ignition coil. With this capability the stock coil is excellent and generally does not require replacement until horsepower moves past the 375 range. If your car is equipped with a capacitive discharge add–on module, the stock coil can handle close to 500 horsepower. Aftermarket high–performance coils typically produce 40,000 volts and should be the first choice when the coil must be replaced. Again, stay with the top high–performance ignition component manufacturers. I have had the best luck with MSD and Accel coils. However, there is very little difference between any of the top units, so go for the best price.

590 EGR VALVE JOB: A rough running engine is a curse. And when it sounds like the valves are popping it often means the time has come for a valve job. But that isn't always the case. It could be a simple matter of a stuck EGR valve. If the valve sticks, it causes the engine to run (and sound) just like a case of bad valves. Lightly tap the outside EGR valve with a small hammer. It should loosen up and function normally. If not, try a new valve. They're cheaper and easier to fix than a complete valve job.

591 PINGS: If your car pings, detonates and rattles all the time, don't be too quick to blame the quality of the gasoline. It could be the vacuum advance line. In many cases, the vacuum hose is routed incorrectly. Vacuum advance is designed to operate on "spark ported or timed spark" carburetor locations rather than direct manifold vacuum. If connected directly to manifold vacuum, there's a good chance that the vacuum advance will be operational all the time. As a result, the canister will be advancing the timing constantly.

592 LEAN OR RICH: How do you know if an engine is running rich or lean at idle? One method involves removing a hose connected directly to manifold vacuum (the engine must be at operating temperature). If the engine speeds up, then the carburetor is too rich. If it stalls or stumbles, it's too lean. Another method involves "hand choking" the engine. Place the palm of your hand over the carburetor. If the engine speeds up, then it's too lean, or worse, it could have a vacuum leak.

593 SPARK PLUG THREADING: Sometimes a car will have a spark plug hole or two that are next to impossible to reach, and it's difficult to finely thread the plug in at the correct angle to get it started. Of course, if you attempt to reach them when the engine is hot, your hand is branded with the name of header manufacturer. In order to solve the problem, try starting the spark plug with a piece of rubber or neoprene hose jammed over the porcelain end. Simply push on the hose and use it as a remote handle to start the plug threads. By the way, a drop of oil on the spark plug threads doesn't hurt installation either.

594 VACUUM LEAKS: If you've tried every known trick in the book to find a suspected vacuum leak—WD-40 on the gasket sealing surfaces; an unlit propane torch over the same surfaces, etc.—try this one. Tape up every "port" in the engine. That means that the PCV opening, the valve cover breather and other vacuum/air ports should be carefully sealed with racer tape. Next, crack the throttle plates open slightly and pin the throttle open (a bolt in the linkage will work). Drop a small vacuum hose through the primary throttle opening with one end above the carburetor inlet. Seal this hose to the top of the carburetor. In fact, cover and seal the entire top of the carburetor with racer tape. Finally, shanghai a buddy who smokes (the brand of cigarette doesn't matter) and have him (or her) literally blow smoke into the engine. The smoke should work its way out of the vacuum leak location.

595 MSD TWO-STEP: Have you ever
wondered how some racers can easily stage their race cars and leave the starting line at a precise rpm? We know that it gets busy behind the wheel during staging, but there is a piece of equipment that makes it easier—the Two-Step manufactured by Autotronic Controls (MSD). Basically, the Two-Step is wired between the ignition control box rev limiter (MSD 6AL & 7AL models) and either the trans brake button or the roll control button. When the respective button is engaged, the Two-Step "switches" to a preset engine speed. When the button is released, the Two-Step then reverts back to the regular rev limiter setting. In simple terms, it allows you to stage "against the limiter" at, for example, 4000 rpm. When you release the button, then the rev limiter returns to the normal setting of, say, 7500 rpm.

596 CLIPPED GAPS: If you are
struggling and can't quite squeeze the ET out of your ride, consider cutting back the ground electrode on your spark plug. But in this case, it doesn't mean a mere file job—it means clipping it so that the ground electrode is flush with the side of the center electrode or shorter than the center electrode.

What this does is to create a massive spark plug gap (about several hundred thousandths of an inch). Be easy on the combination once you have clipped it. You should not drive the car to (and through) the staging lanes if possible. Once you fire it up, do your normal burnout, stage and make your pass. In some cases, the "clipped" electrode will pick up your combination as much as a tenth (in other cases, it won't help one iota). Just be sure your plug wires and ignition system are in top condition, because the wires will eventually self-destruct with this much gap. But remember, this is just a one shot deal. If it works for you, return to the pits and replace the spark plugs with ones that have a more conventional gap.

597 BULK IGNITION WIRE: Instead
of purchasing your ignition wire in kit form, consider buying the wire in bulk. Many companies such as Moroso, Jacobs and MSD offer wire in bulk. This allows you to make up your own wire with the terminal ends that best suit your specific requirements. Although it may not seem economical for a single tune-up, consider the fact that your vehicle will likely require more than one set of wires. Not only does it save you dollars in the long run, it allows you to make up the wires in exact length configurations.

598 HOLLEY DOMINATOR: If you
have a close look at Holley Dominator (4500 series) carburetors, you'll note that fuel can be plumbed from either side of the respective bowls. Also, the Dominator bowls easily interchange with the more common 4150-series carburetors; but be sure to use the rubber Dominator accelerator pump check valve (conventional 4150 carburetors make use of a staked ball check valve assembly in the bowls). The Dominator bowls allow you to plumb a single -6 or -8 line to each side of the bowl (which results in four separate lines to the carburetor). What does this accomplish? It virtually

guarantees that there will be a sufficient supply of fuel to the bowl. Of course, other situations might include two conventional lines to the bowl, but with a psi sender on one side, or fuel delivered to the driver's side only. In any case, the Dominator bowl provides the choice.

599 CHEAP CURVE KITS: Did you
know that the advance weights on a pre-emissions Delco distributor are worth 10° of advance over the weights found on later models? Because of that, it's possible to re-curve a non-HEI smog distributor with early weights—and the cost is negligible.

600 SETTING POINTS: When setting
the points on a GM car with the "window" in the distributor cap, use an Allen wrench and turn the screw in until the car stumbles. Then back off one full turn. Next, turn the screw in 1/2 turn. Why the extra step? Simple. After some use, the screw tends to back out 1/2 turn by itself.

601 COMPRESSION TESTING:
Compression tests are routine tune-up steps, but in a high performance situation, they should not take the place of a leakdown test (see Tip 602). Essentially, the idea of a compression test is to obtain a reading that is close to that specified in a factory service manual. Now, if you have bumped the static compression ratio (high c.r. pistons), messed with the camshaft (changed the lift and duration figures from stock), then the compression test numbers are almost meaningless. But there are two areas where a compression test can be of some assistance. Very low readings can indicate that the piston rings or valves require maintenance. This can be checked further by squirting some medium weight oil into each plug hole. Crank the engine over for a few seconds and then repeat the compression test. If the readings are significantly higher, then you have a problem with the rings, piston or cylinder. If no changes are evident, then the problem is with the valves. A major drop in pressure in one (or more) cylinders can mean several things. The worst could be a holed piston or broken rings. The most common, though, is a blown head gasket. If a pair of side-by-side cylinders show approximately the same compression readings (while other cylinders are good), it's a good sign that the head gasket is blown between the cylinders.

602 LEAKDOWN TEST: Before you can
begin any serious tuning, you must be sure the engine is in solid condition. The most accurate method is with a leakdown test. The test consists of pumping a given amount of air into a cylinder and then measuring how much escapes via the rings and valves. A healthy engine can leak less than 5% while a chronic leaker can exhibit numbers near 50%. Some of the best sealed engines in drag racing are less than 3%. As a general rule of thumb, a high performance car with leakdown numbers of 10% or more should be rebuilt.

603 TOTAL ADVANCE: Almost all hi-po
distributors have mechanical advance. The centrifugal advance system is designed to advance the firing of the spark—typically using springs and weights inside the

distributor body. As engine speed increases, the spark for each cylinder must be triggered sooner to allow time for full ignition of the air/fuel mixture prior to the piston reaching top dead center (TDC). In operation, the distributor shaft speed of rotation builds. As the shaft speed increases, the mechanical weights tend to fly outward, stretching the springs. Pins on the weights act against a plate fitted to the base of the distributor cam. The further the weights fly out (hence the "centrifugal" name), the further the cam position moves, which results in advanced timing. In order to check the mechanical advance system, remove the cap. Hold the rotor and see if you can turn it in the same direction that the distributor shaft normally rotates. There should be some pressure of the advance springs holding back the movement. Release the rotor. It should return to its original position quickly and easily. "Total timing" is the amount of ignition timing (in crankshaft degrees) that the powerplant "sees." Now, if you think about a typical vacuum advance-equipped street distributor, you can easily see that the total amount of timing can approach monstrous levels if not held in check. Look at the variables: Initial, Centrifugal and Vacuum Advance. Too much of each can result in 50° or more of total timing. Initial advance and total mechanical timing can vary from engine to engine (even those that are seemingly identical), and only your own vehicle can "tell" you the exact numbers required. Generally speaking, a hi-po combination can utilize total timing figures ranging from 36° to 46°. This includes initial and mechanical advance.

604 TIMING FOR AUTOMATICS:
Automatic transmission-equipped cars can use more initial advance than their stick shift counterparts, however the total timing should still be the same. This means the mechanical advance will (in most cases) have to be

shortened with an automatic transmission. While this may sound difficult, it can be quite simple (depending upon the distributor you have selected). Inspect your distributor's mechanical advance mechanism. You might be able to shorten the advance curve by increasing the size of the weight stop. Other examples may require minor welding of an advance slot while some aftermarket distributors have provisions to change the duration of the overall mechanical advance curve. Simply stated, it's just a matter of examining your specific distributor and determining how the mechanical advance weights are limited. Generally speaking, the mechanical advance should be "all in" between 2000-2400 rpm for automatic-equipped cars and in the range of 2400-2800 rpm for stick shift examples.

605 INDEXING CAP TO ROTOR:

There's no question that the distributor cap and the rotor must work together precisely to properly and efficiently distribute the spark. There are two areas where cap/rotor fit are critical. The first is the rotor-to-distributor cap clearance. It must be close enough to allow the ignition spark to cross the gap easily. In the second case, the rotor blade must line up exactly with the distributor cap terminal precisely when ignition spark occurs. If the distributor cap to rotor blade

clearance is too great, the spark can easily jump to the next cap post in the firing order. The same thing can occur if the cap to rotor alignment is off—even if it is only off by a tiny amount. Not only will this "jumping spark" result in a poor running combination, it can also destroy the engine if operated for any duration under these conditions. To make it simple, the effect can be the same as far too much initial spark. It's no secret that it is physically impossible to "move" or "adjust" a

conventional rotor. But that isn't the case with the distributor cap. If you look closely at the cap, you'll note that there is a margin of "free play" on the cap mounts. Most caps can be twisted slightly clockwise or counterclockwise even when the mount clips are lined up (but not completely fastened). In order to check and properly phase the system, use the following process:

1. Prepare a "test cap" by cutting a large "viewing window" in the body. The window should be positioned under the cap posts, but high enough so that you can see the body of the rotor. It doesn't matter where (in relation to the firing order) this window is cut. Simply position the window in a spot that is easy to view on your powerplant while it is running.

2. Mark the distributor cap with a series of index marks that correspond with the exact center of each post in the "window." Position the marks at the bottom and top of the window, and be sure that the marks are straight. To make the marks visible on a tan-colored cap, use a fine-tip black felt marker. If your cap is black, lightly cut the marks with a file and fill them with white typewriter correction fluid or white paint.

3. Mark the rotor with an index mark (a light cut with a small file works well). This index mark must coincide with the center of the rotor blade tip. In order to make the tip easy to view, fill the index mark with white correction fluid.

4. Install a timing light to one of the distributor cap posts in your window (it doesn't matter what post, as long as it is physically inside the window). Set the engine speed so that the rotor appears to be steady. Use the timing light to view the position of the rotor versus the distributor cap post. As expected, the timing light will "slow" the rotor speed so that you can spot the location of the rotor tip in relation to the distributor cap terminal.

5. If your car does not have vacuum advance, phase the rotor so that the tip lines up precisely with the distributor cap terminal. To accomplish this with a conventional cap, you will have to note the position of the test cap (mark it with a felt-tip pen). Replace the test cap with a conventional cap but be certain that you have placed it in the same spot as the test cap (be sure to use the same brand of cap as the "test cap"—once you have determined the location and marked the distributor body, you won't have to check the rotor phase again). As indicated earlier there's a slight amount of play available when

installing a cap. In most cases, this play should prove sufficient to phase or index the rotor/cap position.

6. If the car has vacuum advance, you must take into consideration that the advance will change the phasing of the rotor according to manifold vacuum. A distributor with clockwise rotation (vacuum advance disconnected and plugged) should have the rotor just to the left of the "target" distributor cap post. When the vacuum advance is working, the rotor will appear just to the right of the target post. Similarly, a distributor with a counterclockwise rotation will be exactly opposite to the above.

7. If there isn't enough play in the cap to compensate for any misalignment, there are ways to increase the adjustment. Many point breaker plates or magnetic pickup plates found inside the distributor can be repositioned slightly. Coupled with the available movement of the cap, you should be able to properly index the cap and rotor combination.

606 PLUG HEAT RANGE: Heat range refers to a spark plug's ability to transfer heat from the tip of the insulator into the cylinder head. In order for a spark plug to perform satisfactorily for more than a few miles, it must be of the proper heat range. If a plug is too hot, it will cause pre-ignition, but even if combustion is normal, excess heat can ultimately burn the center electrode completely away. On the other hand, a plug with too cold a heat range will have a tendency to foul and misfire and can

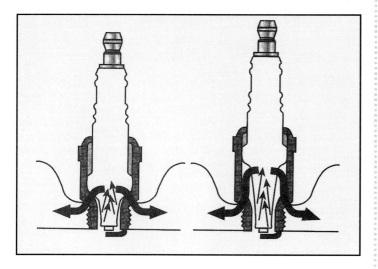

reduce horsepower. Heat transfer rate is largely controlled by the distance the heat must travel through the spark plug body before reaching the head. Plugs that are considered "cold"

have insulators that contact the metal plug shell very close to the threaded base. The insulators in "hot" plugs contact the shell towards the top, which makes for a longer path to the head surface. Keep in mind that the terms "hot" and "cold" are relative—a plug that's "hot" for one engine may be considered "cold" for another. That's because combustion chamber temperatures vary considerably depending upon an engine's state of tune and the conditions under which it is operated. When heat range is properly matched to requirements, insulator tip temperature will range between 700 and 1500 deg. F under all operating conditions. This will provide maximum power and maximum plug life. With a stock engine, it's best to follow the plug manufacturer's recommendation unless there's a good reason to deviate—such as a modified spark advance curve, poor fuel quality, extreme operating conditions or experience with the recommended plug being inappropriate. With a modified engine, standard recommendations can be used as a basis for determining where in the heat chart to start. Raising compression ratio, leaning the fuel mixture, increasing initial spark advance or reworking the advance curve to come in quicker are all reasons to switch to a plug with a colder heat range.

607 WIRE SLEEVES: We've mentioned wire sleeves before. Here's how they work: As spark plug gaps increase and ignition power becomes stronger, the chance of spark leakage through the wire increases. High powered ignition control boxes have become the norm rather than the exception and because of this, almost

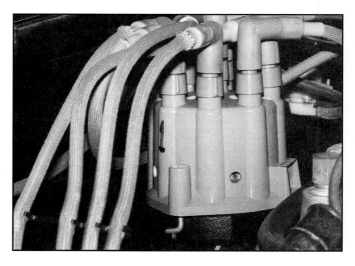

all wires are susceptible to voltage leakage and of course, cross fire. Moroso, MSD and others offer "spark plug wire sleeve" packages. Similar in concept, the sleeves generally consist of a closely woven fiberglass "tube" or sleeve which is sometimes covered with a high voltage resistant silicone material. What's the added wire protection worth? According to the folks at Moroso, their Blue Max sleeve adds 8,000 volts of extra insulation, almost double that figure in cross-fire "insurance" and a profound resistance to heat created by headers.

608 DISTRIBUTOR GEARS: Regardless of the type of distributor you select, pay attention to the gear. Standard iron gears are acceptable if a conventional hydraulic or mechanical camshaft is in charge of valve timing. However, roller cams are machined from SAE 8620 billet steel and the gear on the cam isn't compatible with a cast-iron distributor gear. Whenever a roller cam is in residence, the distributor should be fitted with a high quality bronze gear—with one exception. Steel roller cams with cast-iron gears were developed during the very late stages of the 1980s. These cams can be used with standard cast-iron distributor gears. In a high performance or race engine, distributor gear life isn't always what it should be. While bronze is compatible with steel, it doesn't have the strength of iron, so it wears at a higher rate. The situation can be particularly bad in Chevrolet small blocks because the splash lubrication of the distributor gear is inadequate at low engine speeds. Things are even worse when a high volume oil pump is installed in an engine that doesn't really need one. High volume pumps are designed for use in engines with wide bearing clearances. With normal production clearances, oil doesn't flow as freely through the engine, so the oil pump is working against considerable back pressure. Since the distributor shaft turns the oil pump shaft, the load on the distributor gear caused by a high-volume oil pump can be substantial. That leads to accelerated wear—even with a stock iron gear. Increasing oil flow to the distributor gear significantly improves gear life, primarily because of its cooling effect. This can be most easily accomplished by using a 3-cornered file to cut a .030-in.-deep notch in the lower sealing flange on the distributor housing. For maximum effectiveness, the notch should be oriented so that it is aimed towards the camshaft when the distributor is installed in its normal position. Distributor housings should be notched—irrespective of the type of distributor gear used—in all engines operating under high loads and/or at relatively low rpm, especially if a high-volume oil pump is in place. True race engines rarely experience a distributor gear wear problem because their higher operating rpm provides sufficient lubricant flow, and proper matching of oil pump volume and

bearing clearance eliminate excessively high lubrication system back pressures.

609 CHECKING FUEL PRESSURE: Before you tune the carburetor, you should determine the health of the fuel delivery system. A fuel pressure gauge (either hand-held or plumbed inline) is required for this exercise. Sun, Stewart Warner and a host of other manufacturers all offer high quality units. The engine should be warmed to operating temperature prior to performing this test. A Holley carburetor can normally withstand a maximum fuel pressure of 7-1/2 pounds per square inch before the needle

and seat assemblies are overcome. Any pump reading (hot) under 4 psi indicates a faulty fuel pump, although some vehicles will function normally with as little as 3 psi hot.

610 MECHANICAL FUEL PUMP: When engine speed approaches and exceeds 6000 rpm, the mechanical fuel pump pushrod is prone to floating (just the same as valve float). B&B Performance offers a lightweight fuel pump pushrod with hardened ends to solve this problem (available under P/N 6550 for big and small block Chevy V8 applications).

611 MAGNETOS: The beauty of a magneto is that it generates its own electricity, so it's completely self-contained. That means neither a battery, coil nor alternator are required. Another attractive characteristic of a magneto is that its voltage output increases linearly with rpm. The flip side of this is that at cranking speeds, voltage output is very low, so starting can be a problem. Mallory Super Mags utilize a separate coil so they're more suitable for street and low rpm operation. Currently, automotive magnetos are widely used only in

certain types of race cars such as fuel and alcohol dragsters and Funny Cars, sprinters and the like. Vibration is severe enough in these types of cars to damage a battery, so being able to run without one is a definite advantage—not to mention the weight savings. And since sprint cars spend a good deal of time on their heads, elimination of the battery

removes the potential hazard of battery acid dripping on the driver in the event of a flip or rollover. Magnetos can be used in street engines, but they rarely are. Street cars have to be equipped with a battery for purposes other than operating the ignition, so a magneto offers no weight-savings benefit. And since a street engine spends most of its time operating at low rpm, it rarely spins a magneto fast enough to generate high spark voltage. A third drawback is that it takes a bit of horsepower to spin a magneto, and while it isn't a lot, it represents a power loss that electronic ignitions do not impose.

612 HOLLEY FLOAT LEVEL: The most common Holley performance

carburetors use an adjustable needle and seat assembly. This is used to raise or lower the fuel level in the bowls and is actually accomplished by setting the float level. Carbs with this feature are equipped with a removable sight plug on the side of the bowl. Simply remove the sight plug and check the level. Fuel should gently seep out of the sight plug hole. If fuel pours out, the float level is too high. If the fuel cannot be seen and does not seep out, the float level is too low. Common sense dictates that the car be placed on level ground for this portion of the power tune. In order to adjust the level, simply back off the top screwdriver slot-equipped lock screw and then set the level

with the adjustment nut. Re-tighten the lock screw once the adjustment has been finalized. If the float mechanisms are not externally adjustable, the float level must be set with the fuel bowl removed from the carburetor. Once the bowl is removed, invert the assembly and align the float so that the top (now the bottom since the bowl is upside down) of the float is parallel to

the top of the bowl (not at an angle). The tabs may have to be bent as this is the only method of adjustment available.

613 SINKING FLOATS: Two common problems with carburetors (Holleys and other

types) are internal fuel leakage and constantly "sinking" floats. To cure an internal fuel leak, look no further than the needle and seat assembly. Occasionally, a minute piece of dirt can jam the assembly—causing it to hang open. A sinking float is almost always caused by a float assembly that leaks. While repairs are possible, the "fix" is hardly worth the effort. Simply

pick up a new float from your nearest Holley dealer.

614 PRIMING FUEL BOWLS:
Whenever you change jets on a Holley carburetor, it will take a bit of time for the bowls to prime. To solve the long cranking blues, simply fill an old (and clean) dish soap squirt bottle with gasoline. "Prime" the Holley bowls by squirting gas down the vent tubes with the soap bottle. The engine will fire instantly when the carburetor has fuel in the bowls.

615 READING PLUGS:
The right way to read a plug is via the porcelain inside the spark plug. A ring can be seen where the heat transfer takes place. The closer the ring develops to the tip of the plug, the richer the mixture. The closer the ring develops to the base of the porcelain, the leaner the mixture. By the way, this ring only indicates air/fuel ratio.

616 ROUTING TRIGGER WIRES:
When routing a pair of magnetic trigger wires (from a crankshaft ignition trigger or from a magnetic pickup distributor), always wind the wires around each other. In other words, twist them so that the wires cross in numerous places. In addition, do not route magnetic pickup wires near any plug wires or near high power ignition control boxes. Why is this important? It is very easy for an "alien" signal to provide false information to the trigger wires. In other words, the engine can misfire if the above suggestions aren't followed.

617 COIL LOCATION:
Where is the best location for an ignition coil? It should always be mounted away from direct heat. Many installations have the coil installed in the passenger compartment. Another good spot is high up on the firewall—away from the headers and engine. In either case, be sure to insulate the coil wires from metal surfaces (especially if they have to pass through the firewall). Otherwise you'll be inviting poor ignition performance.

618 DETONATION:
Does your late-model engine rattle or detonate with alarming regularity? The problem could be the EGR valve. If the EGR has been plugged or removed altogether, combustion chamber temperatures rise. The result is detonation and if equipped with an engine management computer, the total ignition timing will be automatically pulled back (retarded). Performance goes away. If you re-install the EGR, then the intake charge will be diluted. This may not be the best for performance, but it does lower the temperature in the combustion chamber. The result is zero detonation and advanced timing.

619 HEAT RANGE & CAM DURATION:
An often over-looked factor when selecting proper plug heat range is cam duration. If no other changes are made, swapping a short duration cam for one with longer duration decreases cylinder pressure, which has the same effect as lowering compression ratio. Shortening cam duration increases cylinder pressure, which has the same effect as raising compression ratio. So even though a long duration cam is designed to produce more horsepower, at higher engine speeds, it will create a condition that calls for a hotter, rather than a colder spark plug under some circumstances. On the other hand, if a shorter duration cam is installed as a means of increasing low-speed torque and smoothing the idle, a colder plug may be required because of the increased heat which is generated by higher cylinder pressure.

620 HOLLEY AIR BLEEDS:
Holley carburetors are very basic and well engineered air/fuel metering devices, but if you don't give 'em any attention, they can cause mysterious maladies. One such trouble spot is the series of air bleeds found along the air cleaner ring. Generally speaking, a plugged bleed will cause driveability problems. To cure the not-so-crisp response syndrome, give the bleeds a shot of carburetor cleaner every three or four weeks. You'll be much happier with the carburetor and so will your car!

621 STICKY VALVES:
Occasionally, a car that has seen a sedate life, one that is caked with internal carbon deposits, will be sold to a leadfooted performance enthusiast. One of the problems that is bound to occur is a chunk of carbon will jam between a valve face and the seat. The result is a stuck valve. Before you tear down the engine to clean up the carbon deposits, try "flushing" the engine with GM "Cleens" (PN 992872). This stuff is poured through the carburetor as the engine is running at fast idle. You'll be amazed at the amount of junk that comes out the tailpipe when Cleens is added.

622 FLOODED FLOATS:
If your carb is experiencing a flooding condition, it could be

caused by a small piece of dirt jamming the needle and seat assembly. To free the needle and seat from dirt, try removing the fuel inlet line from the carb. Plug the line and fire up the engine. When the engine runs out of fuel, remove the fuel filter and either clean it or replace it. Re-install the fuel line and while you have an assistant fire up the engine, use the handle of a screwdriver and tap on the carb body near the needle and seat. In most cases, the incoming charge of fresh fuel, coupled with the tapping, will dislodge the dirt.

623 LOCATING A MISFIRE: If your

car has a point-style ignition system and it has an occasional miss, there is a way to track down the offending cylinder. With a pair of insulated pliers in hand, remove each spark plug boot from the spark plug as the engine is running. If no changes occur on a given cylinder, you can be assured that it's the dead player. Don't try this with a modern electronic

system. It's possible to kill an electronic buzz box since the removal of the plug wire opens a loop in the circuit.

624 PUNCTURED POWER VALVES:

Generally speaking, a Holley power valve will add about 10 jet numbers of fuel to the engine upon demand (it works on manifold vacuum). If an engine has a serious backfire, there's a chance that the power valve diaphragm has been ruptured. To test a power valve, simply hold in your hand (plunger facing away from you). Gently pull on the flat face of the valve. If the plunger moves toward you, the valve is fine. If it doesn't move, the valve diaphragm is punctured.

625 PLUGGED BOWL VENTS:

Does your Holley-carbureted street machine stall or have a lean surge? It could be caused by the air cleaner! Some low-profile air cleaners are so short they seal off the bowl vents. When the bowl vents are sealed, then the fuel in the float bowl will not respond to the pressure differential in the carb venturis. What's the solution? The best bet is to increase the height of the air cleaner lid with a taller element.

If that's not possible, you can shorten the vent tubes.

626 CONDENSER: Believe it or not most

cars with point-triggered ignition will run without a condenser. It just won't run well. It will pop and bang and cause no small amount of general embarrassment and head scratching. The same symptoms arise when a condenser goes away. You can also spot a weak or quickly fading condenser by examining the points. Weird shapes on the points (like sharp hills on one side of the point and a corresponding valley on the other) are sure signs that the condenser is on its last legs.

627 WIRES & CAPS: If at all possible,

don't use spark plug wires with brass terminals along with a distributor cap with aluminum inserts (normally a cheap cap). Why not? Moisture will create corrosion. The result will be poor spark and performance.

628 MARKING WIRES: If you have a

hard time remembering which spark plug wire goes where during a tune-up, try marking a set of wooden clothespins with the respective cylinder number. Then, clip the clothespin on the plug wire when you remove it. No fuss. No mess. And the right wire lead is attached to the right spark plug. By the way, this also works great for other wires and is especially helpful with vacuum hoses on smog motored vehicles. Further to this, if clothespins aren't trick enough for your garage, try one of Crane Cams newest "wire and hose marker kits" (PN 99183-1). Included are ready-made stickers that immediately solve the misplaced wire and hose dilemma.

629 HEAT RANGE & OCTANE: Yet

another factor that influences heat range is gasoline quality. Lower octane fuels burn more quickly and create higher combustion chamber temperatures. In years past, when premium leaded fuels were widely available, octane was sufficient to meet the demands of virtually all high-compression street engines. But with the advent of unleaded gas, octane ratings of all grades of fuel dropped. Consequently, pre-ignition, detonation and run-on became more prevalent problems. If you've been running the same heat range plugs for years, but have been plagued by detonation, pre-ignition or run-on for no apparent reason, it just may be that the plugs you're using are too hot because of lower fuel octane. Many times, a switch to colder plugs will eliminate those ugly knock and ping noises.

630 INSTALLING STUBSTACKS:
Tip #19 told you why you might want to use a K&N Stubstack; here's a few things to watch for if you decide to use one: When installing one, you might find a very small air gap between the base of the stack and the carburetor. The air gap does not affect performance. Because of space restrictions between the choke horn and certain air cleaner base plate configurations, the Stubstack has two thin spots in the casting. When installed, the Stubstack might chip or crack, but this does not hinder performance. And while it looks like it might work, don't use a hammer to drive the Stubstack into place!

631 TIMING LIGHTS:
Did you know that you can install your timing light backwards? Check and verify the position of the trigger clamp when you install it. The jaws can be right side up or upside down. The correct position is the one that provides the most advance—as seen on the harmonic balancer timing tab.

632 MORE TIMING TALES:
When installing the timing light leads, be absolutely positive that number one spark plug wire (the "trigger wire") is well separated from the other spark plug wires. This minimizes the chance of stray signals from adjacent wires (crossfire) triggering the timing light. This happens more times than you think.

633 CARB SPACER TUNING:
When a carb spacer is added to an intake manifold, you're effectively adding to the distance between the carburetor and the floor of the plenum. This weakens the carburetor "signal" which in turn requires a larger jet(s) for

compensation. Carburetor spacers with four separate holes tend to recapture the velocity of the "mixture stream" that is lost when an open carburetor spacer is installed. Simply stated, more exit velocity in the mixture stream creates a stronger carburetor signal than that found with an open spacer. Generally speaking, you'll still have to increase the jet size with a four-hole spacer, but not as much as a single hole job. Keep this in mind if you're playing with spacers.

634 MSD INSTALLATION:
When installing any MSD ignition control box, all ballast resistors must be removed or bypassed. And that includes both OEM and aftermarket models. The one caveat to this rule is a MSD 5. This low rpm street box must use the ballast resistor included with an aftermarket coil (typically, these coils include the resistor as part of the package). Just remember that if you return your ignition system back to stock, all of the OEM ballast resistors have to be replaced in their original locations.

635 DISTRIBUTOR LOCKERS:
Many so-called experts advocate locking out the mechanical advance mechanism completely on a distributor. To be honest, this procedure is a tuning band-aid—used to cover up an inability to limit the mechanical. If a powerplant "wanted" 40 plus degrees of advance during fire-up, Detroit wouldn't have spent the time and effort adding the mechanical equipment to the distributor. Personal testing on a legitimate eight second race car confirmed that a locked out advance mechanism is actually slower than a comparable mechanical advance system. Although the improvement with mechanical advance functioning is small, it is still measurable. Take our advice. Don't lock out the advance curve. Your car will run quicker and faster with the advance operational.

636 HOLLEY FUEL PSI LIMITS:
Today's modern, high-powered electric fuel pumps can deliver copious quantities of pressure and volume. Unfortunately, there's a point where a Holley carburetor will say "enough is enough." At this point, fuel pressure will overcome the needle and seat and pour out of the carburetor vents. Just how much fuel pressure can a typical Holley carburetor stand? A Holley carburetor can normally withstand a maximum fuel pressure of 7-1/2 to 8 pounds per square inch before the needle and seat assemblies are overcome. Keep these numbers in mind when setting an adjustable fuel pressure regulator.

BODY, PAINT, ELECTRICAL, DETAILING & ENGINE COMPARTMENT

637 EASY HOOD REMOVAL:

Removing hoods for access to the engine compartment isn't practical. Removal is a pain and re-installation is worse. An easy solution to this problem is to swap the actual hood hinge bolts for studs. By using a stud/flat washer/lock washer/nut arrangement rather than a bolt, it doesn't take three people to remove or install the hood. Instead, simply install Allen-wrench set screws in place of the bolts. Loctite the set screw into the hood, use nuts and lock washers to hold it in place and before removal, scribe a mark around the various nut/washer locations. The whole setup makes hood removal a lot easier.

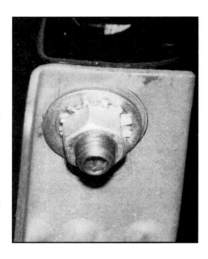

638 LATCHING HOODS:

Hood hinge springs were a great invention—unless your car is fitted with a fiberglass hood. The use of fiberglass generally precludes the use of hood springs. In most cases, springs wreak havoc with the not-so-cheap fiberglass. You have a couple of options: Fit the hood as a lift-off-only piece or make up a hood support rod. Naturally, a hood support rod gets in the way whenever you work on the car with the hood up. And worse yet, if you give it a rap, the hood comes crashing down. Is there a third option? How about drilling a 1/4-inch hole through the hood hinge assembly and inserting a race-bred pit pin through the hole? Due to the internal release mechanism, the pit pin can't wiggle its way loose like a common bolt. If you're worried about toughness, a quick release pit pin such as the 1/4-inch Moroso model (#90390) has a double shear strength of 8,200 pounds—more than adequate for most high performance applications. If you use a steel hood, you can use a pin on each hood hinge, and at the same time eliminate the hinge springs. Fiberglass hoods will

only require a lone pin. Also, using this method allows the hood to be raised further than normal, which helps when working on the car.

639 SCRATCH REPAIR:

Suppose you have a scratch on your car that you've been meaning to fix up, but haven't. Because it has been exposed to the elements for a while, it needs to be sanded. The problem is, it's so narrow that regular sandpaper won't work without sanding surrounding paint. The solution is to Contact Lyons Automotive (P.O. Box 229, Lyons, IL 60543) and ask for a "Paint Chip Fixer Upper." The tool is a pencil-shaped device that features a glass-fiber core. In use, the tool physically burnishes away the rust and rough edges as effectively as sandpaper, but in a much smaller area. After use, the scratch is ready for paint.

640 SPOILER SPEED:

Few will argue that first-generation Camaros are popular racers (even Blue Oval fans). But they were designed and built long before anyone had a handle on aerodynamics. In short, they are the bricks of the nineties (and yours truly has such a racing brick in his garage). But if you have one, all is not lost. Testing has indicated that these old war horses can pick up at least one to two miles per hour in the 1320 just by playing with factory spoilers. If the rules allow it, take off the rear "ducktail" and install the optional front spoiler. Overall drag is reduced and the front snow plow keeps a bunch of air away from the car's undercarriage where it becomes an aero-brake. But if you don't have a vintage Camaro, you can still play the spoiler game. Most old factory muscle machines came equipped with similar spoiler packages. Mix 'n match 'em until the best mph numbers appear on the time slip.

641 PAINT WEIGHT:

When it comes to complete paint and body jobs, the primary goal is usually to achieve perfectly straight body panels along with show quality paint. But in the case of hi-po machinery, there is another target that should be taken into consideration. And that's weight. Plain and simple, a few extra gallons of lacquer, enamel or whatever adds weight (and it could be considerable) to the package. Using a power-speed calculation, it becomes very clear that fifty or sixty pounds added to a 3200

or 3300 pound package can increase elapsed times significantly. So what's the bottom line? Be careful when repainting your car. Too many coats of the shiny stuff can hurt more than they help.

642 HI-PO CAR WASH: What is the best type of soap to use? Automobile, paint and major auto wax manufacturers all recommend that you use as mild a soap as possible. Much of the brightwork and trim parts used on cars today are made of aluminum, making them particularly susceptible to chemicals in strong soaps, and can be permanently stained or etched by them. The safest choice is to select a car wash soap made by one of the major wax manufacturers. In fact, if you're using a particular wax, it would be wise to use the car soap of the same brand.

Hopefully a manufacturer's soap will be formulated so as not to dissolve and remove their wax from the car. Soaps specially formulated for cleaning cars also have non-spotting additives. Westley's Car Wash and No 7 by Borden are popular choices. They are mild enough so they won't harm most waxes. For

those who don't wax their cars, liquid dish detergent is a common choice for soap. Although it's readily available, it is stronger than most car wash soaps. Automatic dishwasher soap is even stronger, and it is definitely not recommended. The soap should not be so strong that it dissolves any dirt or tar spots on the car. It's much better to use a separate cleaning rag with a dab of a stronger cleaner, such as bug and tar remover, to remove the tough spots. To minimize damage to the finish or the wax, use a relatively weak soap solution to wash the entire car and use a stronger cleaner for spot-cleaning any remaining dirt.

643 POLISHING TRIM: A good percentage of the shiny trim (especially window trim and moldings) found on vintage cars isn't

chrome—it's polished stainless steel. And that's good because it is very easy to bring back the shine in the comfort of your own home. Install a couple of buffing pads for your bench grinder, apply some polishing rouge and let it rip. To finish the job, a final pass through the polishing pads with Mother's aluminum polish will make the stainless steel look better than new.

644 SHEETMETAL SCREW: There are a number of small (and maybe not-so-small) components on your car that are held in place by simple sheetmetal screws. Unfortunately, if the screw hole is stripped or becomes oversize, it is an impossible task to tighten the screw. A quick fix is to make use of a paper clip inserted in the hole. The result is, of course, a smaller hole diameter—this allows the sheetmetal screw to grip properly.

645 BOLT FINISH: A good number of the original bolts found on your car are probably coated in a special black oxide finish. This stuff is resistant to scratching and has a unique dull finish. Unfortunately, it's sometimes tough to find replacement hardware and in many cases, it is non-existent. Further to this, it is often difficult to find a company that can re-plate the hardware. To duplicate the finish, try painting the bolts with flat or dull black enamel. After the hardware is dry to the touch, carry the bolts inside the house, place them on a disposable foil cookie sheet and slide the works into the oven. Bake the bolts for approximately twenty-five minutes at about 325 degrees. Allow the oven to cool naturally and install them with a conventional six-point socket or open-end wrench. The result is a baked enamel finish that is virtually scratch-proof.

646 WEATHERSTRIP ADHESIVE: New weatherstrip components almost always require some sort of glue to hold them in place. Unfortunately, many commercial weatherstrip adhesives are sold in an oh-so-ugly yellow color. Luckily, the folks at 3M offer weatherstrip adhesive in black—and it matches the color of weatherstrip perfectly. It's available under part number 80119 and is sold at most automotive jobber outlets.

647 DRILLING HOLES: Sometimes, you have to drill a hole into a section of double-panelled bodywork. But if you don't want to go through the

panel completely, wrap the drill bit with a piece of tape at a depth corresponding to the depth you want to drill through. The drill bit will not go past the tape and when you're finished, you can easily restore the bit to normal by peeling off the tape. For your information, this also works with holesaws.

648 DETAILING DIFFERENCES: Often, the thing that separates good paint jobs from great ones are the little details. Items like new gaskets around the door handles and lock cylinders can be the difference between winning and losing in the show car arena. And it's not tough to pull off the handles and replace the weathered, paint checked gaskets for new examples. The cost is less than a couple of bucks for a complete set of gaskets but the difference in appearance is substantial.

649 REMOVING DECALS: When decals and glue-on body moldings get old, they can become a curse to remove. If you don't want to damage the finish beneath the decals, the work can get downright dicey. A quick (and painless) method involves

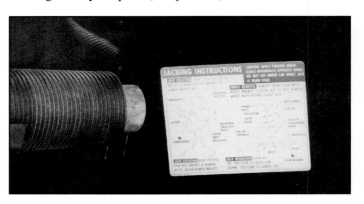

heating the area with a heat gun. As the decal or molding is heated with the gun, the glue warms, which in turn allows you to peel it off very quickly. Don't get too carried away with the heat gun because it has enough power to peel away paint. And no, a common hair dryer won't get the job done.

650 REMOVING MOLDINGS: In all of their wisdom, the GM bunch added windshield and rear window moldings that appear impossible to remove. Not so! Try using one of these little molding tools (available from a number of different body shop supply vendors). The tool slides under the molding, hooks the hidden

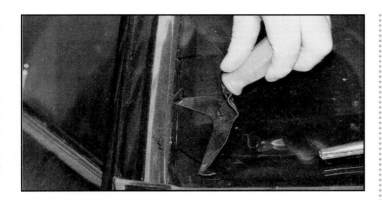

clip and releases it cleanly so that there is no damage to the glass, the molding or the surrounding paint. Best of all, the molding tools are cheap.

651 TRIM CLIPS: Production body shops have a quick 'n dirty way to install emblems.
Instead of taking off the panel to gain access to the backside of the emblem, they use a quick fix with a product called a "barrel clip." These little clips push in from the front of the

panel and then the emblem is literally hammered through them. Although it's a quick fix, it isn't right. Worse yet, the installation process often cracks the emblem. To avoid this problem, use the correct emblem nuts—they're cheap, they look better, they don't cause damage to the sometimes expensive emblems and they are

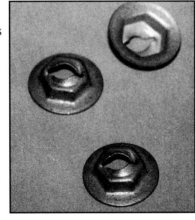

readily available from body shop supply houses.

652 BULK TRIM HARDWARE:
Have you ever noticed how little hardware pieces disappear when it's time for reassembly? If you're missing various trim hardware, visit your local body shop supplier. Many of them offer trim hardware in bulk, such as chrome door panel screws, clips for door handles and window cranks, emblem nuts, captured fender nuts and window molding clips. Since they cater to the professional shop rather than the restorer, the prices often prove to be substantially less than you might think. Of course, these body shop supply houses normally have dozens upon dozens of different items in stock.

653 PAINT DEFECTS: Little things like a small piece of dirt in the paint can seemingly
ruin an otherwise perfect paint job. But instead of repainting an entire panel because of a tiny dirt particle, try using a Meguiar's sanding block to rub the dirt particle down to size. Meguiar's sanding blocks are extremely fine grit (shown here are 1500 and 2000-grit paper) and when used properly (followed up with the right polishing and waxing compound) you won't be able to tell that there was once a defect in the paint. Using fine sandpaper and polishing compound is known as "finessing."

654 PAINT STRIPPING: Can't decide if you should strip the old finish off before
applying another coat, even if it's the same color? Maybe these guidelines will help. You must strip the old paint off if: the paint shows crazing, cracking, bubbling or peeling; you doubt the previous paint work or base coat; the paint is already too thick; if the paint warranty requires it; if you are returning the paint to OEM specs.

655 WINDSHIELD WASHER NOZZLES: Windshield washer nozzles
live in a rough environment. They have water, cleaning fluid and who knows what else running through their internals and

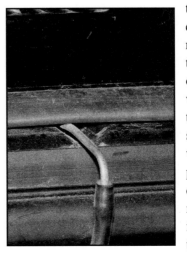

then they're exposed to the elements from the outside. To restore them properly, soak the nozzles in cleaning fluid overnight. Run a thin piece of wire through the nozzle and then buff 'em with a stainless steel buffing wheel. Don't worry about the not-so-stock polished look—the shine will disappear naturally over a month or two but the nozzle finish won't deteriorate past that point.

656 MYSTERY COATING: Do you have parts on your car that look like they

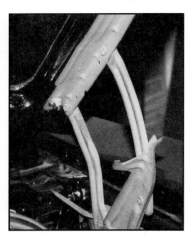

were painted dull or flat grey but you know that it isn't really paint? What you are looking at is grey phosphate plating. It is very inexpensive and was used with regularity on many car parts—hood hinges, hood latches and catches come to mind immediately. ASL Company sells a do-it-yourself phosphate plating kit.

657 MASKING TIPS: Masking is more than just covering up something you don't want paint on with tape. It is a skill, and if not done properly, you'll be working overtime removing overspray. The following tips should help. 1. After laying down a piece of tape, go back and press it tight to prevent paint from blowing underneath. 2. If tape won't stick to a surface, wash surface with wax and silicone remover. If used sparingly, you can also use wax and silicone remover on rubber surfaces. 3. When doing two-tone paint, follow the paint manufacturer's directions so you will know when fresh paint may be masked. 4. Never leave masking tape on a job more than a few days, especially if the car is left in direct sunlight. The tape will dry out, adhere to the surface and is difficult to remove. 5. Do not remove tape from a wet paint job. Give lacquer an hour to dry. Enamel should dry at least six to eight hours, such as overnight. 6. When possible, cut tape when applying it. Tearing will lift and stretch the ends. 7. Never pull "up" on masking tape when removing it. It can lift fresh paint. Peel it back away from the paint and over itself. 8. One more warning on masking tape removal: If masking tape ever gets wet, remove it as soon as possible. In other words, if it gets sprayed by accident during washing, or wet-sanding water falls on the tape, or it sits outside overnight in the dew, take the tape off as soon as possible or it may become so hard that it takes hours to remove. For materials, see Tip #735.

658 REMOVING WAX: When applying a final polish or wax job to your freshly rebuilt car, it's always tough to avoid spreading excess wax into the various nook, crannies and cavities such as body

seams or inside emblems. The solution? Use a good soft-bristled toothbrush to clean up the residue.

659 WEATHERSTRIP TOOL: Many pieces of weatherstrip are installed in a channel. Because of this, the rubber components are installed

after the car is painted. Unfortunately it's difficult to push it in place without the use of some sort of tool that will not mar your high dollar paint job. The solution is to use a popsicle stick or a paint mixing stick. Neither one will scratch the finish and is certainly compatible with the rubber weatherstrip. By the way, some of the flavors aren't bad either.

660 SQUEAKING TANK: If your vintage GM passenger car is plagued with a persistent squeak coming from the rear of the car, it might be originating from a location you never thought about. Many General Motors automobiles were fitted with a special gas tank "anti-squeak kit" from the factory. In essence, this is a section of hard insulation (and sometimes a block of foam rubber) that is glued to the top of the gas tank. When the tank straps are tightened, this insulation is sandwiched between the trunk floor and the gas tank. As the tank moves around while you are driving, the insulation takes up the brunt of the noise—isolating you from the squeaks!

661 DETAILING TANK STRAPS: When detailing the undercarriage of your hot rod, remember the gas tank straps. New straps for vintage iron can either be difficult or impossible to obtain. But you can restore your existing straps with the following process: Strip the straps of all paint, dirt and accumulated crud. Paint remover can be used to remove any undercoating, excess paint and junk, or dipping them in a bucket of water and Drano™ works well too. Work the paint remover into the straps with a common household Scotchbrite® pad (rubber gloves solve the "acid on the hands" problem). The finish will soon take on a natural steel appearance. When that happens, rinse with plenty of water and carefully dry the straps. Paint them with clear enamel and the straps are as good as new.

662 CHAFING WIRES: Both modified and stock vehicles have lots of little wires running in and out of the firewall, trunk and through varied panels. If there isn't some form of protection for these wires, constant movement will eventually erode the wire covering and a short could occur. Most often these mysterious shorts occur only when the car is poised in the staging lanes—next up to make a pass. To solve this potential chafing problem, install rubber grommets at every location where wires come in

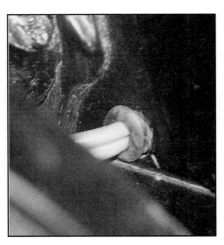

contact with sheet metal. Grommets are available everywhere—but Mr. Gasket offers a neat package that includes a variety of the most popular shapes and sizes. When selecting grommets, the diameter of the hole should be just large enough to accommodate the wire. The hole in the body panel must be just large enough to accommodate the bottom of the groove. And finally, the groove must be just wide enough to fit the thickness of the material the hole is cut in. This usually isn't a problem with sheetmetal, but can be with thick fiberglass. If the fit isn't all that tight, you can seal the edges with silicone. If you can't find a grommet, then wrap enough layers of electrical tape around the wires to wedge them into the hole. Allow enough slack on both sides of the panel so the wires are not strained against the edge of the hole.

663 ADDING PIN STRIPES: If you're adding pin stripes, either painted or tape, make sure you thoroughly clean the surface. A no brainer, right? But make sure you clean with a paint cleaner or polish that contains no silicone, wax or sealant. In fact, you

should use a wax and silicone remover. If the product's label mentions anything about providing protection, select another product. If the label says that it is "paintable" or that it can be painted over, then that's what you want.

664 RADIATOR SHROUDS: Radiator fan shrouds might seem unnecessary on a high-performance car, but if you have an overheating problem, you might consider adding one to your car. Most Detroit-produced cars were fitted with a shroud of some sort as

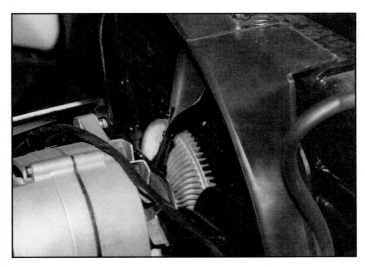

original equipment. Their function is to force any airflow in one direction—through the radiator. So don't be tempted to leave the shroud off when you reinstall your radiator. It has a purpose. Remember that the cooler your engine runs, the better its overall performance.

665 FILTERED FLUID: Most built-in-Detroit vehicles with windshield washers use a filter to effectively strain the big chunks of grit before it hits the motor or the tiny orifices in the washer nozzles. The filters are a simple addition and slip over the end of the pickup hole at the bottle. It sure beats poking holes into the washer nozzles and cleaning them every time you have to use them!

666 PIERCED PANELS: Although it might seem as plain as the nose on your face, don't forget to drill new holes for emblems in fresh sheetmetal before you install it. Replacement and factory sheetmetal isn't "pierced" when it comes out of the box. And if you have to drill the holes, do it before the sheetmetal is painted. Otherwise, you run the risk of ruining the paint surface.

667 NO CHIPS: Many times it is necessary to remove the front end sheetmetal for painting, and paint the individual pieces separate from the rest of the car. This allows for detailing and painting many hard-to-reach areas, including the engine compartment and fenderwells. But sooner or later, you'll have to re-attach the fenders and other front-end sheetmetal pieces. How do you do it without marring the finish with chips and scrapes? Tape the seams on the fenders and the body before you mount up the pieces. A strip or two of masking tape (make sure you use professional body shop masking tape, so you don't peel your paint job) will be sufficiently strong so that fresh sheetmetal doesn't come in contact with other fresh sheetmetal. When everything is aligned, simply peel off the tape.

668 CASE COLORS: Although the best restorations will feature "reskinned"

alternators or new-old-stock assemblies, an inexpensive way to provide a nearly new look is to glass bead the case. Follow this with a very light top coat of clear enamel. Be sure the alter-nator is totally disassembled before you try this! Spraying enamel on the entire alternator will obviously ruin it.

669 FINESSING PAINT: *Finessing* is the process of very carefully sanding and polishing the top surface of automotive paint to remove surface defects, such as hard water spots, bird droppings, acid rain and small scratches, abrasions and rub marks. After determining if the paint is thick enough with a paint thickness gauge (if it's under 4 mils, don't proceed), the paint is sanded lightly then restored with polish. Sanding might be too strong a term, because the new types of sandpaper used in finessing are really more like "polishing papers." The finest grit available used to

be 600-grit, but now grits of 1000, 1500 and 2000 (often called microfine and ultrafine) are common. It is best to use the finest paper possible that will still remove the defect. Start with 2000-grit paper, especially if you are a beginner. If that doesn't remove the defect, then move up to 1500-grit and so on. The 1500- and 2000-grit papers are so fine and they remove paint so slowly that you can actually remove paint faster with a buffer using a wool pad and polishing compound. Then why use them? Control. A few tenths can make the difference between saving a paint job and having to pay for a new one. By using microfine sandpapers with a sanding block, you can remove paint steadily and uniformly. However, if a power buffer is being used for polishing, most professionals will sand with 600- or 800-grit paper. If you haven't much experience, however, be very careful with either 600-grit or a buffer. Both can remove a lot of paint very quickly.

670 T-HANDLED HOSE CLAMPS: How many of you have skinned your knuckles removing a radiator hose? In order to make life easier (especially for your hands), try adding a set of quick release T-handled radiator hose clamps to the hoses. Mr. Gasket and

Moroso offer these conveniences, which actually can be tightened or loosened with the "T" handle, a 3/8-inch hex head or with a screwdriver. Manufactured from stainless steel, the T-handled clamps have a clamping range of 1-15/16 inch to 2-1/4 inch. In addition to easing the maintenance blues, the "T" clamps also ease engine removal and reinstallation—and that's something we can relate to!

671 WATER RESTRICTORS: Commercial (and handmade) water outlet restrictors have been on the market for years. Most are gold anodized donut-shaped discs that replace the thermostat. The idea is to restrict the flow of coolant so that it remains in the engine for a slightly longer period of time (when compared to an open setup). This allows the coolant to absorb as much heat as possible from both the engine block and the cylinder heads and transfer it to the cooling system. Moroso offers a restrictor kit under part number 63440. Included in the kit are three restrictors—all with varied center hole sizes. This allows you to control operating temperature depending on weather and track conditions.

672 TUBE CLAMPS: When the time comes to mount a cylinder shaped object in your car (a good example is a water overflow container or a small "cheater" nitrous bottle), the choices for mounting seem limited or impossible. One suggestion is to use a fire extinguisher bracket. These generally feature a slick dual-clamp design that holds the cylinder securely and can be removed in seconds. The assemblies are inexpensive and easy to mount.

673 REMOVING BATTERY ACID: The next time you have to clean the acid build-up on your battery, mix up a concoction of baking soda and water. Before applying your solution, be sure to cover anything painted that's close to the battery. Once the baking soda has finished bubbling, hose off the works with water. This is an oldy, but it still works better than anything the chemical gurus have come up with, and it costs pennies, if anything at all.

674 KILL SWITCHES: Virtually all race-sanctioning bodies require some sort of "kill" switch at the rear of the vehicle. Now, it's no secret that most of these switches are big and ugly. If you want something more appealing (and perhaps easier to mount), try this on for size: Wire a continuous duty solenoid (don't use a conventional FoMoCo starter solenoid—it will expire in short order. Echlin and other companies offer 12 and 24 volt solenoids designed for continuous use) inline with the positive battery cable. Next, select a high quality "On-Off" switch and wire it to the solenoid. Myriad styles of on-off switches are available, including smooth looking rocker styles. Mount the on-off switch anywhere on the rear of the automobile. Not only is mounting made easier with this remote setup, the looks will improve.

675 BULKHEAD FITTINGS: If you decide to plumb your oil pressure or vacuum gauge with #4 braided line, consider using bulkhead fittings at the firewall rather than routing the line through a grommet. A bulkhead fitting is easier to use and when it comes time to yank the engine, it can sometimes become a blessing. Also, try using the #4 neoprene hose instead of the Teflon-lined stuff if you're on a budget. It's easier to work with, will bend easier and has sufficient pressure capability for gauges.

676 PAINT EXTRAS: If you have someone else paint your car, have the body shop supply you with an extra quart of the mixed paint. That way you'll always have a good supply of touch-up paint that precisely matches your color. Color-matching down the road is expensive and not always possible, especially with some of the complex pearls and metalflake colors currently available. Why take a chance?

677 CHIP DETAIL: Paint chips in contemporary base-clear finishes (or other paint finishes for that matter) are a pain. They're unsightly, but fortunately, relatively easy to repair. In order to fix chips, lightly sand the area (feathering the edges) with a Meguiar's 2000 grade sanding block. Clean all residue. Add a small amount of touch-up paint to the chip, filling it in layers if necessary so that the paint repair is actually  higher than the surface. When dry (usually 24 hours), "grind" down the filled chip with the sanding block so that it's level. Using an electric buffer, go over the repair with Meguiar's No. 2 polish, followed by Meguiar's No. 9 polish.

678 CAR COVERS: When choosing a car cover, make sure you get one that fits snugly. If the cover is loose, wind will whip it against the paint, possibly damaging it. But more importantly, give careful consideration to the fabric. Cotton flannel fabrics breathe, allowing air to circulate through them. They are soft and easy on the car's paint and wax. They have no fluid resistance, so they should only be used in the dry environment of a garage. Cotton/polyester fabrics have poor fluid resistance and they trap heat and moisture. Their stiffness can harm your paint and remove wax and they can also fade. Also, if they are treated with a chemical repellent (such as Scotchgard®) they lose their ability to breathe. Plastic films should be avoided because they don't breathe, trap heat and moisture, and their stiffness can damage the paint. They also shrink in cold and stretch in heat, and they provide only minimal hail and nick protection. Vinyl films should also be avoided for the same reasons. Composite covers made from several layers of material combine the best of each type. An example are covers made from Evolution 3 fabric, which consists of four layers that allow the cover to breathe, repel fluids and provide protection. Another benefit is this material will strongly resist rot or mildew if it is folded when damp. After the expense and effort (especially if you did it yourself) of painting your car, it makes sense to protect it with the best product.

679 DOOR DING GUARDS: To
prevent door dings and paint chips on the edge of a car door when it's in your garage, mount a long, thin board along the garage wall at the height where the door contacts the wall. Tack a section of old garden hose to the board. Now, when you open the door, the first thing it hits is the garden hose.

680 WATERLESS CAR WASH: If
you're like most enthusiasts, you like to keep your car clean, polished and waxed. But all of that hard work can be stripped off quickly with a trip to the local car wash. Hot water and certain soaps tend to strip wax and polish. If you keep your car garaged, then all it may need is a quick wiping down to eliminate the fine film of grime that often accumulates overnight. If this is the case and your car isn't too dirty, then wipe it down with Meguiar's Quik Detailer. This stuff comes in a spray bottle, and it is literally a "spray-on, wipe-off" affair. To apply it, park your car in a cool spot, spray a small mist over a panel and wipe quickly with a soft cotton terry towel. Turn the towel to the dry side and buff the surface. You'll be amazed. Just remember, this is for cars that aren't "heavily soiled."

681 BOWING HOODS: If you run an
aftermarket fiberglass hood on your car and it retains the factory hood latch mechanism, you still might want to add hood pins to the outer edges of the hood. Air pressure has a tendency to bow the corners of the hood out at speed. The higher the speed, the greater the amount of "bowing" at the corners. To tell you the truth, seeing the hood move around at the outer edges is a bit disconcerting.

682 PAINT BLASTING: Sandblasting
and glass beading can remove paint quickly and efficiently, but don't be tempted to do it on body panels unless you're a pro. The sand or glass particles heat the panels and warp them before you realize it, potentially junking the panel. Save the hard material blasting for heavy metal components such as frame members, suspension pieces and so on. For the sheetmetal one of the best methods of peeling old paint is with plastic media blasting. It's a super alternative to chemical stripping and it's much more environmentally responsible and safer. Best of all, it doesn't leave a messy residue like chemical stripper, which can come back to haunt your old finish. If you have to remove paint quickly and with minimal fuss, plastic media blasting is highly recommended.

683 BATTERY POWER: High-powered
ignition systems create added loads on the battery as well as the charging system. When you increase the demand on the battery, it should be capable of handling the load. Batteries are rated by capacity. This is the amount of electrical current or amps a battery can supply for a specific amount of time. While past battery ratings revolved around "Ampere Hour" ratings, the newest "generally accepted" rating system is the "CCA" or Cold Cranking Amps method. The CCA determines the battery's capability of delivering current (amps) under cold conditions. This rating will generally range from 250 to 800 amps, but keep in mind that many (if not all) CCA ratings are rather optimistic. To combat the factory rating game, compare the "RC" or Reserve Capacity ratings of the batteries in question. This rating determines how long the ignition and other electrical components can be operated by

the battery alone (without the generator functioning). The RC rating is defined as the length of time (minutes) that a fully charged battery can deliver 25 amps of power at eighty degrees F (maintaining 10.5 volts). In other words, the higher the RC, the better the battery.

684 RUST KILLERS: If you stumble across some signs of rust in your body panels that is still light and on the surface, try Rust-Oleum's "Rust Reformer," or Turtle Wax's "Rust Eater." Both products chemically render the rust harmless, and stop it from eating the panels.

685 DRIPPING PAINT BUCKETS: When you open a can of paint, punch several holes in the lid groove with a sharp punch or a nail. This will stop the paint from running all over the outside of the can and also makes the lid easier to open. And no, it won't have an effect on the sealing properties of the lid.

686 PLASTIC FILLERS: Follow these simple steps for applying body filler. Make sure the surface is clean, and that you only do small panels at a time. Also, only work with small batches of filler, and apply it quickly. It tends to set up and harden fast if you followed the mixing instructions correctly. Generally, you need at least

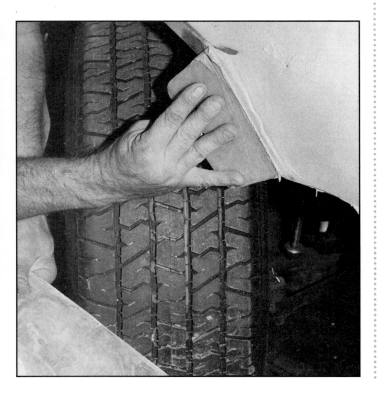

enough filler to cover the area to no more than 1/4-inch thick.

1. Follow the directions on the can of filler to get the right ratio of catalyst to filler. Work the catalyst into the filler with your plastic spreader, overlapping and blending it evenly until filler is a uniform color. Be careful not to get any air bubbles trapped in the filler—you'll create pinholes if you do.

2. Apply over dented area with smooth, even strokes going in one direction only. Changing directions will lift the filler underneath. Overlap the area to be filled, to a depth of no more than 1/4 inch. If you mixed the filler correctly, you'll have about 3-5 minutes before it becomes too hard to work properly. Try not to build it up too high—you'll increase your sanding time if you do.

3. After filler sets up to the consistency of a hard cheese-like texture, use a Surform file to scrap off high spots and excess. Filler should come out of the file like you see here—like shredded cheese.

4. Put on your paper mask and start sanding with 80-grit sandpaper. Sand until it is flat and smooth. If you don't have a power sander, use a long board. Sand in 45° angles to get a crosshatch pattern.

5. When you think you have it smooth, use the "feel" method to check for high spots. You can also use a light guide coat at this stage, like many pros do. You may have to apply another, lighter coat of filler to get that "perfect panel."

6. Do final sanding with 100 grit, then 220 grit. If you're not a pro, you should use a block or board to prevent grooving the filler with the pressure of your fingers

687 PAINT TIPS: First paint job? Try the following to help ensure success:

1. Always wear a professional quality painting mask and long sleeve coveralls while spraying.

2. Lacquer is usually shot at about 35 lbs psi. through conventional guns, and at the full five pounds pressure with HVLP equipment. The pattern adjustment knob (usually the upper one) should be opened fully for the broadest possible pattern. Try 3-1/2 turns open on the fluid control knob (usually the lower one).

3. Keep your gun perpendicular to the surface you are spraying at all times. The width of your hand from tip of thumb to tip of pinkie (about 8") is the distance you will want to maintain between the surface to be painted and the nozzle of the spray gun while spraying. For more spray techniques, see Tip #709.

4. Don't try to wipe off runs or sags. It is easy to sand runs out of lacquer after it has dried.

5.Keep your spray gun surgically clean. Most equipment malfunctions are due to dirty equipment. When you finish shooting paint for the day, clean the paint cup, then put a little lacquer thinner in it and shoot it with your finger over the nozzle to back flush the gun. Disassemble the gun and clean the nozzle orifices with a toothpick. (Never use wire, as it will ruin tightly machined surfaces.) Run pipe cleaners soaked in lacquer thinner down the siphon and vent tubes to clean them. Pull out the fluid control needle valve and clean it. Grease its shaft with a little Vaseline where it goes through the packing gland.

688 WIRE TERMINALS: What's the hot tip when it comes to wire terminals? Always spend the extra money to purchase quality wire terminal ends. When crimping terminals cut away the insulation at the wire end (being extra careful not to damage the wire strands). Use a good quality crimping tool and carefully crimp the wire into the connector "barrel." Too much pressure will break the wire strands while too little pressure will allow the terminal to work loose. Also, the plastic insulator around the barrel is designed to strengthen the connection. Too much of a crimp on the plastic weakens the assembly. Too little pressure has the same effect. While most experts do not recommend it, we have found that small sections of heat shrink added to the plastic terminal insulation makes for a neat, tidy and strong connection.

689 TUBING TEMPLATES: When you are fabricating steel line inside an engine compartment (or anywhere else on the car for that matter), try making a template from coat hanger wire or welding rods. This allows you to mock up the bends before you attack the real thing. It also ensures that the tubing will fit.

690 POSSESSED ELECTRICS: Sometimes it makes you think you're part of a horror mystery: You turn off an electrical item like an auxiliary fan, and even if the car isn't running, the fan still turns. How does this happen? In essence, the fan motor has become a generator. As the fan coasts, it creates electricity, which in turn runs backwards up the power wire. This provides sufficient power for the fan to operate momentarily. To fix the gremlins, try using a relay to operate the fan.

691 WET WATER: Is there something "wetter" than water? The folks from Redline Synthetic Oil (3450 Pacheco Blvd., Martinez, CA 94553) have recently introduced a cooling system additive called "Water Wetter" that actually improves heat transfer, reduces cylinder heat temperatures, reduces pump cavitation, prevents foaming and neutralizes corrosion buildup. There's more, but what does it do for performance? According to some top engine builders, the stuff reduces temperatures to the point that more ignition timing can be utilized, thus improving performance. In addition, the improved heat transfer that results from the addition of this stuff eliminates many engine "hot spots." Water wetter and plain water have been proven to decrease cylinder head temperature by a whopping 45 degrees over a 50% Glycol mixture. Sounds good to us, but try testing it first before you go racing with it.

692 CLEANING BRUSH: Everyone has seen the trick about cleaning used wax residue from body panel nooks and crannies with a toothbrush (see tip 658). It works, for small areas, but it's tedious for big jobs. To make those big jobs easier, run down to your local hardware store and purchase a three-inch paint brush. Cut all but 1/2"-3/4" of the bristles away. The result? An immediate wax residue brush with stiff bristles.

693 BODY CHECK: Everyone knows how to check body panels for plastic filler with a magnet. But there are other things to look for as well. Before you seriously consider any used car for purchase, pull it out into the sun, or better yet, under some bright fluorescent lights, then squat down and sight along the length of each side of the body. Is it wavy or rumpled? Are there funny lumps and bulges? These are indications of collision damage. If so, the panels will need to be fixed. Depending on the extent of the problem a good body and fender repair person may be able to fix it, but it is quite possible that the only way to make the car

look right will be to unbolt or cut off the bad panels and replace them. Such work can get very expensive. Next, check to make sure the doors, hood and trunk lid fit squarely and align properly with surrounding panels. Also check to make sure the bumpers aren't slanted, sagging or deformed. These items could be indicative of extensive damage and a bent frame. Make sure all the trim pieces are there and in good shape. These are some of the hardest items to find for any classic. If pieces are missing, you may want to assure yourself that you can get replacements and find out how much they would cost before you make an offer on the car.

694 BATTERY TERMINALS: If you're fed up with cleaning battery cable terminals, there is another answer other than grease on the terminals. The grease can become as ugly as the green slime with the passing of time. The alternative is to clean the cable ends completely and reinstall them on the battery. Then spray the connections with Permatex high tack "Spray-A-Gasket" (PN 99MA). This

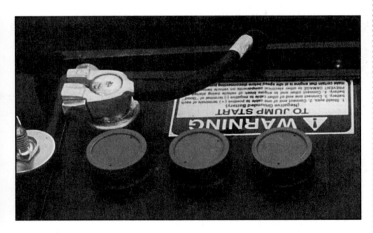

is an adhesive sealant that literally seals out the grime. Just be sure to cover surrounding sheetmetal and engine parts before spraying on the "gasket." The result is a clean battery that will please the most critical car show judge, and one that will also operate properly.

695 BALKY STARTERS: Before you blame a battery or starter for "balky starts," take a close look at the ground cable for the battery. The ground connection should be clean and free of rust, paint and other crud. In addition, the ground should be attached to the engine block if at all possible—even if the car has solid steel motor mounts. At the same time, make certain that the battery posts are spotlessly clean. You'd be surprised at how much battery juice is wasted because of dirt or poor connections.

696 FRACTURED LENSES: Taillight lenses are susceptible to damage because they are so exposed to the elements. One stone or mishit street hockey puck and the lens is cracked. Although a replacement is available, this is an original. If the crack or hole is small, try using Loctite's "Form-A-Lens." It works miracles and only you will know that the lens was once marred. Form-A-Lens is available in red, clear and amber.

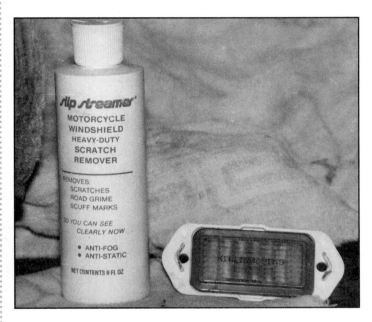

697 MILKY LENSES: If the red on your taillamp lens assemblies isn't red anymore (they fade and often go milky with age), try this: Wet sand the lens assemblies with 600-grit wet/dry sandpaper. Finish sanding with 1000-grit wet/dry and add some plastic polish. You'll be amazed at how red they really are.

698 GRINDING STARTERS: GM starter motors are occasionally plagued with a grinding noise as they engage the flywheel or flexplate teeth. As you know, this isn't good for the health of the ring gear or the starter. Most likely, all the starter needs is shimming to bring it into line. Different shim thicknesses under each of the respective bolts can move the starter

closer or further away from the ring gear. A bit of "fine tuning" and the noise will be gone. If this doesn't solve the problem, there may be missing teeth on the flywheel, which will obviously require major repairs.

699 ALIGNING TRIM: You've installed all new chrome trim on your vintage hot rod. Everything's swell, except for the fact that some of the trim doesn't line up. Do you take everything apart and try again? Not at all. The trim (along with the springy internal clips) can be re-arranged from the outside. Take a small piece of wood, butt it up against the skewed trim piece, and gently tap the wood with the hammer until the trim comes back into line. Remember to use a gentle tap. Body shops use this trick all the time.

700 LUBE RADIATOR HOSE: The next time you need to install a radiator hose, rub a little bit of moly grease or wheel bearing grease on the inside of the hose where it mates with the metal neck. When it comes time to remove it, you'll find the task much easier.

701 OVERHEATING: Does your hot rod overheat—especially in the dog days of summer? Don't be tempted to remove the thermostat. The problem will only get worse. One function of the thermostat is to reduce the flow of coolant so that the cooling system has a chance to properly dissipate heat. If removed, the coolant will flow too quickly, which in turn defeats the entire purpose of the system. To correct the over-heating problem, try different thermostat levels. You might be surprised to find that a high performance car might function much better with a 190-degree 'stat rather than none.

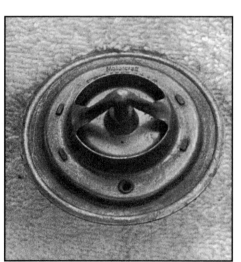

702 HEATERS: While car heaters aren't a big topic in the sunbelt, they are mighty important in other parts of the country. If your driver doesn't deliver the heat, the probable cause is either a plugged heater valve (found in some cars only) or more probable, an engine thermostat that's stuck in the open position. If that's the case, then the coolant will pass through the engine so quickly that it doesn't get hot enough. Check the thermostat before you tear the heating system apart.

703 SQUEALING BELTS: Is your car plagued with a fan or accessory belt that squeals like a stuck pig? Have you tried everything to eliminate the squeal other than a new belt? Before you give up and buy new belts, try adding some belt dressing. Vehicle manufacturers sell the stuff and so do countless auto parts stores. It works and also extends belt life.

704 LEAKY RADS: Small radiator or cooling system leaks are a curse. In most cases, the leak is too small to warrant a complete rebuild, but how in the world do you stop the drips? Check your local GM dealer for "cooling system sealer" under part number 1051687 just for that purpose. And the "installation" is just as simple. Just drop two of the "pellets" into the radiator system and forget about it. The leaks should disappear.

705 QUICK ALTERNATOR TEST: Do you think your alternator is on the fritz? Are you short on tools (or cash) to test the thing? If so, try this: Place a screwdriver blade near the back of the alternator with the engine running. If the alternator is charging, there will be a magnetic field on the backside which will attract the screwdriver blade. If the alternator isn't charging, it won't attract the screwdriver blade.

706 ELECTRICAL GREMLINS: If you've ever flicked the ignition switch and received nothing more than a click, then use this sequence to check for problems: (1) Check the headlamps. If they are glowing, then the trouble isn't with the battery. (2) Have an assistant turn the ignition switch. If the lights dim then the trouble is with the starter. If they don't dim, then the trouble is with the cables, ground connection or starter connections. (3) The trouble could be with the solenoid. You can bypass the solenoid by inserting a large screwdriver between the large battery cable post and one of the small switch terminals. If the starter still refuses to spin, it's time to tear it down for a rebuild.

707 BELT TENSION: Do you have a problem with alternator bearing failure? If so, the most common cause is a too-tight fan belt. If the belt is overtightened, the alternator bear-ings have to absorb the strain. How tight is just right? You should be able to flex the belt approx-imately 1/2 inch for every 12 inches of un-supported span.

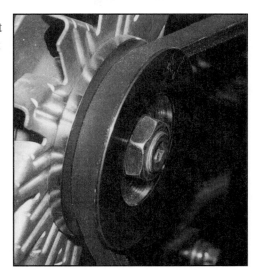

708 BULB SOCKETS: Bulb sockets live in a tough environment. They're exposed to the elements and seldom see any maintenance. After a few years of abuse, they generally become corroded beyond recognition. The end result is usually a taillamp, signal lamp, side marker lamp bulb that doesn't work because of the corrosion. To ensure proper contact, clean the socket with a battery terminal brush. It's quick, easy and gets the job done. Just be sure the lights are turned off before you begin your cleanup.

709 SHOOTING PAINT: Test the pattern of the gun by spraying the paint on a piece of paper first. Adjust the spray, material and the atomizing pressure of your gun to the paint manufacturer's specifications. If you've never painted before, buy an inexpensive quart of paint and practice spraying it, preferably on a spare body panel, but a piece of cardboard will do. Spray guns operate best when held eight to 12 inches away from the surface. If held closer, air pressure will ripple the paint. Held farther away, and the paint will go on too dry (too much solvent will evaporate before the paint hits the surface) and cause orange peel or dry film. It will also affect the color. Begin the first stroke outside of the boundary of the surface to be painted. Pull the trigger and start the airflow, then squeeze it all the way to release the material just before the gun crosses over the surface to be painted. You need to develop this sense of timing. Pass across the surface in one full, long stroke. Keep the gun equidistant from the panel all the way across. Do not fan the gun by waving your wrist—keep it square to the surface. Lock your wrist and arm, using your body and shoulders to pull the gun across the surface. This forces you to maintain the distance and angle from the beginning of the stroke to the end. Move your stroke at a rate of speed that will put down a full, medium-wet, coat. If you go too slow, the paint will run. If you work too fast, the paint will be too thin and dry. The next pass should begin by overlapping 50% of the previous pass, by directing the center of the spray pattern at the lower or nearest edge of the previous stroke. Repeat this procedure, alternating from left to right, right to left, until the panel is coated.

710 BUFF MASTERS: When buffing paint (power polishing with electric equipment), take a tip from the pros: Always use a "wet buff" technique. This means that you stop buffing before the polish dries. Remove the hazy residue and excess polish with a clean, soft, cotton terry towel. Avoid buffing directly over body accent lines, seams or emblems. In any sensitive areas, such as raised door handles or fender corners and door edges where the paint is thin, finish buffing by hand.

711 BATTERY CAUTIONS: You probably already know that it's dangerous to have sparks flying around a battery. But did you know it is much more dangerous just after a battery has been charged? Charging a battery produces extremely flammable gases. Allow an hour or more in a well-ventilated area, if possible, before installing your battery after charging.

712 ATTACHING TERMINALS: Most components will have stud or screw terminals to accommodate a ring terminal on a wire. Generally, the ring terminal slips over the stud and is fastened with a nut and assortment of washers (lock and flat) (a screw

obviously just has the washers). For high performance use, you can buy a little extra insurance by replacing the plain nuts with Nylock nuts, which are thicker and require more stud length, but they hold better. If more length is needed, you can remove the flat washer, but do not remove the lock washer—it prevents the terminal from twisting and placing stress on the wire when the nut is tightened. The correct installation sequence for installing stud terminals is: (1) internal-tooth lock washer; (2) ring terminal; (3) plain or flat washer; (4) nut. For screw terminals, the order is reversed: (1) flat washer; (2) ring terminal on screw; (3) lock washer on screw; (4) screw attached to component. For racers try using a dab of bright red fingernail polish on each connection to act as a mild thread lock.

713 MORE WIRE: Several types of wire covering (insulation) are available—PVC (poly-vinyl-chloride) or Teflon®. Teflon is stronger, but if it catches fire, it tends to give off fumes that are more toxic than PVC. Take your pick.

714 BOILED BATTERIES: If you run into a situation where the charging system in your car is overcharging the battery, the first thing to do is to check the voltage regulator, then the alternator (or generator). That's cool, but what if the thing still boils the battery? The answer could be as simple as a poor ground. The ground between the voltage regulator and the bracket it is mounted on could be the culprit. Check it out.

715 HEAT DELETE: If you have a show car that is only driven in perfect driving conditions (occasionally) and you want to remove a bunch of underhood clutter (and more than a few pounds of excess baggage), think about this: Most of the Detroit carmakers offered "heater delete" options in the Fifties and Sixties. These credit options eliminated the heater and were created primarily for cars shipped south of the border and to Hawaii. Delete parts are available used or as reproductions for many GM-Ford-Mopar vehicles, but more important, they definitely clean up the engine compartment. Just don't try this if you live in Minnesota and you want to use your car in January.

716 HANG PARTS TO PAINT: To do a complete paint job, it is helpful to paint the car in pieces (this only applies to solid color cars—it's impossible with metallics and pearls). Things like doors,

fenders, decklid, hood and other items can be painted individually. It makes sense, but how do you handle bulky components? Items such as doors are particularly troublesome, but if you use several solid strands of mechanic's wire, you'll be able to suspend them from the ceiling of the spray booth.

By painting them in mid-air, complete coverage is possible (including the underside and inner panel of the door—something that is almost impossible using conventional methods). The same method applies to the decklid and other sheetmetal. That was the method used to paint this Camaro.

717 SILICONE SEALANT: Never use silicone to seal glass or to seal holes in metal. Moisture collects behind the silicone and rust begins. And when it comes time to fix the rust, you'll then be faced with the unpleasant task of completely fishing out the silicone. As most of you are aware, silicone and paint don't mix. If any silicone is within a mile of a paint booth, expect fisheyes to appear in the paint.

718 RIBBED HOSES: When adding new radiator hoses to your car, stay away from the ribbed "fits-all" models. Not only are they ugly, they also restrict coolant flow—often by significant margins. Also, the quality of these hoses is usually less than ideal. Use correctly formed hose and you won't have to worry so much about heating problems.

719 CHOOSING BRAS: A front end cover, often called a bra, is an effective means of preventing paint damage caused by gravel and bugs. But beware that air turbulence will cause the bra to abrade the paint to some extent. Choose a bra that is snug-fitting and well-tailored to your car. Examine the paint occasionally to make sure paint abrasion isn't a problem. The bra material can stretch and loosen up so that it flaps around when the car is moving, or dirt and sand can become trapped between the bra and the paint. The minor abrasion of the bra rubbing the paint underneath will just cause the paint's gloss to diminish. If that occurs, use a paint cleaner or polishing compound to bring back the shine. Be careful about using a bra on a freshly painted car. Not only is the paint softer and more easily damaged by wear, water trapped under the bra could cause problems if it bakes in the sun. Another thing about bras is that they do alter the appearance of the car in such a way that it looks unattractive to some people.

720 DASH RUST: Dash rust is something many people overlook when repainting a car or shopping for a prospective project car. In many cases, even low mileage cars will rust because of a poor fitting windshield, but there's also another reason: Rust can be initiated by washing the inside of the windshield! Over the years, excess cleaning fluid or water accumulates in one spot and then sits undetected (and trapped) between the dash panel and the lower section of the windshield. Check the gap between the dash and

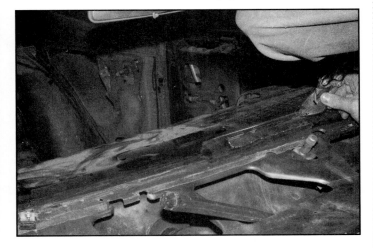

the windshield very carefully. You might be faced with some serious (and expensive) rust repairs.

721 BUFFING LINES: When polishing with a power buffer, never buff directly on top of raised body "character" lines. The reduced film thickness on these areas increases the chance of burning through the paint.

To properly buff these areas of the vehicle, tackle them from either side, and work up to the character line.

722 A-ARM FLAPS: Many vintage cars will either be missing the A-arm flaps or they will be so hard and cracked, they look out of place in an otherwise spotless compartment. Sure you can take them out completely, but the compartment looks naked without them. Help is readily available from the folks at A&M Soffseal. They offer reproduction A-arm flaps that include a set of staples for installation. The special staples are extremely important—the factory staples were installed with a press and as a result, are very stiff. This makes straightening the factory staples next to impossible, and if you do manage to get 'em straight, the re-install process is next to impossible. Just use the repro staples supplied with the flaps—your fingers will be delighted!

723 CANDY PAINT: Want a trick Candy Apple Red paint job? You might not once you consider the following disadvantages. First, it is very difficult to make the candy coat perfectly uniform in its thickness. For one thing, during the spraying of paint, you must overlap the areas being sprayed. And any differences in the thickness of the candy layer where the pattern overlaps can be easily seen in the lightness or darkness of the color. It takes a very skillful painter to apply candy coats without ending up with a blotchy paint job. That, plus the fact that it is a tri-coat process makes it very expensive. If the tinting of the candy coat was very weak such that 10 or more coats needed to be applied, it would be easier to get uniform coverage because the overlapping spray areas and other variances could be averaged out. However, that could lead to a very thick paint job prone to cracking and crazing, especially on a car parked daily in the sun. The second major problem with candy colors is that it is difficult (some would say impossible) to repair any problems. Spot repainting and blending of a candy coat is extremely difficult, because you are seeing through the candy coat, and the line where the old paint meets the new can never be perfectly uniform in thickness. Even if a problem that needs repainting lies on a separate panel, such as a hood or door, it is still very difficult to exactly match the depth of paint previously sprayed. Make sure you weigh these points against your desire for the paint job before plunking down your money.

724 SELECTING WAX: High

performance car nuts generally want the best for their ride, and that includes wax. But like most things these days, the choice is confused by the number of products available. First of all, wax is for protecting paint; it is not to restore gloss or shine. That's the job of a polish. There are many brands of wax available on the market today. Most of them have labels spouting impressive words like polymer technology, pure carnauba, silicones, natural waxes, resins and glazing. All manufacturers have tests that will claim their brand is better than the other. But the best advice is to try several products yourself, then select the one which is easiest to apply, looks the best and lasts the longest. Other suggestions are to ask a trusted fellow car enthusiast or your local body shop which brand they recommend, and then try the product yourself. If a product takes too much effort to apply, you probably won't use it very often. Some of the non-wax polymers and glazes contain silicones and go on very easily. This ease of application makes them very popular, but if you're planning on spot repairs or fixing chips, don't use waxes with silicones or you'll have problems with fisheyes. Another product many experts in the industry recommend highly is one of the oldest—carnauba wax. This wax is made from the carnauba palm tree in South America, and you'll find a product containing pure carnauba wax offered by many of the top names in the car care business. Carnauba wax in its purest form is reported to be the most durable and most protective type of wax. If you're looking for maximum protection, make sure your wax contains carnauba.

725 CHOOSING SPARK: Look under

the hood of many high performance street or racing cars, and you'll likely see one of these in the engine compartment. With all of the aftermarket "buzz boxes" available, how do you choose the best for your application? For anything less than a maximum output, professional race engine, a high output system such as an MSD-6A, 6AL or -6T, or an Accel Laser II, is more than adequate. More powerful systems might produce slightly more power, but considering the operating environment, the added expense isn't justified. Also, some super high output systems aren't designed to run for hours on end. They may be unreliable on the street, or in a

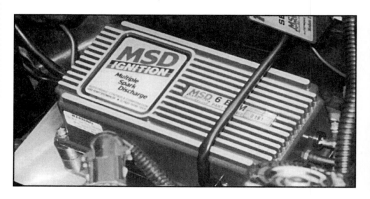

boat or oval track car. Most NASCAR engines use an MSD-6T (also sold through GM as PN 10037378). These are 675 hp engines that run flat out for hours on end, so the -6T should be more than adequate for a street engine. On the other hand, the MSD-7AL2 is preferred by Pro Stock and similar hard-core drag racing vehicles. It puts out 800 millijoules of energy compared to 600 for the MSD-6 series. So yes, there is the potential for more power with the higher end unit. If your racing in a class where every ounce of power is necessary, and you can tune the engine to the max, then yes, go with the 7 series. But for most bracket racers, road racing, short track, marine and street engines, the 6 series is more than adequate.

726 WAXING APPLICATORS: T-

shirts are a good choice for applying and buffing wax. Advantages are that T-shirts are inexpensive, are easily found and are easily cleaned and reused. Make sure the T-shirts don't have abrasive decals, buttons, zippers, rivets and anything else which might cause scratches. Use only soft 100% cotton cloth. Large weave and fluffiness is also a plus because any grit picked up by the cloth will work its way into the weave and thereby not drag along the painted surface. Some car care purists won't use anything but a well-washed soft cotton diaper (available from a diaper service) for polishing. However, be careful of the stitching. I recently bought a package of new "cotton" diapers and found that the stitching was done with nylon thread. The nylon left minute scratches in the paint I was polishing. If you want to test the thread or stitching in any piece of cloth, clip out a short piece of thread. Hold it with tweezers or pliers and bring a match or

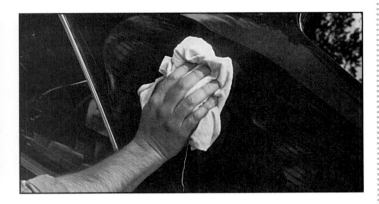

lighter under the end of the thread so that the flame is about an inch away. Nylon thread will shrink up and its end will melt into a ball. Cotton thread will turn brown. Avoid using mechanic's shop rags on paint. Not only are they rough and sometimes contain harsh chemicals, they may have metal particles stuck in the weave. Check with your local autobody supply store to see if it has boxes of rags made specifically for waxing and polishing. Specialty polishing cloths can be excellent. Cheese cloth is just a very loosely woven soft cloth. Terry cloth is a fabric made with short loops of thread on the surface. They all have the advantages of the softest cloths, along with the disposability of paper. The only disadvantage is the cost, which may not be worth the difference to the finish.

727 TRAILER PLUGS: Swapping electricals on any car is a chore. For example, suppose your coil goes out. With a modern high performance electronic ignition system, there are more than a few wires to

disconnect. The same applies to goodies like the starter, the distributor, the electric water pump drive and other odds 'n ends. Removing and replacing these pieces requires time—a valuable commodity for racers. To speed up the process, try adding trailer plugs to the various electrical components that might require attention. The trailer plugs are cheap, waterproof and easily up to the minor electrical loads placed upon them. And when it comes time to yank the engine, snapping open a trailer plug is a lot easier than unhooking a bundle of wires.

728 SQUEAKY SHEET METAL: If you've got an irritating squeak that you just can't seem to locate, it might be the sheetmetal or fiberglass panels, especially the hood. The next time you drive down the road, watch the relationship between the hood and the front fenders. Often, the hinge side of the hood will move considerably, rubbing against the adjoining fenders and causing a squeak. That's one reason why the factories install hood side bumpers on many cars. And, just as important, if the side bumpers are missing, you'll probably have some significant paint

chips on both the hood and the fenders. If your hood bumpers are missing or brittle, it's time to replace them.

729 WIRE INSULATION: When choosing wire, be sure the insulation is capable of withstanding the higher temperatures typical of high performance or racing engines. PVC wire insulation is rated from 176 to 239 degrees F, depending on the plasticizers, stabilizers and sheathing used in its manufacture. The insualtion on wiring sold at most auto parts stores generally has a temperature rating of only 185 degrees F unless otherwise noted. General purpose wire used for race cars (such as for instrument panels and sensors) should have an insulation rating of 221 deg. F. At this rating, the insulation will withstand the rigors of racing without breaking down, unless it accidentally touches a hot manifold or coolant line.

730 BELTING OUT TROUBLE:

Cogged-tooth or Gilmore drives and fans don't mix. Now, we're not talking about the little electric water pump drives. Rather, we're discussing the cogged belt setups that operate off the crank. Accord-ing to the experts at Jones Racing Products (they manufacture combinations of cogged-tooth drives and serpentine systems), you should never mount a conventional fan to the nose of a cogged tooth belt drive. The harmonics will drive the fan crazy and the last thing you need is a five- or six-blade fan exiting the engine compartment via the hood. Jones advises that a high quality electric fan should be used in conjunction with a belt drive.

731 HOOD SCOOPS:

According to Gary Harwood (Harwood Industries), contemporary hood scoops are as much a part of the overall "combination" of a car as the camshaft. No hood scoop is ideally suited to a given race car, but in certain applications, a specific scoop might work better than others. The actual shape of the vehicle, the engine location and other variables easily affect the hood scoop shape and design. Harwood also points out that street-driven cars have similar requirements. Some hood scoops are simply too large and as a result may cause chaos with law enforcement officials. Similarly, air cleaners present problems and so do nitrous oxide systems. Each application is specialized and because of that, Harwood urges individuals to call in regard to specific scoop requirements. Finally, Gary Harwood points this out: "A hood scoop is not a supercharger." In essence, it won't provide any magic, but when properly designed, located and installed, it can improve upon performance. Just don't expect miracles.

732 FILL WIPER HOLES:

If you have a race car and you've removed the windshield wipers, you can fill those ugly holes easily with a set of spring plugs. They're used to fill holes in household electrical junction boxes. Most good hardware or home handyman centers sell them.

733 WIRE SQUEAKS:

A place where you don't expect squeaks and potential hazards is with underhood wiring. But it can happen, especially if the wiring or wiring harness is unsupported and is physically chafing. In order to stop the problem, be sure to support the wire(s) with plenty of plastic ties and if the harness is rather long, consider the use of small ID Adel Clamps. Aside from eliminating small squeaks, they can save bigger repair bills caused by electrical shorts and possibly fires.

734 APPLYING POLISH:

When polishing paint with an electric buffer, use the following procedure to minimize cleanup from sprayed polish: Dispense a thin coating of polish on the buffing pad by hand to help in lubrication and to prevent pad hopping and bounce. Next, dispense a strip of polish on the surface (the surface should be cool to the touch). Each "strip" of polish should be approximately 8 inches apart and should cover an area of approximately 1 foot in length. Place the buffer just to the right and slightly above the strip closest to you with the buffing pad flat to the surface. Lift the position of the foam pad so that it is raised slightly at the beginning of the strip of product. Turn on the buffer and slowly move the pad across the strip of polish. The clockwise rotation of the buffer will pull the polish into the pad and along the working surface. This eliminates almost all of the spray that can make a mess of buffing.

735 MASKING MATERIALS:

Masking tape and masking papers come in many widths. The narrower the tape, the easier it will form around curves. Use expensive tape unless you can afford the time to test less expensive brands. 3M is always a safe choice. Good quality masking tape will not allow paint to seep through, it will stick uniformly to the surface and it will be easy to remove later. The wider the tape, the greater the coverage. Paper comes in several widths. Never use newspaper for masking because it is too porous, and the wet paint can bleed through. Furthermore, the black ink can bleed and contaminate the surface with an oily film. Use 1/4-inch tape for tight curves or hard-to-tape areas. Small items such as door handles and emblems can be masked off with tape only. On large areas to be covered with paper, run a strip of tape around the trim or edges of the area.

Add the masking paper, folding the edges of the paper under to match the contour of the item being masked. When the paper is shaped to the item, apply another strip of tape to the paper edges. This makes an effective seal to prevent overspray from blowing underneath. If you need to use more than one piece of paper to cover an area, make sure you tape the seam. For more masking tips, see Tip #657.

736 PAINTING EMBLEMS: If the original emblems on your car are still in nice shape but the paint is weathered, there's no need to replace them. Instead, paint them with a high quality model car paint such as Testor's enamel. With brush in hand, flow the paint into the recessed areas of the emblem. If you flow the paint with large drops of color instead of physically "brushing" it on, there won't be any brush marks. Let the paint smooth and if you have any buildups in the wrong places (such as raised lettering), remove them with a small piece of 000 steel wool.

737 DRILLING PAINTED SHEETMETAL: If you have to cut a hole in a section of painted sheetmetal (such as to install a set of hood pins or to install a hood-mounted tach), try this: Cover the external sheetmetal area liberally with wide masking tape. Press the tape down firmly so that it all sticks. Then drill the hole with a sharp bit or make a cut with a sharp jigsaw. Proceed slowly with the cutting tool. The masking tape will stop the paint from chipping and peeling. Just be careful when removing it.

738 UNMASKING TAPE: After you've taped a section of sheetmetal (for whatever reason), don't jerk the masking tape off! Instead, the correct way to remove tape goes like this: Peel it back slowly and with a very slight downward movement. This allows the tape to roll back onto itself. It also prevents fresh paint from lifting. Care in removing masking tape eliminates a jagged edge as well.

739 SAGGING DOORS: On many vintage cars, the doors sag whenever they are opened and closed. This results in a door that just doesn't open easily and often proves even more difficult to close. The

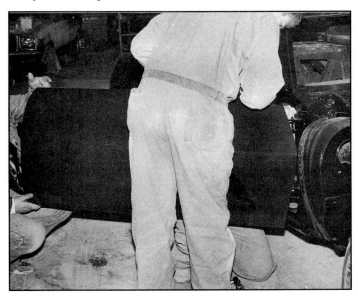

trouble is often worn hinge bushings. A quick test of the hinge pins and/or bushings is accomplished by pulling upward on the door when it is in an open position. If it moves, the bushings need replacement. The job is relatively straightforward—remove the pins and bushings from the door and replace them with quality repro or OEM components. Once reinstalled, stake the pins in place (a small spot weld works well). The job isn't difficult, but the results always create a nice, tight fitting door.

740 SELECTING PAINT COLOR: Selecting the color for your car is pretty much a subjective choice, although if your car is a valuable collector, you should stick with the original color. But if you have a choice, you should also take into account the difficulty of future repairs. This is of particular importance to novice painters because there is a good chance that a mistake will be made at some point during the application and therefore some repainting will be required before the car is taken out of the garage. In fact, that's fairly likely even with paint jobs done by the most experienced painters. Some paints are harder to match and blend when spot repairs are needed. Solid colors are certainly the easiest, with black being the easiest of all.

However, black also shows defects more and is one of the hardest to keep looking at its best. White is another one of the easiest, and like other light colors, more tolerant of minor defects in bodywork and surface preparation.

741 MUSTANG RADIATOR: To improve the cooling of your late-model 5.0 Mustang hot rod, swap the stock radiator for a Ford Motorsport three-core radiator shown. This radiator is

manufactured with three 1/2-inch rows of tubing to improve BTU rejection (cooling) over the stock two-row radiator. The BTU rejection capacity, or cooling ability, is determined by the total area of the radiator, fin spacing and tube size and number. The more rows of tubing, the better.

742 CHROMING CAUTIONS: Before you go nuts chroming components, give this some thought: A major problem with decorative chrome plate is a phenomenon called "hydrogen embrittlement." Due to the use of various forms of acid during the cleaning stages of chrome plating, a hydrogen by-product is released into the tank which is then absorbed by the metal part being cleaned. Additionally, some theories suggest the problem is compounded by the electrolytic process. When a current is applied to a parent metal, it too can create brittleness. As the name implies, hydrogen embrittlement causes the parent metal to become brittle and eventually it can crack under stress. There are methods of heat treating that lessen the chance of hydrogen embrittlement, but for the most part, they are band-aid styles of fixes. In the end, any component that is stressed should not be plated.

743 BUFFER CHOICES: Power buffers generally fall into two categories: orbital and rotary. Orbital buffers are best suited for the application of non-abrasive products that achieve improved gloss without buffer swirl marks. The results created by an orbital buffer are generally similar to those created when applying products by hand. The difference is simply a reduced level of effort for the operator. An orbital buffer will not remove paint defects and

oxidation. The limited action created by these pieces of equipment does not make sufficient friction to remove paint defects. These buffers are so gentle that they will not normally burn through the paint. On the other hand, a rotary buffer is the most commonly used professional tool. Available in a variety of buffing speeds, the correct speed is determined by the type of paint you are working with. Low speed or variable speed "electronic" buffers operate between 1200-1750 rpm. They are most effective on base coat/clear coat paint finishes which are more reactive to excessive heat buildup and static. High speed buffers operate between 1750-3000 rpm. They're ideal for use on acrylic lacquer and acrylic enamel paint finishes. Take your pick, but be sure to match the buffer to the type of paint on your car, or you'll burn through to sheetmetal before you can stop.

744 COOLANT & PRESSURE: As a rule of thumb, the coolant temperature of your car should be in a range between 200 and 210 degrees F, while the internal pressure should be in the area of 20 pounds. If the engine is run at a lower temperature (around 175 to 180 degrees F), you are losing approximately two to three percent horsepower. A 21-lb. pressure cap will automatically raise the boiling point of pure water from 212 degrees F to 260 degrees F. The addition of a 50% solution of aftermarket "coolant" (almost always ethylene glycol, or more commonly, "anti-freeze") will then raise the boiling point to approximately 275 degrees F—high enough for most high performance situations!

745 MORE COOLANT: It used to be that anti-freeze was only added to cars in frigid climates, but all of that has changed. Motor vehicle manufacturers began recommending anti-freeze solutions for vehicles used everywhere. The reasons are quite simple. Anti-freeze solutions that contain ethylene glycol combat corrosion and help to neutralize rust formation in the engine block. In addition, the anti-freeze mixture lubricates the water pump and stops the natural corrosion that slowly destroys aluminum components (such as radiators, cylinder heads, water pumps, etc.). Anti-freeze eliminates the problem of blocks and radiators cracking in extreme cold, but it also raises the boiling point of the coolant (as discussed previously). Unfortunately, if the glycol-based coolant is introduced into the combustion chamber (via a leaking head gasket, cracked cylinder head or whatever), it will quickly contaminate the engine oil. The answer is of course to locate the leak, but if it isn't caught quickly, you can count on some very expensive repair bills!

BODY, PAINT, ELECTRICAL, DETAILING & ENGINE COMPARTMENT

746 MORE COOLING PRESSURE: Here's more food for thought when it comes to radiator caps and cooling system pressure: For every pound of pressure added to the cooling system, the boiling point will rise approximately three degrees. For every 1000-ft. above sea level, the boiling point of coolant will go down about three degrees.

747 TAPING SEAMS: Before you begin a color sand or polish job, consider taping all of the body seams with masking tape. A strip of tape along the door, trunk and hood lines helps to seal most of the residue and mess from entering the crevices. Cleanup is easier and the chance of blowing through a thin section of paint is minimized.

748 BUMPER DETAILS: Before sending off a set of bumpers to the chrome shop, tape the face and then have the back side sandblasted. If you don't detail the backside, it might come back looking rough with huge pieces of flaking and chipped chrome flashing. If the bumper backsides are sandblasted first, then you won't have the problem. When the bumpers come back from the chrome shop, then re-mask the face and paint the backside with aluminum paint. The finish will be superb.

749 FAT FENDERS: Most street cars can accept a L-60 x 15-in. tire mounted on a 15 x 8 to 15 x 9-in. rim with the proper backspace. The real problem is the lip that intrudes into the rear well. The "bulge" of the tire will sometimes interfere with the 90-degree lip at the top of the wheelwell—causing interference as the rear suspension goes through its range of travel. To solve the problem, the upper 90-degree section of the wheelwell lip (found inside the well), has to be cut and bent inward, creating a smooth transition from outer body sheetmetal to inner wheelwell. This may prove to be easier said than done! The best way around this task is via a series of cuts on the inside lip. Simply cut the lip, fold it in with a hammer and dolly and work your way around the entire upper section of the wheelwell. Next, MIG-weld the cut sheetmetal together so that moisture and dirt cannot be trapped between the outer body sheetmetal and the inner wheelwell. In almost all examples, this work will only be required in the upper areas of the well—where the tire's bulge comes in contact with the 90-degree lip.

750 WEATHERSTRIP PUFFING: If you've installed fresh weatherstripping on the doors of your car, you might find that the doors will need adjustment. New weatherstripping is rather "puffy" and as it takes shape with the applicable door or decklid in place, it will take on a slightly different configuration. The only solution is panel realignment after the weatherstrip has taken a set.

751 PLUG WELDING: There is a right way to fill holes in sheetmetal. Here's the drill (no pun intended): First, the area must first be cleaned of all paint. The hole is then filled via a MIG (wire feed) welder, using a "plug" weld (sometimes called a "rosette" weld). Care is taken so that holes are welded at opposite ends of the panel. In other words, a hole is filled on the far left side of the vehicle and the next hole to be filled is on the extreme right hand side of the vehicle. This lessens the chance of warpage. Added insurance comes from cool shop towels (dipped in water and wrung out) surrounding each hole during welding. The idea is to isolate the heat so that the panel does not warp. Once all holes are welded shut, they are ground flush with the factory sheetmetal. The surface should be flush, however most plug welds will require a very light coat of plastic filler and a small amount of final finishing to become flawless. After that, the area can be prepped for paint.

752 HAZY PAINT: If your paint job has a milky, almost yellowish appearance (often called "hazing"), it's because the paint has a solvent and/or wax buildup on the top surface. Typically, the hazy finish occurs over a period of time. The paint is contracting and expanding. As it does, it absorbs old wax and solvent into the top coat. To solve the problem, strip the wax (with a paint "cleaner"), re-polish the car and then re-wax it. Most experts recommend stripping wax at least once a year.

753 SOAKING SANDPAPER: You'll find that many "sanding products" (wet-dry sandpaper or sanding blocks) work better if they are soaked in water overnight. At the very least, they should be soaked in water at least 15 minutes prior to use. In the case of sanding blocks (such as the "Finesse" sanding blocks sold by Meguiar's), they should soak until they sink and then remain in water thereafter.

754 **COOL FANS:** When you have a close look at engine cooling fans, either a flex fan or a "clutch fan" offer considerable advantages as far as horsepower losses are concerned. Obviously, a flex fan is far less complicated than a clutch fan, but it has at least one potential drawback: Many flex fan designs simply take a "set" at a given position following sustained use. The result is too little fan action and reduced cooling. In our experience, the stainless steel units offered the best performance, while the aluminum blade models were the worst.

755 **WIRE GAUGE:** When wiring accessories under the hood of your car, think about the actual size of the wire. Wire gauge is very important. If a wire must be long, try to increase the size of the wire. You can never go wrong with too large a wire—it simply becomes a case of "manageability"—very large wires are hard to route, hard to bend and sometimes hard to wrap. On the other hand, wires that are too small will not be capable of carrying a given load. This is simply a case where too much is better than too little!

756 **JOINING WIRES:** When it comes time to butt two wires together or to make connections, the preferred method is via soldering. The "down 'n dirty" process most often seen on "custom wiring" jobs is a household electrician process—two or three wires stripped bare, twisted together and covered with electrical tape. From an automotive point of view, this doesn't cut it! The right way to join the wires is via a soldered joint. Once properly soldered, cover the joint with a piece of good quality heat shrink rather than black electrician's tape. Eventually the tape will become brittle and unravel, but a heat shrink will remain in place permanently.

757 **PADS & BONNETS:** If you're using power buffers and/or orbitals, you need to know about pads and bonnets. Pads are used with rotary buffers, while bonnets are generally used with orbitals. Cutting pads are woven wool and available in diameters of 7 to 9 inches. Their purpose is to remove paint surface irregularities, orange peel, surface scratches and water spots. The cutting pad will cause swirls in the paint when used with an abrasive compound, so you'll have to follow up on it with a finishing pad. These fall into three types: 100% sheepskin, a sheepskin/synthetic blend, and foam. The 100% sheepskin pads have been the standard for detailers wanting a show car finish, but they are expensive. The synthetics do a good job, and cost less. Foam is popular with pro detailers, especially with clear coats, because it leaves no swirls or swirl marks. Bonnets are usually made of terry cloth, and their purpose is to remove wax, polish or cleaner from the paint surface. Generally, you use one to apply and one to remove the wax. Sheepskin bonnets can be used, but only to remove light coatings of wax or polish.

758 **DUAL BATTERIES:** In many cars (street or strip), you'll often see a pair of batteries in use. From past experience, this is totally unnecessary in a street car application—especially one with a capable charging system. If you insist on running dual batteries, then hook them up in parallel. This doubles their Amperes Hour capacity. To hook up the parallel circuit, route the "hot" starter lead to one battery, then run a line from the (+) post on one battery to the (+) post on the second battery. The second battery should then have its negative post (-) grounded with a cable joining both (-) terminals on the battery. Use batteries from the same manufacturer and of the same capacity. Only use new batteries and do not mix a new battery with an old battery.

759 **BLACK PLASTIC DETAILING:** So, you have a later model car and it has a bunch of black plastic trim (like mirrors, a spoiler or two, louvers and so on) that is looking a little ragged—it's dull, it's scratched and has a lot of bug stains. How do you fix it? Try this: Clean with a soft, damp sponge and a mild fine-cut polish (such as Meguiar's #2). Then hand-polish the plastic with a fine swirl remover (Meguiars #9). In the end, you'll have a finish that is glass-like, shiny and definitely free of defects.

760 **NOT SEAMLESS:** Virtually all cars have body seams. And where there are seams, there is the potential for rust. Before repainting a car, pay some attention to hidden areas (such as the lower door seams, quarter panel seams, etc.). You can seal the seams by pouring in a small amount of rust preventative (catalyzed zinc-based etching primer is a good example). In hard to reach locations, use a clean oil squirt can to apply the primer. Also, take the time to remove production body "plugs" (found in rear quarter panels, in rocker panels and occasionally in front fenders) and clean out the factory "flush and dry" panels. You will be amazed at the amount of garbage that collects under these plugs.

761 OVERHEATING DIAGNOSIS:
Before you condemn the water pump for your overheating problems, check to make sure: there is sufficient airflow through the radiator; that all hoses are clear and not collapsed; that the radiator is not blocked; that the pressure cap is working or is adequate; that the fan clutch is still working; and that there is sufficient coolant. If all of these things check out, then the pump may be the problem.

762 VOLTMETER READINGS:
A voltmeter indicates your electrical system's voltage. When the engine is off, the voltmeter indicates battery voltage, which should be 12-13 volts in a 12-volt system. When the engine is running, the meter indicates total system voltage, which is the alternator and battery combined. A high reading may indicate incorrect calibration of the voltage regulator. If you don't fix this, the life of your battery can be shortened. It may overheat and boil. Excessive voltage also shortens the life of your bulbs in taillamps and such. A low reading may mean incorrect regulator calibration, loose belts, a defective generator or excessive electrical demands. A temporary low reading—as low as 10 volts—is normal when cranking over the engine, especially during cold weather starts.

763 PAINTING PAINT:
Here's the scoop on what paint can be painted over another type of paint: Lacquer attaches with a chemical bond (etching itself into the surface). As a result, it can't be sprayed over enamel or urethane paint. If lacquer is sprayed over these two finishes, the result will often be a big wrinkly mess. On the other hand, enamel or urethane bond to the surface. Because of this, they can be sprayed directly over lacquer or another paint surface (provided it has cured properly).

764 HOOD PINS:
Most race cars should have hood pins installed for easy lifting of the hood in a hurry, and to secure the hood more securely (in some classes they are required). Here's how to install them: First, determine the exact location on the hood that the pins have to go. Next, tape the hood heavily with wide masking tape and re-mark the tape. Drill a pilot hole through the center of the mark on the tape. Using a straight piece of mechanic's wire dipped in white paint, pass the wire through the pilot hole and mark the radiator support. Drill another pilot hole in the radiator support and then use a 1/2-in. drill and enlarge the pilot hole. Apply a couple of strips of masking tape to the bottom side of the hood under the pilot hole (this stops the fiberglass from fraying as the drill bit passes through). Finally, drill through the pilot hole in the glass. If the edges around or through the hood hole look a bit coarse, simply dress them with a small round file. Repeat the process on the other side. Install the hood stud and adjust the height for your application. The last step involves the installation of the scuff plates. Adhesive jobs simply install by removing the protective backing and sticking them on the hood. Screw-on jobs are held in place with self-tapping screws.

765 COLOR SANDING:
When color sanding, keep the paper and the paint wet to keep the paper from clogging. Make sure the bucket is clean, and add a few drops of dish detergent to help keep the paper from gumming up. Dunk the paper and rinse the surface frequently to keep them clean. The last thing you want is a

tiny speck of grit under the paper, sanding scratches on your finish. Use a constant direction for sanding, and in the next step of polishing, you'll sand in the reverse direction to remove any sanding marks.

766 PAINT COATINGS:
You know those "shine for life" permanent polish (or wax) jobs that are hyped almost everywhere? Well, forget about 'em if you really care for your car. Virtually all are actually paint coatings. They don't allow the paint to breathe and if any paint touch up work is required, it's almost impossible to blend. Just as bad is the fact that color matching is extremely difficult once these magic elixirs have been applied. There's no substitute for the standard "clean/polish/wax" procedure for superior paint finishes.

767 PEDAL PADS: When installing a new set of brake or clutch pedal pads, think about adding a dab of silicone to the backside of the pad (or spraying the backside with upholstery cement) before the installation. Why? Invariably, the pad will slide off the second you need to grab a leg-full of brakes (or when you're power shifting). The silicone or cement anchors the pad—even if the pad retainers have been split during installation.

768 GOOFY GAUGES: Do you have a situation where your in-dash gauges read incorrectly when the lights are turned on? It's a common

problem—especially with new plastic dashes or plastic electric gauges. The problem is most likely a poor ground between the gauge and the car. Fix it and your gauges will always work.

769 BLINKING HEADLIGHTS: If your headlights blink on and off—especially when the high beams are on, first check to see if the headlight circuit breaker is the culprit. If it's OK, then check the headlight switch (especially if the switch has an internal breaker). If the switch passes the acid test, then look for a short to the chassis in the wire that runs between the headlight and the dimmer switch. Finally, check the dimmer switch to ensure that it doesn't have a short to a chassis ground.

770 CIRCUIT OVERLOAD: When the time comes to add accessories to the cockpit of your street machine (or even your race car), try routing the various power leads to the fuse panel. A set of marked "open and fused" terminals are generally available for such purposes. It certainly beats hooking the wire underneath an existing fuse or splicing into an already overloaded circuit.

771 DOOR PANEL SHIELDS: Tucked behind most automobile door panels are a set of shields. Some are made from plastic. Others are made from a form of tar paper. If you have your door panels off, don't install 'em without the watershields! If you forget 'em, the door panels will begin to deteriorate the minute they encounter moisture (rain, car wash, etc.). In the end, the inner panels will warp heavily without the shields. And by the way, reproduction shields are readily available for most popular automobiles.

772 DOOR GAP: Wander around a car show or a cruise and take a look at some door panels. In some cases, the panel looks like it grew on the car. On others, you can actually see down inside the door. Why is that? The panel wasn't dropped down completely during installation, which in turn reveals the inner door works (this also applies to rear quarter panels). And in most cases, this improper installation still allows you to attach all of the door hardware. Check your panels for fit.

773 SELECTING GAUGES: The next time you're at a drag race, wander over to the Pro Stock pits and check out the gauge cluster in the cockpit. You'll notice that there probably aren't many gauges. The

important gauges as far as Pro cars are concerned are the tachometer, the oil pressure, water temperature, fuel pressure and perhaps a brake line pressure gauge. The voltmeter might be tucked inside the trunk beside the battery and that's about it. The reasoning is also straightforward and to the point. In a short drag race, how much time do you have to monitor a battery of instruments? Not too much, obviously. Gauges are monitored during the staging and burnout process. Although this Corvette is not a Pro Stock car, the driver is obviously following the same idea behind necessary gauges.

774 ADHESIVES: Spray adhesives are used extensively for interior work. When applying them, wait until they are tacky before joining the surfaces of the respective parts together. That's how the adhesives were designed to work, and if you follow those simple rules, the parts will adhere better.

775 BRAKE LIGHT RACING: Racing against an index or a dial-in takes more than skill, good equipment and luck. Occasionally it takes some slight of hand. By this we don't suggest you cheat, but there are some racers out there who use every opportunity they can get to beat their opponent—and that opponent could be you! One such mind game involves brake lights. Most racers don't worry about 'em but some of the crafty racers have elevated brake light racing to a science. Some people wire the brake lights to a separate shut-off switch so that they don't work on the big end of the track. Simple enough. You can

stand on the brakes and not be noticed. But others have taken on a new dimension. Brake light switches that are again wired to a switch, but in reality, flicked "on"—even when the car is still under power. We even know about a racer who wired his horn button to the brake light switch so his hands wouldn't stray from the steering wheel.

776 SEAT KNOBS: More often than not, the OEM seat track adjustment knobs are often made from chrome-plated plastic. While they were cheap to manufacture, they were (and still are) fragile. Classic Industries has a quick 'n inexpensive solution to the broken track knob problem. The replacement knob is manufactured from solid metal and uses a set screw for retention. Yes, the knob is chrome-plated, but unlike plastic versions the plating does not dissolve during cleaning operations.

777 PLASTIC POLISH: A vast majority of cars come equipped with plastic instrument lenses. And with the passing of time, they tend to scratch and become milky. Although there are a number of products on the market that can cure the "fog," you might try using motorcycle windshield/helmet face mask polish. Most of these cleaner/polishes are inexpensive, readily available and work quickly. Better yet, some are available in simple-to-use aerosols which can be applied with the cluster intact.

778 TRIM GLUE: When the time comes to install soft trim such as carpet, firewall insulation, package shelves, headliners and so on, you'll need some glue to hold the components together. Unfortunately, most glues aren't suited to this task. Trim shop pros use a high-quality spray adhesive called "3M Number 76." This goop is specifically designed for use on soft trim. It dries very quickly and becomes tacky in seconds. With these features, you don't have to hold the pieces together for half an hour while waiting for the glue to dry. There's nothing better

779 GLUE STRIPPER: If you become too aggressive with the above "super glue," you can often create a bunch of overspray. In order to glean it, dip a clean rag in gasoline and wipe off the excess. Use a very small amount of gasoline to remove the overspray.

780 SEAT RAKE: Do you find it difficult to adjust your car's seat to a "perfect" upright position? I'll bet you didn't know that there is a built-in adjustment for seatback rake position on many cars. It is a little bumper stop designed to prevent the seat from going too far

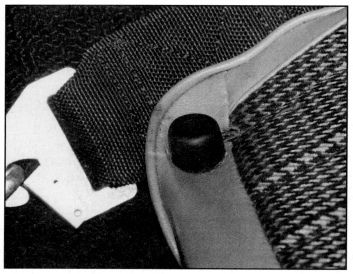

back. Simply trim the seatback bumper if you want the seatback angle more "laid back." If a more upright position is your preference, shim the bumper with a washer or two. Although this isn't a replacement for a set of aftermarket formed racing seats, it sure can help to make driving your factory hot rod more comfortable.

781 FABRIC DYE: In many instances, it's impossible to locate new swatches that match the color of your interior. However, there are plenty of dyes available to match interior fabric. Restoration parts companies are a good source for these dyes, and so are local automotive paint outlets (factory parts manuals often list the correct dye number). By the way, if you clean the vinyl with lacquer thinner before you apply the dye, it will adhere better.

782 CLEANING GAUGES: If you strip the lens assembly from a set of gauges and are about to clean the actual gauge faces with a soft cloth— Stop! The cloth will often marr the gauge faces and smudge the numbers. Instead, use a soft camera lens brush to blow off and "dust" the faces instead.

783 LATCH ACTION: When the door panels of your car are off for a refurbishment, it might be a good time to detail and clean the door latch mechanisms. Remove them from the door (normally there will only be two to four screws holding them in place) and soak them in parts cleaner. After they have been submerged overnight, dry them and buff all of the respective parts with a stainless steel polishing pad and rouge. They won't look like chrome, but the zinc finish will look great for that upcoming car show. Don't forget to lubricate the latches with white grease during installation.

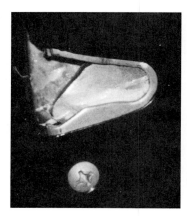

784 DOOR SILLS: Door sill plates take a lot of abuse. In fact, they begin to look rough (and dull) after only a few weeks of use. They aren't called "scuff plates" for nothing. To bring them back up to polished

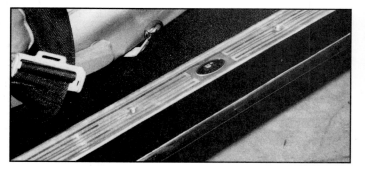

perfection, first rub them with 000 steel wool and lacquer thinner. Then polish them with a good aluminum polish.

785 INSTRUMENT LETTERS: Is the raised, plated lettering on your instrument cluster beginning to show signs of age? A quick fix is readily available. Simply apply a small amount of model-car "chrome" paint to the end of a Q-Tip and gently wipe over the lettering. Due to the small size of the raised characters, it's very tough to tell the difference between chrome-look paint and the real thing.

786 WINDOW CRANK TOOLS: The vast majority of GM products use a little

C-clip to fasten the window crank in place on the window mechanism. The clip is tucked in behind the handle and unfortunately, it's virtually impossible to remove without the use of a special tool. Don't get nervous about the cost—these tools will set you back less than $10.00 and they're very simple to operate.

787 LOCK BUTTONS: When people check out the car, the first thing they see is the paint, and then they usually come closer and check out the interior. One of the first things they see is door knob and lock

ferrule (judges often see this first too). New lock ferrules have a shiny chrome finish along with a tiny gasket that stops the lock button from tipping over to one side. New lock buttons smarten up the interior, and the good news is they are relatively inexpensive. Don't skimp on the details.

788 IRONING HEADLINERS: New headliners are readily available for most Detroit-built cars from a variety of aftermarket resources. All you generally have to do is specify the part number for your car and send in the order. Unfortunately, the tight packing of some headliners creates a spiderweb of ugly wrinkles. To remove them, use a heat gun to unwrinkle the mess before you install the liner. Wave the gun back and forth over an area, careful not to overheat and melt any single spot. This should eliminate the wrinkles and make the installation go easier.

789 MORE HEADLINERS: To replace a headliner, you must first remove all of the accessories such as the sun visors, shoulder harness mounts,

coat hooks and so on. Trouble is, the hardware can get lost easily. You can store it all in a big box or a can, but will you remember which screw goes where? A suggestion is to replace the hardware in the original location immediately after removing the old headliner. Then, remove and replace it again (piece by piece) during the new headliner installation. It saves quite a bit of headache in the end.

790 INTERIOR RATTLES: Nothing is more aggravating than cruising in a trick car that is a cacophony of squeaks and rattles that drives you nuts.

Checking for loose screws helps, but sometimes the problem is a case of the various dash rubber bumpers becoming brittle, falling off or simply being inadequate. Replacing them with with new items is easy enough—if you know where to look. Keep in mind that the bumpers exist in the strangest places—like the ashtray, the glovebox, on seatbacks and in other hidden places. This one's in the glovebox.

791 HIDDEN SHORTS: Tracking down an electrical short can be a long, arduous process. One place where Sherlock Holmes-types seldom look are interior light bulbs. Believe it or not, there is a good chance that bulb filaments can fuse together. The result is often a short that can't be traced. Check all of the lights before you begin searching for hidden shorts.

792 SPEEDO CABLE: For those who are lucky enough to never have done this, installing a speedometer cable into a housing is kind of like pushing a rope through a smaller hole. When the time comes to install a new speedo cable inside the housing, try greasing the thing first. But what if the cable doesn't want to slide in? Try chucking the end in a variable-speed electric drill, slowly turning the cable as it is fed into the housing. This works every time!

793 SEAT BUNS: When you replace seat upholstery, it's always a good idea to replace the seat buns. Unfortunately, that isn't always possible. If replacement seat foam isn't available, you can build up old buns with sections of seat foam (cut from an extra seat) and gluing the works together with 3M "Foam Fast" adhesive. The super glue is available from most upholstery shops.

794 STUCK HEATER FANS: The electric motor that drives the heater/defroster "squirrel cage" in your car can often develop annoying squeals. Often the squeals end abruptly, as does the operation of the heater fan. To avoid freezing your buns over the chilly season, drill a 3/32-inch hole through the raised nipple on the end of the blower motor. This raised bump actually houses the end of the armature. Don't go too far with the drill—the idea is just to break through. Squirt some lube through the hole and cover it with a dab of silicone. The squeal will be banished and the motor will function happily for many more years to come.

795 UNCOILING TUBING: When you buy a new set of mechanical pressure gauges for your car, you will invariably find that the nylon tubing is tightly coiled inside the package. Looks neat, but how in the world do you install the circular mess? Drag it along with you to the kitchen and turn on the tea kettle. As the kettle begins to spout steam, draw the tubing through the steam. Almost all of the coiling will unwind, leaving you with a manageable piece of tubing for the oil pressure line.

796 WEATHERSTRIP FIX: Picture this: You've just installed fresh (and not-so-cheap) weatherstrip in the trunk of your show car. Unfortunately, you park the car in the blazing sun while attending an all-day event. The time comes to leave and you pop open the decklid. Ooops! Because of the heat, part of the weatherstrip stuck to the decklid. It's ruined, and you're out more than a few dollars. But wait! There is a solution! Try cleaning the area and then apply several small beads of 3M Flexible Parts Repair Material (PN 5900). Smooth over the tear and in a few minutes, you'll have a tough time locating the damage. By the way, the folks from Bondo offer a similar product (called "Black Plastic Rubber," PN 902).

797 FLUTTERING TACH: If your electronic tach flutters or takes wild swings on a regular basis, it could be a simple problem with radio noise suppression. In most cases, the culprit is a tach trigger lead that's positioned too close to the coil wire or is resting near a spark plug wire. Your best bet is to isolate the wire. This should settle the tach back down to normal.

798 DIRTY TRUNKS: There is a source of potential water (and dust) leaks inside the trunk that can drive you crazy (we know the feeling from experience). It's the last place you'd look when searching for the source of water in the trunk. Typically, vintage side marker lights consist of a lens, a chrome bezel and a rubber seal. The fit tolerance in this location isn't exactly minute. As a result, a simple movement of the marker lens in the sheetmetal can result in a gaping hole (well, at least it's large enough for dust and water to get through). Check it and adjust the lens assembly!

799 SUN IRONING: If you've installed a new rubber trunk mat in your car and can't get the wrinkles out, simply park the car in the sun on a hot

summer day with the decklid open. Let Mother Nature heat the mat. In an hour or two, the wrinkles should be gone, and your trunk area will look suitable for the judges at the show.

800 FAST FASTENERS: Most car freaks are detail nuts. And some of the slickest hardware available is of the 12-point variety. Trouble is, it's tough to find. And most bolt places will give you the "you're down a quart" look when you ask for it. Fortunately, ARP's 12-pt valve cover hardware is perfectly suited when it comes time to mount other go-fast components. It's easy to find (most speed shops) and most performance parts (automatic shifters, fire extinguishers, ignition boxes) can easily be mounted with 1/4-inch hardware.

801 STEREO WEIGHT:
If you're thinking about filling your street machine with the latest round of stereo equipment, give this some thought: A couple of aftermarket amps, four or six speakers, an EQ and a cross-over or two aren't exactly light. Add in the weight of correct cabling, small diameter wire, the need for a second battery as well as a heavy-duty alternator, and the curb weight starts rising, which translates into a noticeable effect on performance. Things get especially heavy when you start adding sound deadening material to improve interior acoustics and keep the "boom" inside. In the end, it isn't difficult to add a couple of hundred pounds of insulation alone as well as two or three hundred pounds of stereo gear. The end result will be a decidedly slower car with poorer fuel economy.

802 FOOLISH FUEL READINGS:
Does your car seem to run out of steam on the big end of the drag strip even though the fuel psi gauge remains pegged at seven pounds of pressure? There's a chance that the gauge is being fooled. It could be reading air pressure rather than fuel pressure! Some fuel systems that do not feature a separate fuel return or bypass line will in fact pump a significant amount of air through the system along with fuel. And you know what that means—a lack of fuel on the top end along with a not-so-healthy lean condition. So what's the solution? You might consider updating your fuel delivery system with a state-of-the-art setup—complete with a return system and ample fuel volume. By the way, always mount mechanical fuel pressure gauges on the outside of the cockpit (unless you use an isolator).

803 VINYL POLISH:
Vinyl protectants aren't really the best thing for interiors—especially if the protectant is silicone-based. The silicone seals

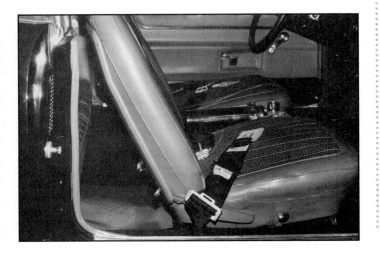

the vinyl, thus stopping it from breathing. Instead, cover the vinyl with good old-fashioned Pledge™ furniture polish. It will gleam, and it will breathe. By the way, the lemon scent smells pretty good too!

804 SEAT BELT ANCHORS:
Finding a correct location for aftermarket seat belt anchors can sometimes be a curse—especially if the car in question is a "for real, built in Detroit" piece of machinery (in contrast to a pro-built chassis). Rather than messing around looking for an appropriate seat belt anchor location, give the

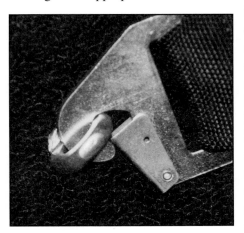

factory setup some consideration. A set of aftermarket eye-bolt anchors are easily installed in the factory seat belt anchor holes. Just add a second nut to the backside of the assembly to ensure that the anchor does not work its way loose. Detroit spent a bundle of money crash testing these vehicles and the factory location is normally braced properly. Besides, it beats drilling yet another hole in the original sheet metal.

805 OIL GAUGE LINE:
Using a common nylon line for your oil pressure gauge is a no-no. The racing association rules makers frown upon it—and for good reason. A sixty or seventy psi blast of oil in the cockpit is no fun. Because of this, some sort of metallic line is mandated by the various racing associations. Now, the first thing you will think about using is a double trick Teflon-lined braided hose setup—and for no other reason than the fact that it looks slick, is extremely safe and it appeases your local tech inspector. But is this the best material for the job? We don't think so. The Teflon-lined hose doesn't like to make bends, it is difficult to work with (from a fitting perspective) and it has pressure capabilities far in excess of an oil pressure gauge. How about using standard neoprene-lined number four braided line? It is far easier to work with, is still indestructible and the fittings are much easier to work with. Besides, the burst pressures are far higher than any oil pressure system is capable of producing.

806 CENTER YOUR STEERING WHEEL:

A worst case scenario in a race car is one where the vehicle gets crossed up at high speed. Everything happens fast—real fast. Because of that, the driver will almost always become disoriented when trying to correct the steering. Inadvertently, you just might crank the steering wheel to what you think is straight ahead, but you're wrong—the steering wheel is actually pointing toward the guardrail. Road racers and a few Pro Stock teams have been using this little tip for years: Point the wheels straight ahead in your car. Note the position of the steering wheel in relation to the front wheels. Take some racer tape or white tape and wrap a couple of turns around the steering wheel—right at the top. By using this system, the driver can instantly center the steering.

807 WIND NOISE:

Hardtops and convertibles can be plagued with wind whistles. One of the first places you should check is the B-pillar seal. Typically, the seal is adjusted in two different locations—the windows and the door mechanisms. Because of this, there are plenty of variables when trying to stop a leak at this location. Generally speaking, it's easier to adjust the door (usually with the latch striker) than it is to move the quarter windows and/or the door glass. Fortunately, the easiest fix might be a simple replacement of the seal (especially if your seal looks compressed or is visibly damaged). If that's the case, then all that's required is to remove one Phillips screw and slide out the seal. Replacement is just the opposite.

808 TRUNK BATTERIES:

Did you know that you can install batteries backwards? Well, not really backwards, but yes, they can be installed sideways. And this is especially important if you've relocated the battery to the trunk. All drag race cars should have their batteries mounted with the plates parallel to the sides of the car. Why? If the batteries are mounted sideways, you run the risk of internal plate shorts—which can occur as the car accelerates. When mounted correctly, the battery service life is extended and you will not get any surprises—such as a dead battery.

809 SPACE SAVERS:

The formula for a traditional musclecar was simple: Slide the biggest engine you had in your arsenal into one of the smallest cars in your lineup. Next, install some of the largest wheels available....and you know the rest. On the down side, those fat wheels 'n tires also become fat spares. What little luggage

space your car might have is eaten up by the spare tire. If that's the case with your factory hot rod, try adding a space saver spare. Not only are they dirt cheap (many new examples can be purchased for less than $20) but they also come in a wide array of bolt patterns. They might not be technically correct, but it sure beats havin' to pack only a toothbrush and a clean pair of socks when take your Ponycar on a road trip.

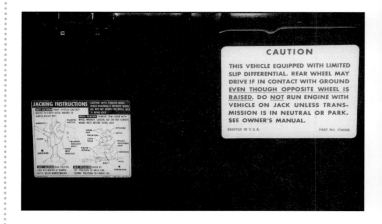

810 DETAIL DECALS:

One of the last details that you can add to a project car is a set of fresh decals. Virtually all cars had decals inside the luggage compartment that detailed jack and spare tire storage, tire pressure and the like. Many restoration companies offer correct decals for various applications. Properly placed, new decals can make a big difference in overall vehicle appearance, and make the difference between first and last place in a car show. Besides, a set of instruction decals beats scratching your head in an attempt to figure out how the jack bolts back in the car!

811 TOGGLE SWITCHES: When

hanging accessory switches inside your street machine or racer, give some thought to the quality and type of switch. Many times you'll need to use a toggle switch. Now, nothing could be more horrifying than to flick the toggle switch labeled "fuel" or "start" while in the pre-staging area, and hearing nothing but a click (due to switch failure). For best results, use aircraft safety switches. They require two separate actions to turn 'em on, but in an emergency, you can just flick the big red switch cover from any angle and it will click off. The switches are available in a variety of ratings and configurations, they are top quality pieces and they only cost a fraction more than their generic counterparts.

812 SHIFTER KNOBS: There are two

basic types of shift handles available—the conventional round ball and the "T-handle." The T-handle may provide more grip, but you shouldn't have your hand resting on the shifter anyway. When driving competively, both hands should be on the wheel as much as possible, and shifts should be quick. When it comes to selecting one of these units for your ride, don't make the selection based upon what your pals use. Instead, try one of each (most shift knobs and T-handles are relatively inexpensive). You just might find that one style fits you better than the other. And at the same time, your driving style and the actual location of the shifter in the vehicle can easily influence the decision. For what it's worth, we prefer the round knobs over the T-handles—even with an inline Hurst V-Gate shifter. In fact, how many race cars have you seen (road race, circle track, etc.) with T-handles?

813 CHOOSING GAUGES: You've

decided to install a set of aftermarket gauges in the dash. After researching a bit, you realize there are many styles and sizes to choose from. When it comes to aftermarket gauges, bigger is better. The large face gauges are far easier to read, and because of the larger area between the markings, they are more accurate. While the 2-5/8-inch Auto Meter models were recently considered huge, Auto Meter has upped the ante with new series of 3-3/4-inch "Monster" gauges. If you can't read these, we suggest you make an appointment with your local optometrist.

814 VISOR BUSHINGS: Believe it or

not, your car can exhibit a bunch of "buzz" coming from the sunvisor(s). Actually, it's not the sunvisor but the rubber bushings or tips that lock the visor to the support at the headliner (or inner rear view mirror). The bushings wear out over the years and as a result, the visors droop and rattle. Reproduction bushings are readily available.

815 INNER MIRRORS: Generally

speaking, there are two types of inner mirrors commonly used on passenger cars—the old setup that bolted to the roof or windshield header and the new package that's glued to the windshield. Old models had a bushing that kept the vibration and consequent looseness to a minimum. If the bushing has gone AWOL, then expect a good amount of sloppiness and noise from a vibrating mirror. Bushings are readily available from aftermarket resto companies for these applications. The newer models usually have a set screw that holds the works to a metal bracket (which in turn is glued to the windshield). If the set screw has vibrated out or is missing completely, then the mirror will shake, vibrate and create a high pitched buzz at speed. In this case, simply tighten the set screw or replace it.

816 SHIFTY BUSINESS: Sometimes, it's

tough to shift gears at the exact moment the tachometer crosses the redline. In super quick cars, there's plenty to do without worrying about the tach. If that problem plagues you, consider adding a "shift light." The folks from Auto Meter have a bunch of shifty solutions to the age-old dilemma—one is built into a tach ("Sport Comp Tach with Shift-lite") while others are available as add-ons. Essentially, the bright red shift light glows when the engine reaches a pre-determined point. Most models have replaceable rpm modules, and as a result, the shift point is tailored to your application. When installed, it's simply a matter of watching for "red." When you see it, grab the next gear.

817 HEADLAMP KNOB: Most

headlamp switch knobs cannot be removed or disassembled from the switch until a button is pressed on the switch assembly. You have to reach behind the dash, press the button, and in one motion remove the outer switch knob. Only then can the switch assembly be removed from the instrument panel.

818 BETWEEN A PILLAR AND A POST:
In many vehicles (vintage and late model), selecting a location for important gauges is next to impossible. A recently introduced new product that should please enthusiasts are "pillar post" gauge mounts. Initially designed by the aftermarket for use on Buick V6 turbos, the post pods mount tightly over the "A-post" (next to the dash) and accept any two-inch gauge. This puts the most important gauge right next to your nose. Unless you're blind, it's impossible to miss. Further to this, a company called "JOE'S" (7409 Cram Rd., Williamsburg, MI 49690) offers both the pillar post mounts and two-inch electric ISSPRO fuel psi gauges that are legal for cockpit installation.

819 EXCESS BAGGAGE:
Everyone knows that light is right when it comes to drag racing. Except, of course, the automobile, which happens to work better with some added baggage in the trunk. Some vehicles work better with as much as one hundred pounds or more of ballast in the trunk. This is a game of experimentation—try your car without ballast, add some weight and keep on adding the weight until the car slows down. Your 60-foot times, along with the ET slip, should be the judge. If you don't know what type of ballast to add, how about using a spare wheel and tire? Many a vintage Super Stock racer was fitted with an LR-78 x 15 steel-belted snow tire in the trunk as "standard" equipment. The ballast was cheap, legal and easily removed. In addition, the ballast can be changed around without any added fuss or muss. As an example, if the car "likes" ballast, but doesn't work right with a heavy full-size spare, try adding a 30-35 pound "space saver."

820 POOR MAN'S COMPUTER:
Can't afford a high ticket drag race computer? Auto Meter has the answer. Called the "LTM" this performance analyzer is tied directly to the tachometer. During a run, it records the tachometer readings and the engine sound. After a run, the unit plays back—complete with the sound of the run and a total recall of the tachometer readings through the entire run. In addition, it has a provision for you to make pre-run voice notations (a neat place to note things like track and weather conditions). Best of all, the LTM won't break the bank.

821 COLOR CODED:
When searching for a special paint color for "accessories" (like a bumper jack base), try your local auto parts store. Many

"generic" paints like C-I-L Grey are perfect matches for factory enamel paints. Simply take the component with you and compare it to the can lid color.

822 CARPET KNIFE:
Before you drill a hole into a panel that's covered with carpet, try slicing an "X" into the location required and peel back the carpet along with any carpet backing or underlay. Then drill the hole. That way, the carpet and insulation won't foul the drill bit.

823 GLOW JOB:
Restoring the needles on gauges, speedometer faces and tachometers is easy if you use fluorescent model car paint. Model car fluorescent paint is available in a wide range of hues and best of all, it's easy to work with. By the way, once the gauge lens is removed, gaining access to the needles and numbers is easy.

824 SPARE LUG NUTS:
If you have mags on your ride and the lug nuts are different than the spare (which they often are), try stringing a set of stock lug nuts on a section of wire and fastening the wire lug nut necklace to the spare tire. That way, you'll never be stuck if you do have a flat. We should also point out that you might need a different size wrench for the spare lug nuts and the mag nuts.

825 CLEAR PLASTIC WINDOWS:
Don't use a chamois to wipe plastic rear windows in convertible tops! If you do, you'll be met with more scratches than you had in the first place. The reason for this is the fact that the chamois holds dirt particles. Use a soft lint-free towel (or diaper) instead. Any light scratches in the

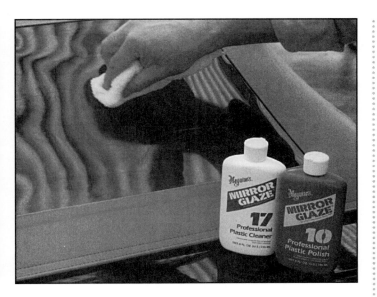

plastic window can be removed with Meguiar's plastic cleaner and polish. If you don't have any Meguiar's handy, toothpaste is a cheap alternative. As an alternative, you might try cleaning the plasitc window with motorcycle windshield polish.

826 VENT-I-LATED: When you install a battery in the trunk, give some thought to ventilation. If you cover the battery up completely, then you don't give the fumes a chance to escape (even sealed batteries vent directly to the atmosphere). If you're real concerned about ventilation, have a look at the special battery vents that were used on vintage (1968-'72) Corvettes. They consisted of a set of special battery caps complete with vent tubes that exited directly to the atmosphere—away from the passenger compartment.

827 MORE TRUNK MOUNTS: If your car has a trunk-mounted battery and you find that starting is difficult (if not impossible), try this: Be sure that the battery ground cable is sound and the actual ground at the frame rail isn't corroded. Then ground the engine to the frame as well. This is a point often forgotten. If the engine isn't grounded, then there's a good chance that the trunk mount installation will cause all sorts of starting grief. By the way, on unibody cars, use the floorpan as the ground location.

828 COOLANT ODORS: If you detect the unpleasant smell of coolant in the cockpit of your car, there's a good chance that the culprit is a leaking heater core. In many cases, the leak will be so small that it can't be detected (except, of course, for the smell). If that's the

case, peel back the carpet on the passenger side and have a close look. If the floorpan is damp, it might be time to remove and replace that heater core.

829 WOODGRAIN TRIM: Many vintage cars came equipped with woodgrain trim on the instrument panel, the center console and other interior locations. The easiest way to repair faded woodgrain

trim is to replace it with fresh woodgrain contact paper (since that's what it was in the first place). Simply trace the shape of the old part on new contact paper and cut it to shape with a sharp knife or razor blade.

830 SCRATCHED GLASS: If you have some light scratches in the window glass or windshield of your car, you don't have to seek professional help. A light polish with 000 steel wool will remove most of them. If you have trouble finding 000 steel wool, try your local hardware store. If they don't have it in stock, they should be able to order a small quantity for you. If that doesn't do the trick, try the glass polishing kit available via mail order from The Eastwood Company. Their ad is listed in just about every buff magazine around.

831 BUMPER SHOT: If you're experiencing a mysterious underdash rattle that's driving you crazy, try checking the rubber bumper that is normally found under the clutch pedal. Most cars have such a component and it can either be mounted directly to the pedal or mounted on an adjoining upright. Typically, these bumpers slip into place or are held in check with a dab of weatherstrip adhesive. If it's missing or loose, there could be metal-to-metal contact, which results in a mysterious and aggravating rattle.

832 LEAKY WEATHERSTRIP: Wet side windows and wind whistles can often be traced to weatherstrip leaks. The most common leak zone is the door weatherstrip. This section of weatherstrip normally takes the most abuse in a vehicle. And if you've ever "entered" the car with a coat hanger, then you can almost be guaranteed

that the weatherstrip is damaged. Occasionally, the whistles and embarrassing wetness can be cured by adjusting the door (moving it in on the hinges and/or rear striker), but this only works if the weatherstrip is sound. If it isn't, it's time to replace the rubber.

833 JACKING AROUND: In many cars, the jack and/or the wheel wrench can be a source of troublesome rattles—especially the rubber sleeve that holds the wrench handle to the jack mast in many GM appli-cations. This is another piece that often bites the dust.

The sleeve holds the jack handle to the mast during storage. Unfortunately, we have never found one lurking in a catalog, but you can either make a replacement or scrounge a suitable example from a "recycling" yard. If you can't find a replacement, the following dimensions should be of some assistance if you decide to fabricate your own: Length: 2-7/8 inches. Diameter: 1-1/2" to 1-5/8". Material Thickness: 1/16".

834 DOOR RODS: Tucked inside most door assemblies are a set of rods which stretch from the inner lock knob to the actual door lock. When new, these rods were often fitted with cloth or synthetic covers (usually a woven, waterproof fabric). The idea was to isolate the rod from the inner door sheetmetal. If the rod(s) are out of

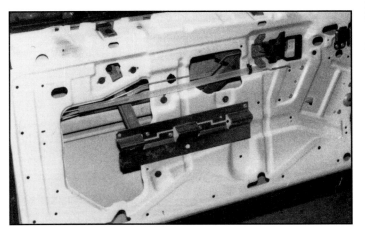

place or if the covers are missing, they can become a source of rattles, buzzes, clunks or the occasional bang. Sometimes, a piece of broken sleeve can jam the lock. Check them first if you have a hidden door rattle or a wayward lock mechanism.

835 HEADREST COVERS: Before installing a set of reproduction headrest covers, you'll find that the vinyl is often heavily wrinkled when first removed from the box. To solve the problem, you can heat the vinyl with a heat gun or a hair drier. But an easier method is to simply toss them into your clothes drier for a few minutes. Not only are they easier to install (because they're soft), but the wrinkles will disappear.

836 SANDWICH YOUR BUNS: If you are covering a set of foam seat buns with fresh upholstery, you'll probably find that the upholstery will often stick to the foam. Because of this, it's impossible to stretch the material tightly. The result is usually a set of wrinkles or not-so-nice-looking seat forms. To solve the problem, wrap the seat foam with plastic sandwich wrap before you install the trim. The upholstery simply glides right over the sandwich wrap. Best of all, the light plastic doesn't have to be removed once the installation is complete.

837 HEADLINER BOWS: When replacing a headliner, you'll find that all of the bows are similar, but not matching. Each bow is designed to fit in a specific location. Before you remove them, tag each bow (first one at the front of the car is "A" and so on). That way, you'll be able to reinstall each bow in the right location with the new headliner.

838 SPEAKER WIRE: A sure sign of professionalism when it comes to stereo installation is how well the wires are hidden and how neatly they are installed. When working with long lengths of lightweight speaker wire, twist them into a single strand to make them easier to hide. To accomplish the task, simply insert one end of your wire strand into the end of a variable speed drill. Give it a few spins and presto! An instant (and good looking) wire harness.

839 TRUNK DETAILING: To detail your trunk, first remove everything that isn't bolted down and then take out all of the stuff that is screwed into place (and that includes the rear wiring harness). Haul out

the vacuum cleaner and clean up any loose scale that exists. Stubborn surface rust should be scraped with a wire brush. Scrub the entire luggage compartment with plenty of soap and clean water. When everything is clean and dry, take the time to mask the various component openings from the outside—the lock cylinder hole, the side marker holes, tail lamp holes, etc. With the masking complete, you can paint. Some vehicles require grey and white while others might be a plain dull black. Splatter paint is available from most automotive paint/body shop supply jobbers. When painting with splatter paint, be sure to clean the nozzle periodically. The basic nature of this type of paint is to spit out chunks of "splatters," and as a result the nozzle will occasionally plug. A small piece of wire and some lacquer thinner can be used to clean the nozzle. How much paint is required? If your luggage compartment is a total hazardous waste area, expect to use two aerosol cans. A more normal situation would use up less than one can.

840 SEAT TRACKS: One item that sticks
out like a sore thumb in an otherwise pristine cockpit is the track that the front seat(s) slides on. If the tracks in your car are rusty and ugly, remove 'em and clean up the rust. Next, give 'em a shot of semi-gloss black (or "eggshell" black).

841 WINDOW CRANK WASHER:
Buried behind most GM window cranks is a large plastic washer (usually grey in color). The purpose of the washer is to keep the crank handle from gouging and ripping the door material. If you remove the crank for any reason, don't forget to reinstall the washer.

842 SOFT TOP CARE: The care and
feeding of a convertible top is no more difficult than any other area of the automobile, however there are certain precautions that should be taken. In order to keep your soft top looking new, it should be washed frequently with neutral soap suds (such as household dish detergent), lukewarm water and a soft bristled brush. Rinse the top with ample quantities of clean water to remove all traces of the detergent. Should the top require further cleaning, first rinse the top completely and then apply a mild "foaming," commercially available soft top cleanser to the entire assembly. Scrub the top with a soft bristled brush, adding water as necessary to maintain a soapy consistency. When you notice an accumulation of dirty or soiled soap, remove it with a damp cloth or a wet sponge and re-apply the top cleanser to

the area. When the entire top has been cleaned, rinse thoroughly with clean water. Due to the fact that the top is inherently "soft," it will move substantially as you scrub it. In order to make the area manageable, it is possible to support a portion of the top from the underside during the scrubbing operation. In addition, do not lower the top until it is completely dry. A wet or damp top that is folded away may cause mildew or wrinkles to form.

843 NEAT FABRIC HOLES: When
you install seat upholstery, you'll find that the job will be much neater (tighter) if you don't cut holes for items like seatback mount studs, head rest supports and the like. Instead, tap the top of each mounting stud with a hammer until the vinyl is broken away. That way, the vinyl will crisply fall around the stud and the rest of the upholstery will remain tight.

844 CRACKED DASHES: If you have a
crack or damaged vinyl dash, don't be too quick to throw it away. A company called the "Newdash Group" (116 N. Roosevelt Avenue, Suite 127-128, Chandler, AZ 85226-3433, PH# 800-283-2744) offers a special dash re-skin service. Recently they have been able to overcome the problem of providing radio speaker perforations in the vinyl skin of the dashpad. In addition, they also offer re-skins for molded door panels, arm rests, center consoles and other interior panels. Further to this, they offer a computer generated color match process (interior dye work, color changes) along with woodgraining, steering wheel repair and general vinyl and plastic repairs. Call 'em for your repair needs. Another outfit that does similar work is "Just Dashes" (5941 Lemona Avenue, Van Nuys, CA 91411, PH# 818-780-9005).

845 GLOVE BOX LINERS: Your
glove box will be much nicer if you swap the grungy old liner for a new one. Over the years, genuine liners were (and still are) readily available from most OE manufacturers. Trouble is, many of these new liners are not

assembled. Working with one was like piecing together a diabolical jigsaw puzzle. And as your can well imagine, assembly is a curse—especially if you're all thumbs. A better bet are the repro liners. Almost all of 'em are completely stapled and due to this fact, the installation is a simple remove-and-replace operation.

846 ACCELERATOR PEDAL: When getting comfortable behind the wheel of your modified car, you might be surprised to find the feel of the gas pedal is important. Yes, a capable throttle return spring (or pair of springs) is mandatory. But some cars are actually "over sprung." In fact, some cars have so much return spring that it's almost impossible to crack the throttle wide open. When working with return springs, make sure that the spring is not mounted in a binding (angled sideways) position. Some carburetors (such as certain Holley Dominators) have massive internal springs. Because of that, they require little "assistance" to close the throttle blades. In addition, you could find that the factory return spring location is best suited for most applications. Try out different spring combos until one feels "right." It might make the difference between enjoying your car and cursing every time you slide behind the wheel.

847 GAUGE PLACEMENT: Before installing a set of aftermarket gauges, it's always a good idea to "test fit" them before you bolt 'em in place. Sit in the "normal" driving position and have someone move the gauges slightly. You might be surprised to find that a bit of angle on the mount hardware can make underdash gauges much easier to read. Similarly, it might be easier to view the gauges if they are actually moved away from the shifter instead of being positioned closer to the driver. With this setup, you might be able to view the gauges by moving your eyes instead of your entire head. The result is less time taken away from watching the road or the track.

848 GRABBING GEARS: In the "old days"—before planetary transmissions became the norm in professional doorslammer racing, the manual four-speed was king. And as expected, some drivers were better at wheeling a "speeder" than others. One of the secrets of the good drivers was the relationship between the seat and the shifter. Although it isn't quite as comfortable for cruising, movement of the seat one or two notches closer to the steering wheel (and consequently closer to the shifter) can improve your chances of grabbing the gears quickly and

cleanly. This works especially well for conventional shifters. You'll note that the race-inspired shifters such as the Hurst Super Shifter move the mechanism further back, higher and slightly to the left of a standard manual shifter. This puts the shifter in a position of better leverage. Moving the seat forward does almost the same thing.

849 ROLL CONTROLS: Roll controls (line locks, stage locks, etc.) always have an "on" lamp included with the assembly. The lamp is normally wired into the system via the wire that goes to the valve assembly. Whenever the system is engaged, the light comes on. Simple as that. Unfortunately, some people don't bother to include the warning lamp during an installation. This is a mistake, especially from a safety perspective. With a roll control system, there is a remote possibility that in a panic situation, you might click the button on while braking hard. When you release the brake pedal, you could still have your sweaty fingers wrapped around the roll control button. The result? Locked front brakes. Rather than using the stock bulb mount, try mounting the "on" lamp in a gauge panel. The lamp looks more integrated and since it's in a place that you normally "monitor," it won't go unnoticed when you need to see it most.

850 CRACKED WHEELS: If you've got a classic original plastic steering wheel on your musclecar but it's cracked, here's how to recondition it. First, remove the wheel, then hog out the cracks with a Dremel motor tool fitted with a file bit. After cleaning the crack, fill it with Bondo or plastic filler. Overfill it to leave room for sanding. When the filler is as hard as cheese, sand with 60-grit paper. Finish with #360 grit. Wipe down with lacquer thinner and paint with the lacquer or enamel of your choice.

851 ASHTRAY: If you're rebuilding (or restoring) a car and the ashtray is double scruffy, try this: Have the receiver (the removable part) chemically stripped. Then ship it off to a plating shop and have 'em zinc or cadmium plate it. Not only will it look like new, it'll add some flash to the dash.

GENERAL TIPS & TECHNIQUES

852 SOCKET STARTER: When working on your car, there are many instances where it's impossible to start a bolt with a socket because the bolt is too short. And at the same time, you can't physically reach the bolt to start the threads with your hands. To solve the problem, fill the socket with a small amount of soft foam rubber. The threads are now exposed, but the bolt hex is still contained inside the socket. Starting the bolt is easy and the socket can be easily returned to normal duty.

853 SCREW GRIT: Have you ever tried to remove a screw that is so tight the screwdriver keeps slipping out of the slot? The result is either a set of bloody knuckles or a rounded fastener slot. To solve the problem, try adding a dab of valve grinding compound to the slot. The compound grips the screwdriver, allowing you to spend your energy turning out the screw.

854 BULB HOLDER: Swapping light bulbs in tiny taillamp housings or dome interior light housing is often a pain—especially if the bulb is hard to reach (or worse yet, broken) and your fingers are bigger than a child's. To save agony and physical pain, take a section of old 3/4-inch garden hose (about six inches), make several cuts in the end and carefully slide the hose over the bulb. The result? A quick and effective way to remove and replace fragile bulbs. Of course, this is only for interior light bulbs, or taillamp bulbs and such.

855 CLEARING ZERKS: If you have a zerk fitting in some chassis component that won't accept grease, there is an easy way to clear the obstruction (short of removing the zerk). A small Allen key will fit inside the zerk opening. Run the key in and out several times to clear the gum, varnish and grit, and the zerk should be clear enough to accept grease.

856 CLEANING DISTRIBUTOR CAPS: Anyone who has hosed down an engine at a high pressure car wash knows that the distributor cap can get soggy. If that situation occurs, be prepared! Remove the cap immediately after the hosing, wipe off the inside of the cap and spray the internals with WD-40 or CRC

556. Both of these lubricant sprays are non-conductive and repel moisture. The car will start every time if you take the time to wipe and spray the distributor cap. The lubes will also repel the moisture and keep it from rusting the ignition components.

857 ANTI-SEIZE SUBSTITUTE: There's nothing worse than pulling an all-nighter to get that race motor assembled in time for the next race, and finding out in the middle of the night that you need some anti-seize compound. Trouble is, the auto parts stores are closed. An effective alternative could be in your very hands, or at least in your medicine cabinet. If you dip the bolt or nut into a solution of Maalox™, the hardware will be covered with a dry powder that doesn't burn off. Just as important, the Maalox solution prevents the bolt from seizing.

858 COOLING FLUSHES: When the time comes to flush the cooling system in your vehicle, there are some things to consider. Ice cold water flushed through a searing hot powerplant can spell big trouble. The temperature difference can crack a block or cylinder head (especially where late-model thin-wall castings are concerned). You should either wait until the engine is completely cooled and use tap water or (and much easier), flush the engine cooling system with warm water from your house hot water heater. You can either use a garden hose plumbed into a tap (water bed stores sell tap adapters for hoses) or simply plug the hose directly into the hot water heater.

859 HOME MADE THREADS: It's a sickening feeling when you've stripped a thread and the parent piece, such as a trick aluminum head, is too difficult to remove (or too expensive to replace). Other than a heli-coil, is there another method of repair? You bet! Loctite offers a neat thread repair kit that actually works. Included in the kit are a two-stage epoxy and a special release agent. To use the stuff, simply clean out the area in and around the damaged threads. Mix the epoxy and insert it in the hole. Cover the bolt or stud with the release agent and insert it in the hole. Several minutes later, the epoxy dries and you can remove the bolt. The bolt or stud can be screwed back into the hole. Best of all, the repair is extremely strong and can withstand torque readings that were once impossible with conventional thread repairs.

860 PLUGGING LINES: When working with brakes, it's often necessary to remove things like wheel cylinders so that you can rebuild them. If that's the case, the brake lines and hoses should be plugged to avoid contamination. But how do you do it? Try some golf tees (the cheaper the better). They fit right in the line and prevent dirt from entering the now-open system. By the way, golf tees are also great for temporarily plugging vacuum hoses.

861 LOCTITE COLOR CODED: What color of Loctite does what? It's hard to check because Loctite puts the instructions on the package, not on the tube. What's even worse is the fact that the tubes are all red—no matter what color of Loctite is inside. Here's an easy way to remember what the strengths are: Red Loctite (#271) is the strongest common type of thread holder. Blue Loctite (#242) isn't as strong as red. Meanwhile the green stuff (#290) has the same strength as Blue, but it also has an agent that penetrates threads that have already been assembled.

862 FROZEN BOLTS: If you encounter "frozen" bolts in locations such as the exhaust manifolds, take a break before you break off the bolts. While you're waiting, spray the stuck bolts with GM "General Purpose Penetrant & Heat Valve Lubricant" (PN 1052627) and let it soak through for about 1/2 hour. Most of the time, this magic penetrating oil will unstick the frozen hardware. This saves you from having to dig out a broken bolt stud in a delicate cylinder head or something like that.

863 SENSITIVE TPS: When washing under the hood of your late-model ride, be careful with the water around the throttle position switch (or sensor or "TPS"). These pieces are very sensitive to water and if it does get wet, expect the engine to run rough for a while. Unfortunately, drying out the sensor does little to help the rough running problem. To solve the problem, you'll have to purchase a new sensor. Better yet, simply cover the thing before you soak the engine with water.

864 SILICONE SPILLS: Silicone is nice stuff to have around (unless, of course, you operate a body shop—silicone is a major cause of "fisheyes").

Trouble is, if it spills in liquid form, then your shop floor will be forever slippery. To soak up a slippery spill, add some vinegar from your kitchen to the contaminated area. The vinegar neutralizes the silicone.

865 CHIPPED FITTINGS: If you use run-of-the-mill tools on shiny new anodized AN fittings, you'll find that they will be marked and chipped before you know it. While the right method of working with these fittings is with special aluminum wrenches, you can fix the blemishes. How? With common felt marker pens. Use a common red for the red anodizing and a standard bright blue for the blue stuff. It works and the only way you'll notice the scratches is with a very close inspection.

866 MEGA DRAIN PAN: Most conventional drain pans don't have the capacity to catch a radiator full of coolant. Try using a plastic baby wash tub. They are low enough to fit under most cars, but just as important, they have the capacity to handle a large heavy-duty radiator. Just be sure to dispose of the coolant properly. The stuff is most definitely hazardous to the health of both humans and animals.

867 INITIAL STARTUP: When starting a newly assembled engine for the first time, you have to be sure that the timing is as close as possible, that the valves are relatively close (in terms of adjustment) and that there is fuel in the carburetor. As well as your plan is orchestrated, there is always a good chance that the engine will backfire, which in turn can create a carburetor fire. Not a way to make your day and certainly not very effective with a flawlessly detailed engine compartment. Rather than grabbing the first available fire extinguisher, simply smother the flames with a damp shop towel (which should be nearby where you can grab it easily). Make sure the towel is clean—meaning free of grease and oil.

868 WRINKLED GASKETS: Don't you hate it when you buy a new gasket (particularly the skinny types used on carburetor bases, rear end covers, etc.) and find that they are bent and wrinkled. And that's just after you opened up the sealed package. In order for them to seal properly, they must be straight and flush with the surface. So, the best thing to do is to iron them with a conventional steam iron, just like you would a shirt. Make sure you use high heat and plenty of steam, and keep the iron

moving back and forth. A folded shop towel on a bench makes for a good ironing surface.

869 CARB CLEANER: If you have the good fortune of getting water in your gasoline (and consequently in your carburetor), you'll find a nice collection of alkali. This stuff builds up in the fuel bowls when the water evaporates rapidly. Unfortunately, alkali is immune to conventional carb cleaners. The best bet is toilet bowl cleaner. Soak the offending components in the cleanser for several minutes and then rinse with carb cleaner. Amazingly, the grunge will be gone.

870 PILOT LIGHTS: So you've decided to paint your car yourself in the garage. You've basically turned it into a paint booth, you've got vent fans, and covered everything up. But wait! Before you start spraying paint and blowing noxious and flammable fumes and overspray all over the place, did you remember to extinguish the pilot lights from the water heater (or gas dryer, furnace, etc.)? Are the fans "spark proof"? Make sure that you take care of these items, otherwise your garage will become one big combustion chamber.

871 LINE CAPS: When timing a car, you almost always have to remove and plug a vacuum line. Instead of fumbling around looking for an adequate plug, stuff a pencil in the vacuum line. You'll never forget to reinstall it either! On a similar note, if you have to plug a neoprene fuel line (e.g. you're checking mechanical fuel pump pressure), then grab the closest junk spark plug. It fills the gap perfectly.

872 CONTACT CLEANER: Some bolts absolutely must stay put. A good example are ring gear bolts or flywheel bolts. To ensure that they stay where you left them, they should be installed with plenty of Loctite. But the Loctite won't work well if the surface is grungy. To clean the oil and grime away, first spray the area with a specially formulated compound called "contact cleaner," which may be marketed under various brand names. VHT and other companies offer it.

873 GORILLA SNOT: If you've snuck the engine back in your car to the point where it almost kisses the firewall, you'll gain some performance (more weight on the rear wheels). Unfortunately, it's almost

impossible to start the bolts which hold the bellhousing in place. But the problem can be alleviated in two different steps. Instead of standard hardware, use 12-point bolts. The heads are smaller and easier to reach. Before you install your new bolts, coat the back ends of the threads lightly with "Gorilla Snot" (a.k.a. yellow weatherstrip adhesive). The adhesive will keep the bolts affixed to the bellhousing as you install it. Once you torque them down, the Gorilla Snot dries up and doesn't have an effect upon the hardware.

874 RACER'S CHECKLIST: Credit this tip to an old pro racer from the east coast. Instead of trying to remember what to do between rounds at the track or what maintenance is required between events, make a permanent list and tape it to the windshield. Include things like valve lash, spark plugs, jetting, timing, tire pressure, clutch adjustment, oil and fluid checks, and countless other variables. You can make up a sheet and have your local print shop run off a couple of hundred copies. Keep them in your toolbox and check off the items that require attention between rounds or during the week.

875 PESKY PIPE THREADS: Pipe threads almost always require a good application of Teflon tape to thwart leaks. As you know, that particular type of tape isn't exactly fun to work with. It slips off

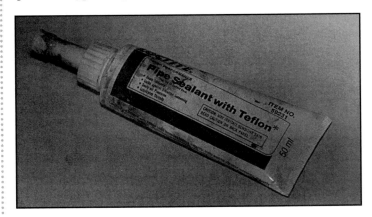

the thread. It gets tangled in your fingers and it always seems that the thread you are sealing is upside down and under a hot header. The good news is that there is an alternative. Instead of messing with tape, make the switch to Loctite's "Pipe Thread Sealant With Teflon" (part number 59241). This stuff is a high performance miracle. When properly applied it doesn't leak. It isn't messy and it never falls off. Finally, it's not terribly expensive. What more could you ask for?

876 STORING FUEL: Believe it or not, the way you store your fuel (race or otherwise) can have a decided effect on its combustion

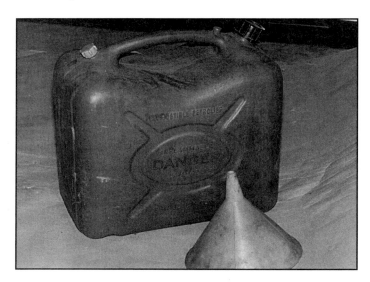

characteristics. As an example, fuel that is stored in clear or semi-clear containers for long periods of time tends to lose its punch. In a nutshell, it goes stale. Hi-po fuels are like night creatures. They're at their happiest when stored in a cool place, out of direct sunlight. Besides, storing gas in red containers and using the white or semi-transparent containers for water makes more sense.

877 BAGGING NUTS & BOLTS: When disassembling a car (restoration or otherwise), don't put all of the various little parts in one big box. Use Ziploc bags, label them with a felt marker and store all of the parts in order. Better yet, hang the freshly bagged parts on a sheet of pegboard. The parts will be easy to find and if you're even partially organized, very easy to locate when the time comes to clean them up and reinstall them.

878 HELPFUL MANUALS: A vehicle assembly manual can prove to be a major asset during a restoration (or any rebuild for that matter). While the assembly procedures found within are worth the price of admission, there is an added bonus: Many of the part numbers listed within are still "good" or can be changed up via the dealership cross reference manuals. Additionally, most of the illustrations are not generally depicted in the dealership parts catalogs. If you are looking for obscure parts, simply take your assembly manual with you to the dealership and use it to

show the parts person the item you need. Besides, the manuals are a great piece of reference material when you are junkyard scrounging—it sure beats sorting through a pile of bumper brackets, hoping that the one you found is right. Okay, so you're convinced, but where do you get an assembly manual for a car built 25

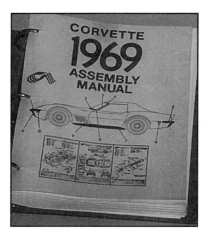

years ago? Try *Hemmings Motor News*, for one. Or, you might contact Helm, Inc., P.O. Box 07130, Detroit, MI 48207 (313/865-5000).

879 HANDY BOLT TRAY: When painting hardware items such as bolts, make

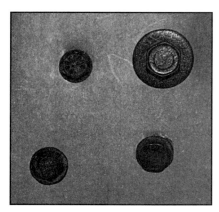

up a cardboard "tray" to retain them. Simply pop the bolt through the cardboard and squirt the new finish on the bolt heads. The threads don't get painted and it sure beats holding them with your left hand as you paint them with your right.

880 GARAGE SPACE: Planning on building that race car in the home garage? Make sure there is space to open doors without hitting anything. You'll need room to get a floor jack under the front, sides and back. Planning to pull the engine? Leave room to wheel in that cherry picker. Front-end sheet metal coming off? Leave plenty of real estate to wield those unwieldy fenders and hood, and to store them out of harm's way. Devote another area to storing seats, soft trim, chrome trim, glass and small boxes and cans for small parts such as screws, clips, nuts and bolts. Do you have enough light? Adequate power and power outlets? What about ventilation? These are all considerations you must make before turning the family garage into your race shop. You and your family will be much happier.

881 STORING SLICKS: According to the folks at Goodyear, you should never store drag race tires near sources of high temperature. Direct sunlight or garage rafters can sometimes create temperatures that exceed 100 degrees. Extended exposure to high temperatures can destroy the slicks. On a similar note, don't stash them near high voltage electric motors or near welding operations. The high voltage can also raise havoc with your pricy race rubber.

882 HEARTY PAINT: Does you engine stand (cherry picker, axle stands or other big shop equipment) look a bit rough around the edges? You know—chips, scrapes and all of the other stuff that comes from the hard use of hot rodding and/or racing. But before you rush out and grab the first can of available enamel, think about painting the equipment with epoxy paint. This paint is very resistant to chemical spills and is particularly resistant to chipping. Because of that, it's gained widespread acceptance for use on drag race and street rod chassis. Of course, it's immunity to abuse also makes it a likely candidate for your engine stand and other shop equipment.

883 METRIC MIXUPS: It seems like more and more vehicle fasteners are metric. Trouble is, some cars have both metric and conventional fasteners. Now, can you tell the difference between a 14mm open end wrench and a 9/16 open end with a quick glance, lying on your back under a car on a creeper? We can't. Because of that, consider adding a blob of bright paint (red?) on the end of the metric wrench. This will help you spot it quickly in a pile of wrenches.

884 ALUMINUM WRENCHING: When working with AN aluminum hose fittings, the advice has always been to use aluminum AN wrenches so that the aluminum fitting isn't damaged. But in

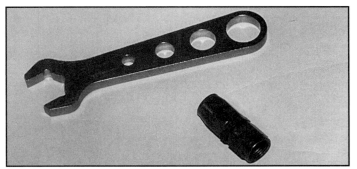

some cases, torque on the wrenches will cause them to physically open. Use a "fits-all" Crescent wrench and you won't have this problem.

885 RIVET HOLES: Going to be doing some pop riveting? There's a procedure you should follow to ensure a solid, tight rivet. To make the right size rivet hole, first mark the location of the hole with a center punch to keep the drill from wandering. Then drill a hole about

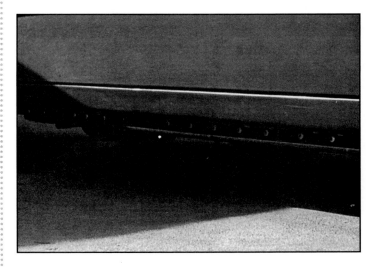

1/32" smaller in diameter than the intended rivet diameter. This is called a pilot hole. Then drill the pilot hole out to the correct diameter. Deburr the hole, removing rough spots, without enlarging it. To secure the part, use Clecos or vise grips to keep it securely fastened while you rivet.

886 CHROMING PREP: Don't bead blast any component that is to be chrome plated. Why not? Simple. The blast will create small pock marks in the material and the plater will have a bear of a time polishing the surface before actually chroming the part. Instead, let the plater chemically strip the component.

887 HANDY JACK: We've discovered a dirt-cheap and low-profile jack that comes in real handy in our shop. It's the standard production scissor jack used on almost all '82-'92 Camaros and Firebirds. The jack is very low, is relatively strong and uses a ratchet up-and-down mechanism. Best of all, they're available at junkyards for little cost. However, they definitely are not meant to support the car without jackstands. Don't even think about it—never crawl under a car that isn't properly supported at all four corners.

888 RELOCATING BATTERY:

To improve weight distribution for your Saturday night drag racer, consider relocating the battery to the rear of your car. Just make sure it is securely tied down and that the wiring is attached firmly.

889 SCRIBING:

If you're fabricating a lot of sheet metal, don't mess around with your critical measurements. Cover it with machinist's blue (it's available at most large auto parts jobber outlets under the brand name Dykem). Next, use a metal scribe to mark the area

to be cut. When you're working on the part, you'll always see your mark. It won't fade in glare or rub off like marker. When the machining is complete, wipe off the blue with lacquer thinner.

890 STEEL SECURITY:

Garage security is a big problem. Here's something that will make life easier for you and tougher for a potential thief: Slip a big bicycle lock through the overhead door channel (inside of the door) when you leave the garage. Even if a would-be thief manages to gain entry into the garage, he (or she) now has to contend with a hardened steel lock. They might steal some parts, but it will be difficult to remove the car without first removing the lock.

891 BIG DRIPPER:

When you're assembling an engine on a stand, one of the biggest curses happens to be the mess. Oil gets everywhere—especially on the shop floor and on your shoes. And if you lay down "kitty litter," then you run the risk of having the granular "goop" contaminate your pride and joy. Thanks to the folks at Jaz Products (1212 E. Santa Paula Street, Santa Paula, CA 93060), there is a solution. It is a formed plastic drip tray that fits on the legs of your engine stand. It works with both three and four leg stands and the cost is minimal (less than $30.00).

892 EASY-OFF GASKETS:

Scraping old gaskets is a pain. Not only is it tedious, the process can damage the parent materials. Instead of sharpening your favorite putty knife, try using Permatex Gasket Remover (PN 4MA). The stuff simply sprays on. Let it sit for a while, then peel off the gaskets quickly and easily. It's even effective on those especially sticky carburetor gaskets.

893 BETTER LIGHTING:

If your garage is a bit on the dark and dingy side (and you can't afford a battery of fluorescent fixtures), don't despair. Go to the local hardware store and buy a few 110-volt, clamp-on light fixtures. Instead of using conventional bulbs, plug in flood lamp bulbs. Arrange the clamp on fixtures wherever you need 'em. You'll be amazed at how bright the old garage can become.

894 SOFT JAWS:

Soft jaw accessories for your bench vise are neat additions. But what if you're in a bind and don't have any? Help is on the way! Simply stack a couple of cheap note pads on either end of the vise. The paper acts like a cushion and the part you're securing won't be damaged by paper.

895 BOTTLE WASHERS:

If you have a handful of bolts and other small hardware to clean, but there's not enough to warrant the price of a gallon of solvent, try this: Clean a couple of used quart oil bottles (the "new" plastic jobs that have superseded cans) with solvent. Rinse them out and fill halfway with solvent. Drop the bolts and hardware in the bottle and shake vigorously. Repeat the process every half hour or so (while you're doing other garage chores). Before you know it, the bits and pieces will be squeaky clean. By the way, 1-gallon plastic milk jugs work great for bigger jobs.

896 SQUEAKY CLEAN: After you've cleaned wheel bearings (before a repack) with solvent, the film remaining on the bearings should be cleaned. The solvent will leave a residue on the wheel bearings if allowed to air dry. It must be removed before re-greasing them.

Otherwise, the new grease won't adhere to the bearing surfaces. In order to clean off the solvent residue, blow dry the bearings before the solvent dries, then place them close under a 150-watt bulb. In a few minutes, the residue will be gone.

897 FLUORESCENT FIX: The new style fluorescent trouble lights have certainly improved lighting when you're working under (or inside) your car. Trouble is, dirt and grease can quickly foil the lamp surfaces (or worse yet, kill the bulb). To keep the fluorescent tube bright and clean, wrap it a few times with plastic sandwich wrap. When it gets dirty, simply replace the wrap. The fluorescent bulb shouldn't heat up enough to melt the wrap, so you needn't worry about that.

898 CLICK TORQUE WRENCH: Click-type torque wrenches, the ones that offer an audible click when the desired torque is reached, are probably the most common in enthusiast tool boxes. As time goes on, however, you might find that your clicker has lost its "click." Before you rush out to the tool repair house, try spraying the moving parts with WD-40. Over time, it is not uncommon for the moving parts to dry up or seize. Without adequate lubrication, the click will disappear. Adding the spray lube should bring it back.

899 SCRAP SCRAPER: If you must scrape gaskets, there is an alternative to the sometimes pricey gasket scrapers. Try shortening the blade on

a cheap hardware store putty knife. By removing all but 1-3/4" from the blade and then sharpening the end, you can manufacture your own gasket scrapers.

900 "J" HOOKS: The "J" hooks used to hold stuff on pegboard sheets work great, until you have to remove the tool or part that is held by the hook. Quite often, the "J" hook will slip out of the pegboard and will vanish on your garage floor. To stop the hooks from making a quick disappearance, add a dab of silicone to the backside of the hook and the pegboard hole. They'll remain on the pegboard until you decide to remove them.

901 CODING JACKSTANDS: If you frequently use jackstands in your garage, this tip's for you. Color code the various notches or pin holes in your stands. By having, say, the third notch white, you can always set the vehicle level quickly, easily and safely. It beats counting notches or holes in the jackstand while you're jockeying underneath a 4000-pound car supported by just a single jack.

902 STICKER STRIPPER: If you ever have the good fortune of having to remove a drag race (or other event) credential sticker from your car or tow vehicle, this is a tip for you. Try using 3M'S General Purpose Adhesive Cleaner (PN 08084). This stuff immediately cleans away the glue after you pull away the label. Best of all, it doesn't hurt paint. Perhaps just as important, this stuff also removes weatherstrip adhesive spills—from both your car and your fingers.

903 MOISTURE PACKS: Next time you're about to throw away a medicine bottle, save the little silica gel sack (the thing with the large disclaimer stating that it's not medicine). A couple of these little sacks inside your tool box drawers can do wonders for rust and oxidation accumulation on the tools. Also, larger quantities of the stuff are usually packed inside your favorite stereo or computer shipping container.

904 RECYCLING PAINT BRUSHES: Old paint brush handles (especially the smaller ones) can easily be recycled as handles for files. Before you toss those old brushes, try removing the bristles, cut the bristle receiver end to length and slip 'em over your files. Once you hammer them home, they work great and cost

nothing. They also make working with files much more pleasant.

905 BLOCKING PORTS: The next time you have to scrape gaskets from the intake side of a cylinder head, stuff the ports with foam rubber (the kind used in upholstery) before you begin scraping or peeling the gasket. The foam expands to the size of the port, preventing gasket junk and debris from entering the port. It makes life easier and from the engine perspective, safer. When you're done, simply remove the foam fillers.

906 SUPPORTING STANDS: Jackstands are used to support a vehicle, but did you know you need to make sure they are supported? This is no problem on the concrete floor of your garage. But in the gravelly pits or on soft ground at a car show, the stands may wobble or sink if they are not supported. To solve the problem, try cutting out four 3' x 3' sections of 1/2" plywood and using them under the jackstands. It's the safest thing to do, works and is especially handy for racers who have to pit on grass or gravel.

907 HANDY FUNNEL: Need a cheap wide mouth funnel? Take a look at the top of a plastic five gallon water jug (the kind they use for bottled drinking water). Whack the top off the bottle and you have an oh-so-cheap wide mouth funnel. And don't forget to pay the bottle deposit.

908 TAPE RESTORATION: It's no secret that masking tape dries out. And when it dries out, it's next to useless. Instead of tossing a big roll of "dry" tape in the trash, toss it in the microwave instead. Fifteen or twenty seconds on high will make the tape nice and pliable. It'll be sticky too!

909 SAFE SAFETY-WIRE: If you have parts that are safety-wired on your car, take the time to add a dab of silicone to the end of the wire twist. You'll find that the "joy" of having your skin pierced every time you come near the sharp safety wire will all but be eliminated. When it's time to remove the wire, the silicone won't get in the way either.

910 HOSE LUBE: When you're working with braided AN hose and the associated

fittings, the instructions for assembly often call for the end of the "nipple" to be coated with oil. Don't bother spraying the disassembled hose end with light lube. Instead, open a can of 10W oil and dip the entire disassembled fitting in the oil. Not only does the assembly process go much faster, the chances of galling the aluminum fitting is all but eliminated.

911 CUTTING WIRE: When you use a set of wire cutters (side cutters, pliers, etc.), there's a good chance that the short piece of wire you've just cut will go flying—at exactly the same time as you snap the cutters closed. It can be a bit unnerving (not to mention dangerous). To stop the flying wire, simply close the cutter and fill the gap with silicone. Once the silicone has dried, slice it down the center, allowing the cutting pliers to open. The next time you use them, the stray section of wire will be cushioned by the silicone. And you don't have to worry about a piece of wire in your eye.

912 CUTTING TUBING: Making a straight cut on a piece of exhaust tubing is a curse. More times than not, the cut will be crooked. And it seems that it's always off target when you don't have any more room to cut. To solve the problem, wrap a conventional hose clamp around the tubing, tighten it and use the hose clamp as a cutting guide. The cut will be square every time. By the way, this tip also works on roll bar tubing and other round stock.

913 DRILL PRESS:
If you have problems with components moving around on your drill press table, try stretching a section of old inner tube over the table. Slice a hole for the table center hole and you're ready to go. Nothing will slip and slide when it sits on the rubber surface.

914 MORE TUBES:
When you toss your tool box into the bed of your pickup truck (or in the car trunk or on your trailer), it probably moves around a lot, even if you've tied it down. To keep it protected, wrap the tool box with a partially inflated rubber tire tube. It will keep other parts and equipment from rubbing up against and scratching it.

915 TAPE TALES:
Sometimes it's tough to read a beam torque wrench—especially when you're lying on your back torquing something like a lower shock absorber mount. To make the torque wrench easier to read, simply mark off the beam (at the appropriate torque level) with a small strip of masking tape. As the needle reaches the tape, you can easily see when to stop yanking on the handle.

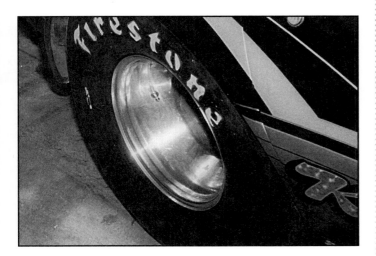

916 DRAG MATS:
Don't be too quick to throw away worn out drag slicks. Instead, cut the sidewalls off along the circumference of the tire and save the slick tread. Slice the tread in half with a sharp knife and you have an instant rubber mat. It works great under your feet at the workbench and is equally suited to use under the car, under a drill press stand or in any place you need some extra foot and knee comfort. By the way, this doesn't work that well with conventional radial tire treads!

917 PRESSURE TESTING:
Looking for a cheap way to pressure test your cooling system (and that includes blocks, heads, radiators, hoses, etc.)? Try drilling a hole in the center of a radiator cap (sealed system caps only—they don't have a relief spring) and add a tubeless tire valve stem assembly. Install the cap on your radiator and pressurize the system with an air compressor. At approximately 25-30 psi, you should be able to find any leaks. Best of all, this can be done with the engine cold so there's no hot water to escape and make a big mess.

918 SEAL DEAL:
Removing a radiator hose can sometimes be a curse—especially if it's stuck firmly on the radiator. Too much force and you could easily damage the soft radiator necks. Too little and the hose simply won't budge. If that's the case, try using a bearing seal remover to peel the hose off. It works every time and neither the radiator nor the hose will be damaged.

919 HANDY HOT WATER:
If you're looking for an instant supply of very hot water to wash a car or parts, and you don't have a tap in your garage, try this: Virtually all contemporary hot water heaters found in houses have a drain port/valve combo at the base. Simply run a garden hose from the hot water tank outdoors. The water supply will be ample and yes, it will be hot! By the way, this tip works great if you live in a locale with snow and ice in the winter and need to wash your car. But don't forget that the hot water will eventually turn to ice.

920 GREASE GUN:
Typically, the nozzle of a grease gun will fill with dirt and junk even when it's sitting idle. The normal solution is to pump out a bit of grease before using it to clear the nozzle, but this is a messy job. In order to keep the nozzle clean between grease jobs, simply cover it with a plastic (or vinyl) 9/16-inch vacuum cap. The grease gun will always stay clean.

921 QUICK CALIPER:
Baffled by sizes of small tubing or hoses and you don't have a caliper handy? Try slipping an open wrench over the tubing or hose. Use a "go-no-go" system and the wrench size will tell you approximately what the outside diameter is.

922 FILTERING FUNNELS:
If you need to filter gasoline, coolant, solvent or almost any other liquid, try adding a paint strainer to the

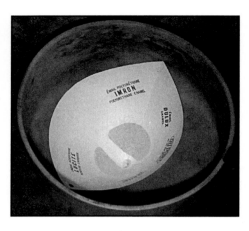

funnel. The strainer separates the junk and goop and when you're done with it, it can be dried, cleaned and re-used. Coffee filters can be used in a pinch, but they aren't as reliable as a paint strainer.

923 LEAKY LIFTERS: It's no secret that new hydraulic lifters should be filled with oil prior to installation. Trouble is, it's a curse (messy too) to fill them by pumping oil through the plunger. Instead, try dropping each lifter inside a partially full plastic one quart oil bottle. When all sixteen lifters are inside the bottle, fill it with oil and let them soak. In a few hours, the lifters will be filled with oil. Simply cut the bottle apart and the lifters will be ready for installation.

924 HOLDING VALVES: If you have to change a valve spring and you don't have compressed air handy to keep the valves from dropping into the cylinder, remove the spark plug and crank the engine until it approaches TDC for the appropriate cylinder. Slice a section of soft 3/8-inch nylon line and tie a couple of knots in one end. Feed the loose end through the spark plug hole (two or three feet of rope should suffice) and rotate the engine to Top Dead Center. The rope jams the valves up and doesn't damage the cylinder wall or the piston.

925 HANDLING WHEEL GREASE: I don't know what you think, but wheel bearing grease has to be one of the stickiest, messiest things known to the car enthusiast. And every time you work on wheel bearings, it seems the grease gets everywhere, especially when hand-packing bearings. To stop some of the mess, try placing your hands inside a pair of clean bread bags (the type without holes that fresh bread is often packaged in). There's enough room to move your fingers freely and the grease is on the bag—not on you. When you're done, you turn the bags inside out and toss them. The grease stays in the bag and doesn't end up all over the shop floor.

926 HOT LICKS: If you cut a radiator hose, you'll find that the white reinforcement strands that remain are tough (no, make that impossible) to remove. To make the hose nice and clean, simply burn the excess white strands with the flame from a lighter. Wipe the hose off and you have a nice clean cut.

927 ALIGNMENT EASE: If you do wheel alignments at home or have to work on the front steering of your car when it's on the garage floor, you'll know how difficult it is to move the wheels. Naturally, a wheel alignment table is the correct tool for the job, but few of us have such luxuries in our home workshop. If that's the case, try this: Fold a heavy-duty plastic garbage bag several times so that it fits under the tire contact patch (one for each side of the car). The plastic allows the wheels to be turned freely (and easily).

928 GOLDEN RULE: Instead of trashing a broken steel tape measure, try this: Nail down a length of the tape measure to a section of your workbench or

table. The "ruler" has countless uses and doesn't take up any space. Besides, it cost nothing and recycling can't hurt.

929 TIE-DIES: Everyone uses plastic or nylon wire ties. After all, they've been called the mechanic's wire of the 90s. Trouble is, they're often as sharp as wire once the tails have been cut off. To solve the problem, simply touch the cut-off end with a hot soldering iron. The end will be blunt, will never work loose and best of all, won't cut you when you least expect it.

930 AXLE COVERS: If you have a set of axles in your garage and you're worried about (a) damaging the splines or (b) infuriated because the greasy ends are always messing up your clothes, try this: Slip an old heater hose over the splined end. It protects the spline and keeps the gear lube where it should be—on the splines.

931 BELT BLUES: Trying to measure the length of a belt for a custom application is a curse. String works, but you can never be sure if the depth of the grooves has influenced the measurement (in other words, you'll probably have to go to the parts store twice). A better system involves the use of an old, long belt. Just be sure that it's the right width and pitch. Cut the belt in half and wrap it around the pulleys in the normal fashion. Mark where the ends overlap and measure the belt. You'll get the right one every time.

932 PORTABLE AIR: If you need a portable air tank, take a close look at a common gas barbecue tank. Yup. They make great air tanks—especially if you rig up a common air compressor valve on the neck. Best of all, they are cheap, available and capable of withstanding considerable air pressure.

933 CAM KEEPERS: In order to keep cam journals fresh and free of nicks during storage, try slipping them inside a section of 2-inch foam insulation (available at air conditioning supply houses). In a pinch, the cam can also be stored inside a spare section of race car roll bar padding.

934 HARD DAY'S NIGHT: Storing tires is often a problem since they can harden (vulcanize) over time. To keep the rubber in good shape, simply coat the tires with rubber protectant and place them in large black plastic garbage bags. Remove the air from each bag with a vacuum cleaner and tie the end tight. The tires will be healthy whenever the time comes to remove them.

935 GASKET CLAMPS: If you need an extra pair of hands to hold a gasket in place while it's drying (e.g., glueing a valve cover gasket to the valve cover), use a set of old-fashioned clothespins. They work great as "gasket clamps" and best of all, they cost next to nothing.

936 FRAY FIXER: When cutting braided hose, you'll often find that the end of the wire braid can become frayed. If that happens, then it becomes a real chore (not to mention painful on the fingers) to fit the frayed ends inside the fitting. Try adding a small hose clamp over the frayed ends. Tighten the screw and the braid will shrink enough to fit into the hose end. Once the hose end has started inside the fitting, remove the clamp and continue with the hose assembly.

937 RAZOR SHARP: Razor blades have numerous uses in the shop. Trouble is, they often go missing. And when you do find them, the search usually ends with a trip to the Band Aid box. To solve the problem, remove the magnet from a discarded radio speaker and glue (or silicone) inside your toolbox. Keep the blades on the magnet (with a strong magnet, laying them close will work) and you'll never lose your blades or have a need for emergency finger repairs.

938 OIL FILTER WRENCH: The old band-type oil filter wrenches probably occupy a spot in many enthusiast toolboxes. Trouble is, they lose their grip when they get old. To renew the clamping power, simply fold a section of emery paper over the band (a piece two to three inches wide will work). The emery paper grips the filter and the wrench. As a result, it never slips and you never have to resort to hammering a screwdriver through the filter to remove it.

939 CHUCK KEY HANDLE: Drill chuck keys are short. Because of that, they sometimes don't offer enough leverage to tighten drill bits inside the chuck. If you've run into a similar situation, add a file handle (available from any tool supply house) to the end of the chuck key. You'll be amazed at the difference in leverage and how tight you can get the drill bit.

940 KITTY LITTER: If there is a major spill (oil, coolant, gasoline, etc.) on your garage floor, the first thing most enthusiasts run for is the bucket of shop towels, which don't work very well. Some savvy guys have a bucket of *floor dry,* which works really well. Simply cover the spill with the floor dry, and sweep it up. But what if your shop floor dry is all gone and the stores are all closed? Try the corner grocery store. Kitty litter works just as well as floor dry. In fact, it even looks the same!

941 CAP TRAP: Those kid-proof caps on today's aerosol paint cans are pretty adult-proof as well. It's really irritating when you're in a hurry or a foul mood to try and get one of these things off. They always require a screwdriver to open. If you're tired of the jam-the-screwdriver-under-the-lid routine, try this: Snip a couple of notches into the internal ring using a set of diagonal cutters.

The lid will snap on and off—without the use of a screwdriver.

942 MEASURING FLUID: Some people use automatic transmission fluid to measure volume in engine parts (like port volume or the combustion chamber c.c.'s). But the trouble with ATF is that it takes forever for air bubbles to disappear. Not so with rubbing alcohol. Unfortunately, alcohol is tough to see since it's clear. To solve that problem, add a couple of drops of food coloring. Besides, alcohol is easier to clean from head ports and combustion chambers, and it's a lot less expensive. Another solution is to use colored parts cleaner solvent.

943 LUG WRENCH: If you regularly use a cross-pattern lug wrench in your garage, give this some thought: We've used these wrenches on a regular basis, but some cars in our personal "fleet" have 13/16" lug nuts. Others don't. To make things easier, we simply dip the 13/16" end into a can of red paint. Saves going around the wrench to find the right end.

944 TIMING LIGHT MELTDOWN: Nothing is worse than frying the wires on your timing light. It's easy to do, especially when tight engine compartments are cramped with hot headers and manifolds. If the wires on your timing light drop too close to the headers for comfort, try wrapping the wires with spark plug wire insulating sleeve material. No, it's not immune to melting, but it's a lot tougher than the timing light wire.

945 MORE TIMING LIGHT: If the above system of protecting timing light wires doesn't work, try this (it's not so "clean," but it works). Use a couple of wooden clothespins to keep the timing light wire away from headers and other heat sources. You might have to tie the clothespins to the timing light wire with string, but otherwise, it's a good alternative.

946 DRILL GUIDE: If you have to drill a hole in sheetmetal and the drill bit "wanders," even though you've used a good center punch, try drilling a small pilot hole a size smaller than the intended diameter. If the bit still wanders (or if you don't have a drill bit one size smaller than the hole you want to drill), try this: Use a flat washer (sized similarly to the hole you need to drill) as a guide. Hold it in place with vise grips. This works great, unless of course the vise grips don't have enough "reach" to hold the washer. If that's the case, try racer-taping the washer to the sheetmetal. It beats the mess that normally occurs when a drill bit bounces and wanders across sheetmetal, and it's safer too.

947 GEAR TOTE: If you have to carry a 9" Ford center section anywhere, you'll know just how heavy and bulky (not to mention messy) it can really be. If that's the case, try this: Use a plastic milk crate to help carry it around. The plastic is durable, it has handles, and the center section fits in it pretty good (depending on the size of your milk crate).

948 HEATING PARTS: Some press-fit parts go on easier if they are heated first. A 500 watt heat lamp is absolutely perfect for warming things like bearing assemblies or other press-fit components prior to installation (we've used one to heat oil pump bodies before installing the pickup tube). Place the part a couple of inches from the lamp and turn it on. Just remember: A heat lamp is HOT! And the parts get hot quickly. You can buy heat lamps from most hardware stores, electrical supply companies or auto supply stores.

949 BULLET HOLES: If you like to save money by cutting your own gaskets, you'll appreciate this tip: In order to make holes in the gasket, use an empty brass bullet casing as a hole punch. Simply place the open end of of the casing over the gasket and tap it with a hammer. Different calibers have different diameters. For tiny holes, use a leather punch (available in different sizes from hobby shops).

950 VIBRATING GRINDER: If you have a bench grinder bolted to your workbench, we'll bet you're familiar with this situation: The moment you turn the thing on, little hardware that's on the workbench does a frantic dance—directly onto the floor and out of sight. The remedy is easier than you might think: Remove the attaching bolts. Add a set of old shock absorber bushings between the grinder base and the bench top. Tighten the works down again. Most of the grinder vibration will be absorbed by the bushings.

951 CLOGGED SAW BLADES:
Many of you novice sheetmetal fabricators know that a jigsaw works well when cutting aluminum (sheet, tubing, etc.). They work great, especially when you use the correct blade. Trouble is, even the right, fine tooth blade becomes clogged with aluminum. Then you have to spend ten minutes cleaning out the blade teeth. To solve this puzzle, coat the blade with soap. It stops the aluminum from sticking, but you'll have to re-coat the blade occasionally while you work. By the way, this also works on more exotic equipment such as a band saw.

952 METAL CHIPS:
If you have to tap a hole in a location where you can't remove the chips, try this: Coat the cut out areas of the tap (the name for these cut outs is "volutes") with grease. As the threads are cut, remove the tap occasionally and clean off the grease and the chips. Re-coat it with grease and continue. Work slowly, keep the tap clean and greased and you'll have no cleanup woes.

953 BRUSH OFF:
If you're looking for a decent brush to clean axle housing tubes, look no further than the bathroom. A good old-fashioned toilet bowl brush is perfectly sized for the job (most automotive brushes are far too small). And not only that, they're cheap and easy to find.

954 WELDING SPLATTER:
When using a good old-fashioned stick welder, you'll find that welding splatter seems to cover every piece of metal within five feet. To save cleanup time, try this: Coat areas around (but not on) the areas to be welded with a light coat of grease. It won't stop the splatter, but it will stop it from sticking on adjacent areas.

955 PLUG DRIVER:
Sometimes installing soft plugs in engine blocks (and heads) can be a curse. The reason, of course, is that a special

soft plug driver is often required. If you don't have one or two of these seldom used tools in your collection, try using a socket. Select a socket that is just large enough to fit inside the soft plug. Appropriately sized plug drivers are no further than your toolbox.

956 FLOOR CRACKS:
Don't you hate it when your creeper wheels jam inside a crack on your garage floor? An easy solution isn't far away. Clean the garbage from the cracks in the concrete and fill the crevice with body filler. Smooth it with a trowel and let it dry. You'll be surprised at how tough the stuff really is.

957 LOST & FOUND:
Maybe it's a case of poor organization, but we often lose track of little items in the toolbox. One of the smallest (and one that seems to go missing the most) is the tire valve stem core removing "tool." In order to keep track of the thing, try screwing it onto a spare valve stem. It's about 100 times larger and much easier to spot in a cluttered tool cabinet.

958 WINCHING:
How many of you have a project car in your garage that doesn't run? Isn't it amazing how easy it is to push the car out the garage door down that sloped driveway, but difficult to push back in? What a pain! A slick trick that saves a bunch of grunting and groaning is the installation of a hand winch on the front wall of your garage. A boat anchor winch is strong enough to yank that old project car back inside (a used hand crank boat trailer winch is cheap too). But if you have the money, the best way is to go with a 12-volt trailer or offroad winch.

959 PUMP PRIMER:
Although special-built engine priming tools are readily available, here's a cheaper method: Take a stock, used up distributor and remove the drive gear and replace it with a spacer (a piece of tubing will suffice). Remove the point plate, vacuum advance cannister, mechanical advance mechanism and other hardware. Now you have an instant pump primer. Just add a 1/2-inch drill to drive it and you'll have immediate oil pressure.

960 HEAT WRENCH:
This is an old tip that's worth mentioning. If you have a rusted bolt or fastener (a real good example are the block drains found on Chevy V8s) that is virtually impossible to remove, try this: Heat the area around the fastener before you round the

GENERAL TIPS & TECHNIQUES

head off of the bolt with too much wrench abuse. Melt candle wax around the threads. This acts as a lubricant, which allows the stubborn fastener to be removed. A propane torch also works as well.

961 SOFTEN THE GRIP: If you have to clamp delicate components such as pistons in a vise, try wrapping the part with an old piece of inner tube. The rubber keeps the part from being marred by the vise jaws but it also has another purpose: The rubber "band" keeps the component from moving around in the vise as you apply pressure.

962 TUBE CAPS: Have you ever noticed how the pointed caps on tubes of silicone always end up hardening after use? But don't despair, there is a cure (no pun intended). Take a used straight spark plug boot and cover the pointed silicone tube applicator. You can seal the end of the boot with slicone, but they even work better if a piece of the old ignition wire is left attached to the boot.

963 SPIN TIGHT: When tightening bolts, you'll often find that using a socket extension (without the ratchet) works great until the bolt begins to seat. Often, the end of the extension is hard to grasp (even worse if your hands or the extension is covered in grease or oil). To solve the problem, try adding a shock absorber bushing to the top of the extension. It slips over the end of a 3/8-inch extension and increases your grip considerably.

964 SCRIBE SOLUTION: If you often fabricate your own parts from aluminum, you probably use machinist's blue for the layout. If you're like us, the time you need the blue is when the bottle is empty or the machine shop supply house is closed. An inexpensive alternative is the use of a fat felt tip "permanent" marker. Use it to make your layout and then scribe the lines. Once the cutting, sanding and filing is complete, the "permanent" marker lines wipe off with lacquer thinner to remove it.

965 NITROUS FILLING: With the popularity of nitrous oxide systems, many enthusiasts are filling their own small car bottles at home from readily available large tanks of nitrous (tanks like those on acetylene welding systems). When refilling small bottles, keep this in mind: Never attempt to speed the process by heating the big stationary bottle with a torch! The heat creates

localized stress on the bottle and can easily cause an explosion of major magnitude! Be patient and follow the manufacturer's recommendations!

966 STICKY NUTS: If you have a tiny nut that's hard to reach, let alone start, try this: Wrap one of your fingers with two-sided tape. Stick the nut to the tape on your finger and presto! You have a cheap and reliable method of starting an "impossible" nut.

967 LOWERED CARS: Many of today's street machines are so low, you can't even slide a conventional floor jack underneath them. In order to get the jack under the car, try making up a set of low ramps. Stack a couple of two by tens (or 2 x 6) together in a staggered pattern and nail them together. Drive the car onto them. The low ramps will raise the car enough that you'll be able to slip your floorjack under the car.

968 BOLT VACATION: Have you ever noticed how the attaching bolts on your engine stand always disappear when the stand is not in use? These are the bolts that attach to the engine, ones that normally don't have nuts. The next step is usually one more trip to the local hardware store for a handful of grade five fasteners. Unfortunately, that can get old in a hurry. Try this: Simply put nuts on the quartet of fastening bolts when not in use. That way, the vital bolts always stay with the engine stand.

969 CUSTOM WRENCHES: Everyone knows the tip about heating a wrench and bending it to fit a special application (you know, the one where you need a trained monkey to reach a "special" bolt). Instead of permanently molding your new and expensive Snap-Ons, buy a set of cheap wrenches and modify them as you see fit. Most auto parts stores sell these cheap wrenches by the bucketful.

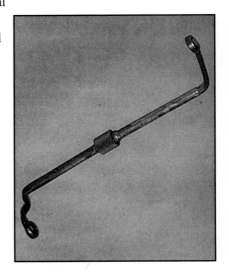

970 RECYCLE WOOD PALLETS:
The next time you purchase a major item that arrives on a wooden shipping pallet, take the time to disassemble the wood work. Cut to various lengths, the cheap boards can be used in a variety of shop applications—"cushions" for jacking under an oil pan, custom short ramps, pounding blocks and the list goes on.

971 FREEZING PARTS:
We've already discussed the tip (#948) about heating press-fit parts. There is another way to make those tight tolerance tasks easier though. While one of the parts (e.g., a connecting rod) is heated, try throwing the "sister" component (such as a wrist pin) in the freezer for an hour or two. The cold makes one part contract while the heat obviously makes the other expand, so it should slip together easier.

972 CRUSHING BLOW:
Never trust a floor jack or a hydraulic bottle jack—no matter how expensive or how high the quality. When working

under a car, always be sure that the jack is supplemented by quality jackstands or a high quality ramp. All it takes is for a tiny, ten-cent seal to fail and the fluid leaks out of the jack. When that happens, it no longer works, and the car comes down rather quickly. Take the time to place jackstands under the car.

973 RAG SAFETY:
Instead of tossing your greasy, oily shop rags in the corner of the shop, place them in a metal container, preferably one with a tight fitting, steel lid. You never know when a spark can ignite a flame, and old shop rags are a prime candidate for spontaneous combustion, meaning they don't always need a spark to ignite.

974 RECYCLE BUFFING PADS:
Don't throw away worn out buffing pads from a high speed polisher. Even if they're worn out, wash them and re-use them as cushions for the tops of floor jacks. Their shape fits rather well with the round head of a hydraulic jack, and most have ties that can be used to secure it to the jack head. The soft surface won't mar a detailed undercarriage.

975 ROOM TEMPERATURE:
Many chemical products (including paint, RTV sealers, plastic filler, etc.) are very sensitive to temperature. In other words, the environment has to be correct for the product to work properly. Because of that, it's a good idea to mount a reliable thermometer in your garage. Watch it carefully when working with sensitive products such as paint.

976 TRASH BAG COVERS:
There are some cases where you have to cover wheels and tires when you're working on your car (a good example is if you do body or paint work). The idea is to keep the wheels and tires from getting dirty. And sometimes, commercially available dust covers create more dust and debris than they protect. Try using a large plastic garbage bag instead. The large jobs cover just about any wheel tire combo and when you're done, the bags can be recycled to hold trash.

977 SCUFFED STUFF:
Instead of using steel wool to clean items, consider using Scotchbrite pads. They work great for cleaning oxidized metal and are equally at home as small sanding pads. Best of all, they don't scratch the surface as deeply as steel wool, nor do they tend to leave slivers of steel in your hand.

978 STEEL SUPPORT:
If you insist on using steel wool for your cleaning jobs, your hands will appreciate this tip: Cut an old tennis ball (or any hollow rubber ball) in half. Stuff the steel wool inside the ball and use it as a "backing plate." Your hands will appreciate it.

979 FLAME OUT:
If you have to remove undercoating from a car, don't bother firing up the propane torch just yet. Instead, use a heat gun to soften the tar. It's a more efficient (and safer) piece of equipment. A typical heat gun will operate anywhere from 600 to 1,000 degrees and there's no flame to worry about. But you still might need to use the torch in tough places.

980 SHOP COMPRESSORS: Looking for a ready supply of compressed air for your home shop? There are several types of compressors available, and most are either a single-stage or two-stage type. Without getting into too much technical detail, suffice it to say that the smallest two-stage compressor will meet your air needs (especially for painting) better than the largest single-stage compressor. It will supply enough air to power most pneumatic tools as well. Whatever you decide, make sure the compressor has enough volume and pressure. A good professional spray gun requires 8.5 cfm to run right, so make sure the tank delivers it. A general rule of thumb is to purchase the largest compressor you can afford. Base this on the cfm consumption of the tools you're going to use and the length of time you wish to use them. Nothing is more frustrating than to have the air cut out when in the middle of laying down a layer of paint.

981 SETTLING STANDS: Once you've placed a car on jackstands, give it a few up and down shakes on the bumpers. This ensures that the jackstands are fully engaged, and that they are secure and steady. Nothing is worse than climbing under a car and finding out that your ratcheting jackstands aren't fully engaged!

982 CLEAN WIRES: If you're stuck on a way to clean ignition wires and wiring harnesses, try this: Wipe the wires carefully with lacquer thinner. Once they are clean, you can spray them with Armorall. If the silicone-based stuff is too shiny for your tastes, wipe the wires with hand cleaner. They'll look like they just came out of the box.

983 MAGNIFYING PARTS: If you need to carefully examine parts for minute cracks or damage, try using a photographer's "loupe." Available in different magnification numbers, an 8X job will easily enlarge small defects. Best of all, the loupes are inexpensive, durable (most are plastic) and easy to find at your local camera store.

984 SAND QUALITY: Remember the old saying "you get what you pay for?" It even applies to sandpaper. The cheap stuff will almost certainly wear out quickly and shred. Worse yet, it just doesn't have the cutting power of the better name brands. Buy the professional sandpaper that is available from auto body paint supply shops.

3M and Meguiar's sell the good stuff.

985 BATTERY BOOM: When charging batteries on the workbench, be very careful with sparks (or even cigarettes). It's not the charger or the battery that you have to worry about, it's the fumes that are given off by the charging battery. Not only are the fumes toxic, they're highly explosive. And you know what's inside batteries.

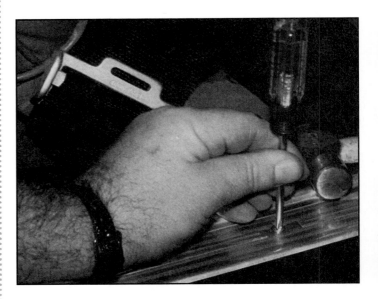

986 PHILLIPS FIX: Phillips head screws are found everywhere on a typical passenger car (or truck). Of course, they can sometimes be next-to-impossible to remove—especially if they haven't been touched for two or three decades. To solve the problem, insert the screwdriver in a normal fashion. But before trying to turn the stubborn screw, give the end of the screwdriver a quick tap with a small hammer. This dislodges any corrosion and at the same time, makes the screwdriver fit the head of the screw perfectly.

987 HANDY CLEANERS: If you have problems cleaning your hands after a messy day under your car (and even the best hand cleaners don't work all the time), try this: Before you begin a major project that involves grease and grime, apply a small amount of hand lotion to your hands (arms and whatever else will become dirty). This keeps the real grime from deeply penetrating your pores. When you're done, use hand cleaner as you would normally, and you'll find the grease and grime comes out much easier.

988 HANDLE THE JACK: Floor jacks
are wonderful pieces of shop equipment. That is, until you accidently slide the jack too far under the car and whack the hand-rubbed lacquer paint job with the handle. If jack handle door dings are driving you crazy, try slipping a length of roll bar padding or air conditioner insulation over the jack handle. When installed, the padding will cushion any wayward blows and your sheetmetal will always look perfect.

989 TUBE EXTENSION: When you
have to add glue, weatherstrip adhesive, caulking, silicone or other product to a hard-to-reach location, try adding a section of rubber hose (windshield washer hose or small vacuum hose works) over the end of the tube. This extends the nozzle enough to allow the goop to reach a previously inaccessible location.

990 MIGHTY MICS: Micrometers are
almost always supplied with the standards used to set them. They are exceptionally sensitive instruments calibrated to read in thousandths (or smaller) of an inch. Consequently, it doesn't pay to sling them around in a toolbox that gets tossed around in a transporter or around the garage. Keep your mics away from extreme heat and cold, and store them in a protected case, secure (preferably packed in foam rubber).

991 FENDER COVERUPS: Sometimes,
commercial fender covers are the best thing invented for the protection of paint, but some people prefer a large, soft terry towel (a beach or bath towel is perfect). It works better, doesn't wound the paint and is easily cleaned. If you want to get trick, add several velcro strips to one side and glue the opposite velcro fastener to the inside of the fender. Then the terry cloth cover will never fall off.

992 SOLDERING CLAMP: Trying to
solder two wires together usually requires a third hand. We're not personally equipped with that feature (you too, we hope). If that's the case, try this: Take the plastic lid from an aerosol paint can, flip it upside down and cut a slit in it so that it holds the wire. You can actually put both pieces of wire in the cap, one on each side so they meet in the middle. Not only does this contraption hold the wire, it also catches any wayward solder.

993 HOT GLOVES: Removing and
replacing spark plugs that are close to hot headers is a job for a masochist. Although there are special gloves designed for the job, try using a pair of household gardening gloves. They're thick enough to keep the heat away, and not so thick that you won't be able to work the plug wrench. Besides, they're cheap and readily available.

994 BASTERS: Believe it or not, a standard
household baster, like the kind used for turkeys, is a great tool for odd jobs like filling a battery or better yet, sucking the gas out of carburetor float bowls. And, it can even be used for ugly jobs like filling rear ends or manual transmissions. Run down to your local kitchen supply store and buy a couple. You'll be amazed at how useful they can be.

995 CAPTURED CANS: We've
mentioned before that carburetor jets are best stored on commercially available jet boards, but what about the large quantities of O-rings, mini-circlips and other carburetor hardware that go along with your standard high performance four-barrel? If you toss pieces like these in a workbench drawer, you'll never find them. The best bet for storing these tiny components is a used 35mm film canister. Not only are they air tight, they're also waterproof. If you don't shoot much film, ask for a dozen or two at your local camera store.

996 SHOT BAG: Occasionally, you'll need
to hammer metal panels into shape. This is especially true if you're a racer and like to fabricate your own metal parts, like dashes and stuff. The best way to stretch

metal is to strike it on a surface that will yield to the blow. A shot bag is a leather bag filled with lead shot (#9, the same used in shotgun shells, is best) and sewn shut. The metal is struck on top of it, and the bag gives some support yet yields enough so the hammer can form. The shot inside the bag conforms to the hammer's face, and the metal stretches. You might be able to find one (U.S. Industrial Tool Supply makes them), or you can go to your nearest sporting goods store (one that sells hunting gear and guns) and purchase some high quality leather. Then have it expertly sewn shut.

997 MIXING TOOL: If you have to mix up a bunch of Bondo, paint or especially fiberglass resin, this tip's for you: Make a mixing wand from a coat hanger. Bend the rod into an "S" shape and insert the straight end into your 3/8-inch drill and you've got a power mixer for paint products.

998 HEADER HELPERS: A lot of people have a spare set of headers in their garage, and they are always underfoot. They are difficult to store because of their awkward shape. If that's the case, try this: Bolt the flanges together with (you guessed it) a 3/8-inch header bolt or two. Then hang them high up on the garage wall. They'll never be underfoot again.

999 KITCHEN DEGREASER: If you run out of degreaser in the shop and the auto parts stores are all closed, don't despair. Check out your supply of kitchen and bathroom cleaning chemicals. Spray-on oven cleaner works wonders as a replacement for engine shampoo. Be sure the engine is hot. The oven cleaner works better when the surfaces are scorching. And for lesser jobs, try some aerosol bathtub cleanser. It works great for spots that are more delicate, such as painted inner fenders or the firewall.

1000 SMOOTH AS GLASS: A thick piece of glass is almost mandatory in most shops. It's perfectly flat. As a result, you can use it to test pushrods for wobble. You can also use it to sand parts flat. When sanding on the glass, first cover it with emery paper and sand the part with a figure "8" motion. When buying the glass, get the thickest possible. The thicker, the better.

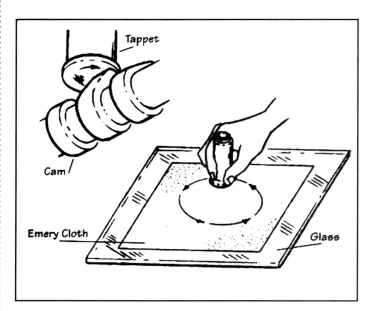

1001 ALUMINUM CUTTERS: Anytime you use a die grinder or other carbide type cutter to work with aluminum, we'll guarantee that the cutters will clog—likely sooner than later. To solve the problem, dip the cutter in a small container of automatic transmission fluid frequently as you cut. The ATF lubes the cutter, which in turn allows the work to proceed faster. Better still, the cutter teeth don't fill with aluminum shavings. And as an added benefit, ATF is much cheaper and easier to find than special fluids "designed" for the job.

NOTES

NOTES

ABOUT THE AUTHOR

Wayne Scraba was born and raised in a small, rural community in the midwest. Automobiles and motorsports played pivotal roles in this life, even in the early years, which explains his massive personal collection of Hot Rod, Popular Hot Rodding and Car Craft magazines (dating back as far as 1961). On his seventeenth birthday, he purchased his first "factory hot rod"—a new 1970 SS454 Chevelle sport coupe. In retrospect, the Chevelle was just the very beginning. Some fifty different vehicles would follow—most of which were modified to go extremely fast! The die was cast, and Scraba was hooked on quick cars and competition—an element of his life that would remain a constant in the decades to come.

By the mid-eighties, Scraba's high performance interests and expertise led him to journalism, and he has appeared in the very same magazines he so religiously collected over the years, as well as a few others. He has written over 800 technical articles and several books on high performance, and has served as the editor of a musclecar magazine.

Although Wayne has performed drag tests, written feature articles and reports on products, he's happiest writing about technical matters. In simple terms, he's a gearhead with gas in his veins. Tips and shortcuts make things easier in his garage too. And that has formed the basis for this book.

HANDBOOKS

Auto Electrical Handbook: 0-89586-238-7
Auto Upholstery & Interiors: 1-55788-265-7
Brake Handbook: 0-89586-232-8
Car Builder's Handbook: 1-55788-278-9
Street Rodder's Handbook: 0-89586-369-3
Turbo Hydra-matic 350 Handbook: 0-89586-051-1
Welder's Handbook: 1-55788-264-9

BODYWORK & PAINTING

Automotive Detailing: 1-55788-288-6
Automotive Paint Handbook: 1-55788-291-6
Fiberglass & Composite Materials: 1-55788-239-8
Metal Fabricator's Handbook: 0-89586-870-9
Paint & Body Handbook: 1-55788-082-4
Sheet Metal Handbook: 0-89586-757-5

INDUCTION

Holley 4150: 0-89586-047-3
Holley Carburetors, Manifolds & Fuel Injection: 1-55788-052-2
Rochester Carburetors: 0-89586-301-4
Turbochargers: 0-89586-135-6
Weber Carburetors: 0-89586-377-4

PERFORMANCE

Aerodynamics For Racing & Performance Cars: 1-55788-267-3
Baja Bugs & Buggies: 0-89586-186-0
Big-Block Chevy Performance: 1-55788-216-9
Big Block Mopar Performance: 1-55788-302-5
Bracket Racing: 1-55788-266-5
Brake Systems: 1-55788-281-9
Camaro Performance: 1-55788-057-3
Chassis Engineering: 1-55788-055-7
Chevrolet Power: 1-55788-087-5
Ford Windsor Small-Block Performance: 1-55788-323-8
Honda/Acura Performance: 1-55788-324-6
High Performance Hardware: 1-55788-304-1
How to Build Tri-Five Chevy Trucks ('55-'57): 1-55788-285-1
How to Hot Rod Big-Block Chevys:0-912656-04-2
How to Hot Rod Small-Block Chevys:0-912656-06-9
How to Hot Rod Small-Block Mopar Engines: 0-89586-479-7
How to Hot Rod VW Engines:0-912656-03-4
How to Make Your Car Handle:0-912656-46-8
John Lingenfelter: Modifying Small-Block Chevy: 1-55788-238-X
Mustang 5.0 Projects: 1-55788-275-4

Mustang Performance ('79–'93): 1-55788-193-6
Mustang Performance 2 ('79–'93): 1-55788-202-9
1001 High Performance Tech Tips: 1-55788-199-5
Performance Ignition Systems: 1-55788-306-8
Performance Wheels & Tires: 1-55788-286-X
Race Car Engineering & Mechanics: 1-55788-064-6
Small-Block Chevy Performance: 1-55788-253-3

ENGINE REBUILDING

Engine Builder's Handbook: 1-55788-245-2
Rebuild Air-Cooled VW Engines: 0-89586-225-5
Rebuild Big-Block Chevy Engines: 0-89586-175-5
Rebuild Big-Block Ford Engines: 0-89586-070-8
Rebuild Big-Block Mopar Engines: 1-55788-190-1
Rebuild Ford V-8 Engines: 0-89586-036-8
Rebuild Small-Block Chevy Engines: 1-55788-029-8
Rebuild Small-Block Ford Engines:0-912656-89-1
Rebuild Small-Block Mopar Engines: 0-89586-128-3

RESTORATION, MAINTENANCE, REPAIR

Camaro Owner's Handbook ('67–'81): 1-55788-301-7
Camaro Restoration Handbook ('67–'81): 0-89586-375-8
Classic Car Restorer's Handbook: 1-55788-194-4
Corvette Weekend Projects ('68–'82): 1-55788-218-5
Mustang Restoration Handbook('64 1/2–'70): 0-89586-402-9
Mustang Weekend Projects ('64–'67): 1-55788-230-4
Mustang Weekend Projects 2 ('68–'70): 1-55788-256-8
Tri-Five Chevy Owner's ('55–'57): 1-55788-285-1

GENERAL REFERENCE

Auto Math:1-55788-020-4
Fabulous Funny Cars: 1-55788-069-7
Guide to GM Muscle Cars: 1-55788-003-4
Stock Cars!: 1-55788-308-4

MARINE

Big-Block Chevy Marine Performance: 1-55788-297-5

HPBOOKS ARE AVAILABLE AT BOOK AND SPECIALTY RETAILERS OR TO ORDER CALL: 1-800-788-6262, ext. 1

HPBooks
A division of Penguin Putnam Inc.
375 Hudson Street
New York, NY 10014